SOVEREIGNTY AND ITS OTHER

FORDHAM UNIVERSITY PRESS NEW YORK 2013

COMMONALITIES
Timothy C. Campbell, series editor

SOVEREIGNTY AND ITS OTHER

Toward the Dejustification of Violence

DIMITRIS VARDOULAKIS

Library of Congress Cataloging-in-Publication Data

Vardoulakis, Dimitris.
    Sovereignty and its other : toward the dejustification of violence / Dimitris Vardoulakis.
        pages ; cm. — (Commonalities)
    Includes bibliographical references and index.
    ISBN 978-0-8232-5135-3 (cloth : alk. paper) —
    ISBN 978-0-8232-5136-0 (pbk. : alk. paper)
    1. Sovereignty.   I. Title.
    JC327.V36 2013
    320.1'5—dc23   2012049119

Printed in the United States of America
15   14   13   5   4   3   2   1
First edition

For Amanda Third

CONTENTS

PREFACE

This book was a product of a series of accidents. In 2009 I found myself teaching philosophy at the University of Western Sydney in a major called "History, Politics and Philosophy." To acknowledge the historical aspect of this major I wanted to design a new course that would look at the development of an idea. But it was not going to be simply a history of ideas. For it so happened that when I arrived at my new department, I had also finished a first, rudimentary draft of a book in which I was trying to investigate the possibility of a "logic" of sovereignty through a series of reflections on the word "stasis." The manuscript required an introduction to contextualize the concept of sovereignty. Thinking that combining them would be the most expeditious and efficient strategy to dispense of my didactic and authorial duties, I decided to present the introduction as a course. This proved neither expeditious nor efficient for the completion of the manuscript on "stasis," but by the end of the semester I realized that I had another manuscript in my hands. These serendipitous circumstances determined the topic and the disciplinary balance of *Sovereignty and Its Other*.

As for the tenor of the book, that was determined by another set of accidents. As a new university that was formed by the amalgamation of a number of higher education institutions, the University of Western Sydney had been seeking rapid expansion of its student population. But this was difficult due to the challenge posed by the fact that the campuses of the amalgamated institutions were located in a large geographical area and were often far apart. To provide lectures to students located in different campuses, a recording system was put in place for students to listen to the lectures if they were unable to travel to be physically present. There were also, of course, tutorials where face-to-face teaching took place, but still I had to present my lectures to a large student audience that was only going to have access to the recordings—and indeed would never have met me in person, since the large numbers of students meant that teaching relied on assistants. Daunted by this present/absent audience, I decided to write my lectures. Or, rather, because I did not have the time to write them fully, I had to structure each lecture around a series of quotations that I annotated and then synthesized during the lectures. In 2010, as I was repeating the course, these lecture notes became a complete first draft of *Sovereignty and Its Other*. The notes provided the textual analysis of the book. Meanwhile, having to present lectures that would have been accessible to students listening to them on their iPods, I had to construct a narrative voice that was different from the seminar environment that I was more used to. This voice was instrumental in the rapid writing of the manuscript between July and November of that year.

It is not because of the healthy, even philosophical, irreverence toward institutions advocated by Spinoza—a crucial figure in the book—that I cannot thank the university as such for this book. It is rather because institutions are made from the people working in them, and I was very fortunate to be surrounded by stimulating colleagues. I would like to thank, then, Chris Fleming and Chris Peterson, Judith Snodgrass and Anthony Uhlmann, Allison Weir and Jessica Whyte, Cristina Rocha and George Morgan, Gail Jones and Magdalena Zolkos, Charles Barbour, and Alex Ling, and Paul Alberts and Tim Rowse. I also thank Peter Hutchings and Mike Atherton for the institution's support in the arduous editing of the draft manuscript in 2011. I am grateful also to Norma Lam-Saw for assistance with the manuscript and for her insights.

Presenting parts of the book at different research seminars, I was very fortunate to discover a challenging and demanding community of scholars with whom I let my ideas contend. For this privilege I can mention here the following: Kiarina Kordela, Cesare Casarino, and John Mowitt; Stathis Gourgouris, Gil Anidjar, and Andreas Kalyvas; Eleanor Kaufman and Amir Mufti; Justin Clemens; Arthur Jacobson, Peter Goodrich, and Stanley Fish; Peg Birmingham, David Pellauer, and Tina Chanter; Peter Fenves and Bonnie Honig. Andrew Benjamin supported the development of the ideas in too many ways to enumerate, but primarily by being *the* most challenging and demanding audience of my arguments.

The decision to actually write the book was made possible by Helen Tartar, who strongly encouraged me to embark on this project. The conception of the book took place while I was enjoying the generous hospitality of Tina Weller and Flemming Lembech. The actual writing of the book was influenced primarily by two people. The first is Alexis Vardoulakis, my son. I can still point to the sections of the book that were written during my trips to see him in Melbourne. The other is Amanda Third. Her generosity of intellect and spirit enriches both my thought and my life.

SOVEREIGNTY AND ITS OTHER

PREAMBLE, OR POWER AND ITS RELATIONS

The present examination of sovereignty rests on the axiom that the operation of sovereign power consists in the justification of violence. Justification is determined—for reasons that will become clear later—in terms of a means-and-ends relation.[1] Thus the question that structures the present study entails that both a descriptive and a normative extrapolation of sovereignty are outside its purview. Rather, the examination of sovereignty proceeds through the construction of a relational ontology of power that interrogates the way that means relate to the ends of power. The thesis I defend is that there are two distinct forms of relation.[2] The first, sovereignty, consists in different modalities of the justification of violence. The second is a kind of relation that is incommensurable with a means-and-ends relation and hence cannot be reduced to justification. This relation is democracy, the other of sovereignty.

An important reason for examining sovereignty through such a relational ontology of power is that such an approach mediates on an ambiguity that seems to suggest that there are two incompatible ways of propounding a theory of sovereignty. The first concentrates on the epochal differences that structure power, whereas the second endeavors to derive a logic of power without a reliance on chronological ruptures. A rapprochement between these two different approaches is requisite to delineate sovereignty's relation to its other—namely, democracy. Or, more emphatically, a relational ontology of sovereign power incorporates both a typology of sovereign power—distinctions can be drawn as to how the means-and-ends relation of justification operates—and a logic of sovereignty that distinguishes it from democracy. I will present some of the salient features of the relational ontology of power by starting with the distinction between the two approaches to sovereignty. This will lead us to show how justification can be understood as a means-and-end relation, as well as to how sovereignty is distinguished from democracy.

The most prominent philosopher to have adopted the first, epochal approach to sovereignty is Michel Foucault.[3] His archaeologies of sovereignty rely on separating classical power from disciplinary power and then from biopower and so on.[4] This approach also permeates the vast majority of the literature on sovereignty from political science and international relations.[5] This is not to discount the significant diversity of views in the approach that concentrates on different epochal determinations of power. For instance, one of the most commonly held views in this approach is that sovereignty is a modern configuration of power whose main principle is the separation of national from international politics—or internal from external power.[6] The corollary to this view is that sovereignty is power exercised by the state.[7] This view is almost axiomatic in international relations, but it is not shared by Foucault. So what I have referred to as the "epochal" approach does include a wide variety of often competing perspectives.

Jacques Derrida and Giorgio Agamben have been the most prominent proponents in the past couple of decades of the approach that seeks to identify a logic of sovereignty. In *Rogues* Derrida identifies "ipseity," or the self-referentiality of one power, as the main characteristic of sovereignty.[8] In the lectures published as *The Beast and the Sovereign*, the figure of animality is identified as the other that animates sovereignty's power.[9] Agamben observes that Roman law defined subjectivity in relation to sovereignty as "*homo sacer*," or the division of the individual into a political and a biological part. He contends that this same division applies diachronically, from Aristotle's separation of *bios* and *zoe* to the contemporary biopolitical world.[10] The provenance of these attempts to discover a logic of power may not be strictly speaking Friedrich Nietzsche, but Nietzsche's work has been instrumental in propagating this approach. One crucial feature of this approach is that power—and hence sovereignty—are not confined to the state.[11] Rather, as Georges Bataille showed in his influential *The Accursed Share*, power is a matter of "economy," or the sets of relations that permeate community and sociality.[12]

There have been some attempts at a rapprochement of these two approaches to sovereign power.[13] The most important is Michael Hardt and Antonio Negri's *Empire*.[14] Hardt and Negri both develop a historical typology of sovereignty and argue that the different forms of sovereign power rely on a single logic—namely, repression of the creative forces in society or the "multitude." The crucial common denominator of their typology and their logic of sovereignty is the distinction between constituent and constituted power.[15] They offer illuminating insights based on this distinction, but ultimately their logic requires constituent power to overcome constituted power. The "multitude" is expected to rise above, take over, and thereby abolish government—in Hardt and Negri's words, "the multitude banishes sovereignty from politics."[16] This proffers a vision of an occlusion to power. I criticize elsewhere such a utopian conclusion.[17] Suffice it to say that I seek to avoid such an occlusion of power in the present book. To do so it is necessary to construct a logic of sovereign power that, unlike Hardt and Negri, does not depart from the opposition between constituted and constituent power.

The rapprochement that I am proposing here develops a logic of power that derives from an insight at the beginning of Walter Benjamin's "Critique of Violence."[18] Benjamin notes that power, or violence (*Gewalt*), can best be described through the way that the law relates to justice or, in other words, in terms of how violence is justified.[19] He further describes the relation of law and justice as a means-and-end relation: "If justice is the criterion of ends, legality is that of means."[20] Investigating sovereignty in terms of justification in general or the justification of violence in particular is nothing new.[21] And even though it is less recognized, articulating legality and justice as a means-and-ends relation is not particularly novel, either— for instance, we will see later that Spinoza, a crucial figure for this book, had arrived at a similar conception.[22] The novelty in Benjamin's argument consists rather in combining these two insights in order to draw distinctions about how power operates—moreover, distinctions that allow for a typology of power. Specifically, the central characteristic of modern conceptions of power is the privileging of means over the ends: "the central place [in this study] is given to the question of the justification of certain means that constitute violence," writes Benjamin in order to delimit his article to the study of power or violence in modernity.[23] Thus Benjamin implicitly asserts that the privileging of legality—or what he refers to as "positive law"—is the essential characteristic of modern power.

Benjamin's articulation of the justification of violence through the use of a means-(law) and-ends (justice) relation can be expanded to provide a typology of power based on the ways in which such a means-and-ends relation is articulated. If the relation of means toward ends is the defining feature of modern power, then there can be two further modalities of power. In particular, there can be a power where the end justifies the means—that is, the reverse of the modern conception of power. I will argue here that this relation characterizes ancient sovereignty. Further, there can be a power that is characterized by a perceived lack of ends, or more precisely, by a justification of means with reference to further means. The present book refers to this kind of power as biopolitics. Schematically, the typology of relations of power that I derive from Benjamin's essay will unfold as follows:[24]

In Chapter 2 I argue that *ancient sovereignty* privileges the end over the means. For instance, Augustine argues in *The City of God* that the aim of mankind is to enter the "city of God." The "pagans," however, hinder the "pilgrims" from achieving this just end. Therefore, Augustine argues, violence is justified against the pagans. In other words, the end (entry into the "city of God") justifies laws and institutions that function as the means to that end, including the exercise of violence against those who are opposed to that end. *The end justifies the means.*

Chapters 3 and 4 will show that *modern sovereignty* reverses the relation between means and end. When Machiavelli writes in Chapter XVIII of *The Prince* that a prince observing moral rules may be honorable, but will thereby lose power, he is not simply granting license for the exercise of unlimited violence. Rather, he provides a different justification of power—namely, that the sovereign must use the laws and institutions of the state to remain in power. The means (law and institutions) justify the end (the just aim of the perpetuation of sovereignty). In other words, it is just for the state to desire its self-perpetuation because *the means justify the end.*[25]

Biopolitical sovereignty was a term coined by Foucault in *Society Must Be Defended* to describe, as I will outline in Chapter 5, the exercise of power through the control of populations. Biopolitics justifies itself in terms of the betterment of the lives of the people. With biopolitics issues such as the control of sexuality become central to the operations of power, as Foucault's unfinished project on the history of sexuality makes clear. Biopolitics blurs the distinction between means and ends. For instance, sexuality is not regulated primarily by creating new laws, but through campaigns that aim to change how people think and act. Biopolitics describes a dispersed sovereign power that *blurs the distinction between means and ends.*

Understanding sovereign power in terms of the justification of violence, where justification is explicated in terms of a means-and-ends relation, enables a rapprochement of the two approaches to sovereignty. The logic of sovereignty is one of justification, whereas its typology is given by the differential relation between means and ends. The corollary to this rapprochement is that the three modalities of justification—ancient, modern, and biopolitical—can be distinguished, but not separated. Ultimately, as it will be argued throughout the book, this means that the three modalities of justification do not exclude one another, but rather are mutually supportive. This is a crucial point, since it makes possible a thinking of power without being based on a logic of justification—indeed, as I will argue shortly, the possibility of democratic judgment depends on recognizing that the different modalities of justification are distinct, yet inseparable.

We can represent the mutual support of the three modalities of sovereign justification in the form of a triangle—or the "trinity of justification," as it will be called in Chapter 1. Each corner of the triangle indicates the privileged point of each form of justification (see figure on p. 6). The different forms of sovereignty indicate the direction in which justification proceeds. Thus ancient justification proceeds from end to means, whereas modern justification moves from means to end. A central thesis of the present study is that justification as such includes all three points of the triangle. The three modalities of justification—ancient, modern, and biopolitical—are mutually supportive. Or, more emphatically, the three justifications are *cosupponible.*

I will use the concept of the "neighbor" to illustrate in rough brushstrokes the cosupponibility of the three modalities of justification. As I will argue in Chapter 2, ancient sovereignty culminates in the universalism propagated by Christianity. One of the crucial figures in this context is Paul. His injunction to "love thy neighbor" is not merely a law, but rather the justice that underlies any sense of legality. As Freud observes in *Civilization and Its Discontents,* such a sense of neighborly love functions as a justification of violence.[26] Violence is inevitable, since Paul's logic relies on

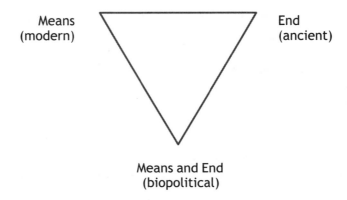

Means
(modern)

End
(ancient)

Means and End
(biopolitical)

a dichotomy between "us" who love and "them" who do not: "They which are the children of the flesh, these [are] not the children of God" (*Romans* 9:8). If neighborly love creates a community under God, those who have earthly desires are excluded from that community. It is a small step from here to more systematic elaborations of just war—it is simply a matter of developing a system that defines what the "flesh" is. Notions of nationalism can be understood as the transfiguration of the Christian neighborly love into the modern justification of violence. Modern sovereignty can privilege the realm of means or legality because of the insistence on the independence of a state from other states or of the separation between one state's system of laws and another system of laws in modernity. The universalism of neighborly love is now constrained within the borders of a nation state. Thus the fellow citizens who share the same ethnic and/ or religious identity now become the territorially determined neighbors, and their other is now the foreigner. With the advent of "postmodernity" and high capitalism, territorial integrity is undermined. From the perspective of biopower, ethnic and/or religious identity is no longer the essential criterion that determines one's neighbor. Rather, now the criteria are being constructed through the control of populations—or what Hardt and Negri call a "right to police."[27] From health to housing to work, conduct is regulated, and whoever deviates from the justified norm is no longer a neighbor. The figure of the "smoker" can be taken as an example of biopolitical control of conduct. Smoking is regulated on the grounds that it is harmful to personal and public health. The ban on smoking extends across public spaces, across territorial borders—no smoking is allowed on airplanes—and even to private places—for instance, the state of Tasmania in Australia recently prohibited smoking in the presence of minors, even in one's private home.[28]

A number of inferences can be drawn from the different configurations of the neighbor according to ancient, modern, and biopolitical forms of justification. First, violence is justified by identifying someone who is not a neighbor—someone who is other. Differently put, there is a logic of sovereignty that relies on the justification of violence. Second, the other can be determined in different ways. The logic of sovereignty can be expressed in three different modalities. Third, the three different modalities of the justification of violence are distinct, but they do not preclude each other. Paul's "children of the flesh," the "foreigner" of the nationalist discourse, and the "smoker" of biopower have a family resemblance, which is not merely a lapse into identity politics.[29] Rather, it moves toward a relational ontology of sovereignty according to which one modality of justification does not preclude either of the other two modalities. The "smoker" can be castigated not simply on health grounds. Smoking can also be constructed as a marker of identity—it is "these foreigners" who smoke more than "us." Or smoking can be linked to immoral behavior—to the sin of lusting after earthly pleasures or the sin of harming (not loving) others.

The mutual support of the three forms of justification as a result of asserting both a typology of sovereign power and a logic internal to it is indispensable in recognizing the other of sovereignty. To say simply that the sovereignty's other is he or she against whom violence is justified is not really to say very much. The cosupponibility of the different modalities of justification entails that potentially—if not de facto—everyone can be positioned as the other. The multifarious forms of justification can be applied to every situation. Sovereignty is omnipresent because being a subject means being subjectable to violence.[30] Consequently, a form of relating that does not privilege justification—the other to sovereignty—cannot be sought simply in the other that sovereignty subjects, precisely because everyone is subjectable. Instead, the other of sovereignty has to be sought in how its logic is disrupted by altering its defining relation—that is, justification. It is this disruption of justification that is called here judgment, which is a different kind of relation, as I will argue in Chapter 1. In addition, judgment is understood as the defining feature of democracy. In this sense, democracy is the other of sovereignty.

Without a recognition of the cosupponibility of the different modalities of justification—or a recognition that sovereignty can assume three forms—judgment cannot counter justification. I will illustrate this point with a specific example: namely, the Australian government's justification of violent actions against refugees as it was expressed at the height of the debate in the lead-up to the 2001 general elections. The anti-refugee stance of the incumbent Liberal government was encapsulated in Prime Minister John Howard's statement, made for the first time on October 28, 2001: "We will decide who comes to this country and the circumstances in which they come."[31] This statement summarized the government's attitude to asylum seekers arriving by boat and was regularly repeated during the rest of Howard's tenure as prime minister. By adjusting the emphasis this statement can be used to justify the government's violence against asylum seekers in accordance with the three modalities of justification that correspond to the three forms of sovereignty—ancient, modern, and biopolitical. As I will demonstrate, each modality of justification can be countered individually, but sovereignty can still slip from one form to another. To interrupt justification and to arrive at the possibility of judgment, the logic of justification as such must be countered.

The most obvious meaning of the statement "we will decide who comes to this country and the circumstances in which they come" is the assertion of territorial sovereignty. A sovereign nation must retain control of its borders. This corresponds to the modern justification of violence—those who enter illegally are subject to punishment. Hence the government called the refugees "illegal immigrants." The main argument to counter this form of justification relies on human rights. According to the Geneva Convention, a refugee is a person who is subject to prosecution on political or religious grounds in his country of origin.[32] Australia, as a signatory to the convention, is obliged to provide asylum to refugees. Therefore, from a legal perspective, the asylum seekers posed no challenge to the border integrity of Australia. An argument based on the rights of the refugees can deal with the claim about the undermining of Australian sovereignty where sovereignty is understood in the modern sense.

Confronted with the rights discourse, power can shift to a justification of means through an end—that is, to ancient sovereignty. In fact, the statement "we will decide who comes to this country and the circumstances in which they come" was mobilized in precisely this manner. Three weeks before Howard made this statement, the infamous "children overboard affair" had unfolded. A sinking boat carrying asylum seekers was rescued by the Australian navy on October 6, 2001. The government released photos of children in the ocean, purporting that their parents threw them in the water so as to be rescued by the navy, thereby effectively reaching Australian territory. Although it was later revealed that children were not actually thrown overboard, the rhetoric of not wanting to take into Australia "the kind of people who put their children in danger" was widely used by the Howard government.[33] The condemnation of exposing one's children to harm became a moral denouncement of all refugees who were seeking passage to Australian shores on leaky boats. Behaving in such a way was explicitly framed as "unaustralian." This posited an end, "australianess," that was used to aggravate fears about the potential of a large wave of refugees on Australia's northern doorstep to inundate the country and corrupt its moral substance. This justification was used in direct contravention to the Refugee Convention in order to transport asylum seekers to a remote Pacific island, where they were effectively incarcerated while their refugee claims were processed. A response to this moralizing justification was provided by the "We are all boat people" campaign.[34] The campaign concentrated on dispelling the myths about refugees—for instance, by publicizing the facts of the "children overboard affair" as well as by challenging the perception that it is "unaustralian" to arrive by boat to Australia. However, debunking the moralistic argument directly could not deal with a third modality of justification.

This biopolitical justification of the violence exercised against the refugees interpreted the statement "we will decide who comes to this country and the circumstances in which they come" from the perspective of regulation. The asylum seekers arriving on boats in order to reach Australian shores were termed "queue jumpers." They were portrayed as too impatient to await their turn to be processed offshore. Their supposed disdain of the norm was magnified to inflate yet more fears about refugees as a threat to a smoothly functioning Australian system of regulation—for instance, by making claims on the welfare system, thereby asking the Australian taxpayer to "reward" them for their impatience and dismissiveness. Again, it is not difficult to counter such biopolitical justifications of violence against the refugees with facts. For instance, the Australian government had to expend much more significant resources to establish the various detention centers for refugees than it would have needed to care for their welfare. However, sovereignty would counter such arguments by reverting to either the modern or the ancient form of justification. Thus, it was claimed, the detention centers were "sending a message" that Australia is serious about the protection of its borders and that the Australian government was concerned to preserve the "fair dinkum" Australian way of life. The slippage among the three distinct modalities of justification was so rapid in the political speech around that time that the public rhetoric completely obscured their distinction. Ultimately it is that slippage itself that guards justification—a slippage that is symptomatic of the cosupponibility of justifications that protects sovereignty.

Justification, as I will argue throughout the book and as the above example illustrates, can be disrupted only by adopting a double strategy. First, it is necessary to distinguish and counter the three modalities of justification in any specific case. I call this judgment "dejustification." The strength of dejustification resides in concentrating on the specific—the particularity of the case or the detail of the argument. In this sense dejustification has a particular historical character that allows it to tackle the distinct modalities of justification. Its limitation is that it does not account sufficiently for the slippage of justification—the cosupponibility of the three modalities of justification. For this a different kind of judgment is needed: what I call "democratic judgment." This concentrates on showing that the function of all modalities of justification is the same—namely, the justification of violence. The role of the democratic judgment is to describe forms of commonality that counter violence. The basis of the democratic judgment is welcoming of the other as a way of disrupting the cycle of sovereign justification.

The rapprochement of the two approaches to sovereignty—the epochal approach that leads to the distinction of different forms of sovereignty and the approach that identifies a logic of sovereignty—achieves its full significance at this point. The rapprochement of the two approaches to sovereignty shows that the two kinds of judgment are in fact the way that judgment is registered in response to the two different approaches to sovereignty. Dejustification responds to the distinction between the different modalities of justification, while the democratic judgment counters the justification of violence that indicates the logic of sovereignty. This double aspect of judgment is recognized, *mutatis mutandi*, by Jacques Derrida in an address to

Pantion University in Athens.[35] Derrida identifies an unconditional thought that he associates with freedom and the democratic imperative to hospitality and the welcoming of the other. The unconditional is distinguished from sovereignty's assertion of frontiers and of the processes that identify the foreigner. Derrida acknowledges that the unconditionality of a free, democratic thought and the absolute power of sovereignty resemble each other. This leads to the question of how it is possible to distinguish them. "It is ultimately [because of] a theologico-political history of power," answers Derrida.[36] According to Derrida, then, the logic of sovereignty that operates through justifying the violence against whoever is deemed to be a stranger is interknitted with the historicity of the concept of power that has led to the formation of the modern concept of sovereignty. Thus any democratic thought, or the unconditional, in Derrida's terms, has to do two things at once: to assert the freedom of hospitality, but also, in tandem, to do so while being mindful of the theologico-political history that determines sovereignty. The former corresponds to the kind of relation to the other that I call democratic judgment, and the latter to the kind of relation opposed to the various modalities of justification that I call dejustification.

How is it possible, then, to make a choice between sovereignty and democracy? Are there any criteria that will help us decide between the two? Framed this way the questions are misleading, because they imply two things. First, they imply that it is possible to have democracy without sovereignty, judgment without justification. Nowhere in this book do I make such a claim. The reason is that I regard as the ultimate utopian illusion to believe in a politics where the justification of violence will be de facto completely eliminated. Second, they imply that a choice or decision is possible, presumably because of some preestablished, secure rule or law that dictates right from wrong. I regard this moralistic desire for secure criteria as a corollary to the aforementioned political utopia. Instead, the questions can be answered by making two observations. First, if it is in practice impossible to definitely separate democracy from sovereignty, then there is all the more reason to remain vigilant and proactive in exercising judgments. Democracy requires that endless task. Second, part of this task is the recognition that sovereignty's absoluteness—that is, its circularity and self-referentiality that articulates itself through the cosupponibility of the different modalities of justification—this absoluteness that appears to present sovereignty as omnipotent is, in fact, an assertion of the inferior position of justification in relation to judgment.[37] The reason is that it is only in order to avoid judgment that the logic of sovereignty lapses into slippage, allowing for the cosupponibility of justifications. This slippage is a defensive tactic against judgment. Obscuring judgment is sovereignty's only chance in perpetuating the operation of its logic. Or, differently put, it is only because of its other, democracy, that sovereignty can operate. Thus it is not a question of what prevails—democracy or sovereignty, judgment or justification—but rather of describing the ways that sovereignty dissimulates its reactive stance against democracy. The task is to recognize sovereignty's reactive relation to democracy. Another name for this endless task is "judgment."

1

JUDGMENT AND JUSTIFICATION

JUSTIFICATION OR JUDGMENT?

The distinction between judgment and justification points to the aporetic link between law and justice at the heart of the concept of sovereignty. The reason that a delineation of the relation between law and justice is needed for a conceptualization of sovereignty is that there is no sovereignty without the establishment and exercise of a legal framework. But law for its part requires justice because, as Walter Benjamin succinctly expressed it as the axiomatic principle of his critique of power (*Gewalt*), "the most elementary relationship within any legal system is that of ends to means."[1] It may be that the end is conceived of as co-terminus with its enactment—that the justice of sovereignty is the imposition of its power. Or, alternatively, the legal framework may be conceived of as being reliant upon and defending a preexisting just foundation, such as the blood ties of a nation, the progress of civilization, or the welfare of the people. These two conceptions of sovereignty—as either an executive power on its own right or as a power executing some preexisting foundational right—both presuppose that any body of laws that forms into a system such as a state that aspires toward justice relies on a pursuit of means toward certain ends. This coordination of legal means and just ends can also be expressed in a different way— namely, as the immediate connection between law and justice. Justification signifies that immediate connection, as well as the rhetorical, conceptual, and technoscientific discourses that support it in theory and in practice.

Judgment, on the contrary, will be described here as the severing or interruption of the immediate connection between law and justice. Two elements are necessary in order to grasp the interruptive power of judgment. First, one must discern the ways that law and justice are first separated in order subsequently to create a narrative that immediately connects them. This process of separation and connection, exclusion and inclusion can take different guises, a typology of which will be offered in this book. It is crucial to recognize that these exclusions and inclusions assume a means-and-ends relation—that is, the form of justification. As already intimated, the means-and-ends relation is constitutive of a determination of justice. Judgment performs a critique of this logic of sovereign justification. Judgment interrogates the discourses and the narratives that both create and support justification. For it is an axiom of the present study that justification is never natural, but rather always created, generated out of human interaction and community, and hence always historical and transformable. The logic of sovereign justification is always an articulation whose various rhetorical strategies need to be transformed through critique. To the extent that judgment proffers a critique of justification's immediate connection between law and justice by recognizing its instrumental presupposition and its narrative aspect, judgment can be here provisionally described as the power of dejustification. It will be argued throughout the present study that dejustification deconstructs particular instances of the logic of sovereignty and its justificatory articulations.

Judgment, in addition, has a positive function—namely, it makes possible democracy and justice, where justice is no longer understood as immediately connected to law. Judgment presents justice as disjunct from law and expressed in such narratives that free themselves from justification. Through an alternative understanding of justice, it will be possible also to consider how the democratic can be constructed. It will be argued that democracy is profoundly related to the enactment of judgment. The relation between judgment and democracy is introduced by a host of questions about how to regard the other. How does one dispense of one's democratic responsibility toward one's fellows citizens? How are determined the limits of what is allowed to be expressed in public discourse? How to deal with those who do not belong to the sovereign state? An answer to such questions would be to argue that sovereignty draws its legitimacy by instituting rational procedures that protect the rights of its citizens, establish freedom of speech, and deal respectfully with those foreigners who respect the sovereignty of the state and international law. This determination of the other under the condition of the law of sovereignty encounters, however, a persistent obstacle. What if the other has inimical intentions? This is a major problem for the understanding of democracy since ancient Athens. To grasp its complexity and magnitude, I can simply indicate here that the problem of the enmity of the other is merely displaced when it is dealt with in terms of international relations between sovereign states. The reason is that enmity can also be internal, as Aristotle recognizes in the fifth book of his *Politics*.[2] Even more dramatically, enmity manifests itself between members of the same family, as is shown by the fratricidal narratives—of, for instance, Cain and Abel or Romulus and Remus—that seek to account for the genesis of the political.[3] There are two ways of responding to this problem that correspond to the distinction between justification and judgment. To determine democracy by justifying its legality, the other—as the fellow citizen, as the voice of a dissenting opinion, and as the foreigner—is welcomed within the sovereign state under certain conditions determined by law. There are norms linked to universality that are the means to identify the correct legal avenue of dealing with the other. These norms aspire to the order, peace, and stability of the state. (I will expand on the universality of "order, peace, and stability" shortly.) Ultimately, justification consists in the identification of the subject that threatens order, peace, and stability—the identification of the enemy—and the use of violence against them. Conversely, judgment can be defined as the understanding of the other in such a way as to not be regarded as an enemy. Judgment is not the application of prefabricated criteria on given situations, but rather the process that transforms enmity. The possibility of democracy depends on not regarding the other as an enemy. This does not mean, naively, that enmity and violence are to disappear. Rather, it means that for democracy to come into play, the universal is the other. Hence it is by responding to the other that justice is possible.

Before proceeding any further I need to clarify the connection between democracy and judgment. There are well-known theories of democracy that do not conform to the notion of judgment that I am developing here, but rather are related to justification. In terms of political theory in the past few decades, the best-known exemplars of this approach are theories of deliberative democracy. The work of John Rawls, Seyla Benhabib, and Jürgen Habermas spring here to mind. Despite the differences among these theorists, what they all have in common is a commitment to the exercise of reason as the basis of claims to legitimacy. Legality is conceived in such a way as to open up a space where the giving of reasons is linked to the creation and maintenance of institutions that function as guarantees of popular sovereignty. This link is described as a procedure or, in the vocabulary I am using here, as justification: it is the immediate connection between the means (deliberation) and the end (legitimacy). In other words, deliberative democracy understands law and justice as connected, whereas the starting point of this study is that the link between law and justice is aporetic because the two are separated and reunited in ways that reveal the dispositif of power. Thus the perspective adopted here—namely, the necessity of sustaining the disjunction between law and justice—is incompatible with deliberative democracy. But there is also a second significant difference that pertains to an aspect of theories of deliberative democracy that has also attracted significant criticism—namely, the way that interpretation figures in the giving of reasons and in the processes of legitimation. For instance, in reintroducing a Heideggerian perspective to the debate, Nikolas Kompridis has argued that claims to legitimacy are still underwritten by the creation of meaning.[4] Reason is not autonomous, but rather supported by narratives of justification. Taking into account such criticism, my own approach pays close attention to the rhetorical strategies employed in the formation of justifications. Thus methodologically it is incompatible with the model of deliberative democracy. Instead of engaging directly with theorists of deliberative democracy, I have opted instead to interrogate the idea of justification by giving it a historical grounding—for reasons that I will be explaining shortly.

Some of the most significant figures that have influenced the idea of democracy as it will be presented in this book are opposed to theories of sovereignty as justification. These are political theorists of agonistic or plural democracy, such as Ernesto Laclau, Chantal Mouffe, William Connolly, and Bonnie Honig, as well as philosophers such as Michel Foucault, Gilles Deleuze, Jean-François Lyotard, Antonio Negri, and Jacques Derrida. There are two features that are common in the works of these figures and that play an important role in the thinking that develops in this book. First, there is a recognition that legitimation is not a sufficient ground for sovereignty. For instance, what Hardt and Negri call the "juridical tradition" simply presupposes legitimation and fails to ask for its value for the political.[5] A forceful critique of legitimacy was already developed by Carl

Schmitt in the early twentieth century.[6] And even if it led Schmitt to shy away from developing a theory of democracy and to interpret sovereignty in terms of a theory of dictatorship, still his critique of legitimacy contains *in nuce* an agonistic notion of democracy, as Andreas Kalyvas has perspicaciously shown.[7] Second, and just as importantly, all these theorists pay attention, in one way or another, to rhetoric, expression, judgment, to all various kinds of strategies employed not so much to deductively reason, but rather to persuade and convince in the public realm. In other words, what matters for them is not only reason, but also its other side—the irrational that is just as constitutive of the political. The recognition that the political processes that generate meaning, understanding, and interpretation are never fully rational was already acknowledged by Aristotle, who defined rhetoric as moving in the opposite direction (*antistrophos*) of dialectic.[8] Because the theorists mentioned have paid close attention not only to institutions and law formation, but also and primarily to how power represents itself, it is a common feature of their approach to use art and literature in order to analyze power.[9] It is not as an homage to this methodology, but due to a conviction of the ineradicability of interpretation, that the present study of sovereignty turns to four literary works—Sophocles's *Antigone*, Shakespeare's *Hamlet*, Heinrich von Kleist's *Michael Kohlhaas*, and J. M. Coetzee's *Life and Times of Michael K*—in order to perform critiques of political theorists.[10]

One objection needs to be forestalled. Is it not self-contradictory to object to the space of reasons using reason? And how is it possible to negate justification—that is, the giving of reasons—without presupposing an alternative justification and hence an alternative basis of justification, even if that remains unstated, hidden, dissimulated? In other words, what justifies the rejection of justification? What can be the criteria of judgment against justification? The response to such questions points to one of the unanswerable questions of democracy—namely, the question of what is proper democratic speech. Democracy is agonistic only so long as it maintains responsiveness, and hence responsibility to the other cannot be assimilated—and that includes justification. This means that judgment is not the opposite of justification. Judgment is not a determinate negation of justification.[11] Instead, judgment is distinct from justification precisely because it adopts a different attitude to its other. Chantal Mouffe has aptly expressed this point by saying that "the aim of democratic politics is to transform an 'antagonism' into an 'agonism.'"[12] The other is not rejected, but rather allowed to have its voice.

The two main aspects of judgment are dejustification as an engagement with and deconstruction of acts of justification and the acceptance of otherness as a manifestation of the democratic. Before I can expand on these two aspects of judgment, a clearer determination of justification is needed. For this I will use the figure of discomfort because it allows for an extrapolation of how particular acts of justification rely on an immediate connection between law and justice, or means and ends. It is necessary to delineate the immediacy that characterizes sovereignty and its various modalities of justification prior to examining how dejustification can deconstruct them.

SOVEREIGN DISCOMFORT: THE IMMEDIACY OF JUSTIFICATION

It was a routine presidential visit to a school, Booker Elementary, on an autumn Tuesday morning to promote children's literacy. In front of the lined-up cameras, George W. Bush was listening to pupils reading stories when unexpectedly his chief of staff, Andrew Card, entered the room, walked up to the president and whispered in his ear. This lasted only a few seconds, but the message conveyed—that a passenger plane had crashed into the World Trade Center—left the president decidedly puzzled, with a clear demeanor of discomfort. As the saying goes (and I will be returning to this saying from different perspectives), "the rest is history": the announcement of a "war on terror" in order to defend values such as freedom and democracy, the "preemptive strikes" against sovereign nations in the Middle East that were deemed to be threats to the West, and the countering of the panic about additional attacks with the introduction of draconian laws that increased the powers of policing. The figure of sovereign discomfort can explain how sovereignty uses justification to establish a nexus of means and ends—an immediate connection between law and justice.

There are three important aspects in the way that the immediate relation between law and justice is posited through the justification that followed on from the moment of sovereign discomfort. The first consists in that, by controlling the relation of law and justice, sovereignty claims a monopoly on violence. This does not have to be "explicit" violence.[13] Violence can take several guises, including violence against the law, or the suspension of the law in the service of a just cause. Carl Schmitt expressed this succinctly in the famous first sentence of his *Political Theology*: "Sovereign is he who decides on the exception."[14] The sovereign authority appears or emerges by being able to act out in exceptionally dangerous circumstances that cannot be circumscribed within the law. In other words, sovereignty exists only so long as a violence against the lawful existence of a state is possible *and* so long as this threat can be answered by acting violently, including doing violence to the law, in order to defend the state. The structure that constitutes the justification of sovereign violence is one of violence against violence, of force against force, or of one anti- or super-legal authority against another authority that is outside the law. In other words, the monopoly on violence that sovereignty seeks to justify consists in the inscription of violence at the limit that signifies legality's reach—but always in the name of and for the sake of the law that defines that limit. The sovereign is said to be above the law in the sense of both grounding legality and transcending its limits.[15]

This reliance on the law instead of an inherent justice entails that the sovereign monopoly on violence is never justified in itself. After that morning of September 11, the U.S. administration did not go to the United Nations or to the Security Council requesting a license for the exercise of violence as such. Nor has there ever existed a theory of sovereignty that justifies violence for the sake of violence. The justification of violence never posits violence as a universal value. Instead, violence is always posited as a response to exceptional circumstances, a reaction to something unpredictable that places sovereignty in a position of discomfort. We will see later that Heinrich von Kleist is well aware of this point in *Michael Kohlhaas*, where every sovereign decision is preceded by involuntary signs of discomfort, such as the blushing of the holder of power. This point is also clearly acknowledged by Carl Schmitt, who defines the exception thus: "The exception, which is not codified in the existing legal order, can at best be characterized as a case of extreme peril, a danger to the existence of the state, or the like. But it cannot be circumscribed factually and made to conform to a preformed law."[16] The danger that calls for a violent reaction arises out of *the* law in the sense that it is a reaction to the threat to the existence of the state as the guarantor of legality. But it can never arise out of *a* law in the sense that the exception points to the limit of legality; it is extralegal—which also means that it can never be codified in rule; it can never be universalized; it is always historical. (Hence the violence that was justified after the president's discomfort was historical—the "rest" was indeed "history." There is no such a thing as an "end" to history.) The extralegal is related to justice through violence only ever instrumentally—it is always the means for the attainment of pragmatic goals on the historical plane. Violence can only ever provide a justification of means.

The second aspect is that the justification of sovereign violence takes order, peace, and stability as the universal. To return to our example, the sovereign discomfort captured on camera that Tuesday morning at Booker Elementary resulted in an appeal to the community of sovereign nations as well as to international institutions such as the United Nations and the Security Council to use violence against particular states so as to ensure that order is restored. "Order, peace, and stability" is the comfort of the sovereign discomfort. I will use in this study the syntagm "order, peace, and stability" to signify the universal aspect in the justification of sovereignty. This is not to say that order, peace, and stability are actually universal. Instead, as I will demonstrate, order, peace, and stability take specific historical determinations, often by configuring the three substantives—order, peace, and stability—in different ways. For instance, since the Enlightenment there have been two predominant ways to conceive of peace as a universal. Following Kant, peace may be conceived of as an ideal that becomes the guiding principle of a politics that aspires toward universal order and stability.[17] According to this approach the instrumentalism that characterizes violence is overcome. If violence is a means toward the attainment of a goal, then peace is the "absolute," as Hannah Arendt calls it, that suspends violence's instrumentalism.[18] Conversely, the instrumentalism of violence, or enmity, as Carl Schmitt calls it, can be thought to support order and stability between sovereign states: "[A] world in which the possibility of war is utterly eliminated, a completely pacified globe, would be a world without the distinction of friend and enemy and hence a world without politics."[19] The political is violent, instrumental, and historical because, according to Schmitt, the political cannot be translated into a universal value. There is either universal peace or universal order and stability. Regardless of the different determinations of peace in these two formulations, peace is conceived of as a universal.[20] And this means that peace aspires to be ahistorical, transcending the tumult of *Realpolitik*. If violence is the justification of means, the universal—order, peace, and stability—aspires to a justification of ends.[21] The justification of means and the justification of ends need to be separate for justification to show their immediate connection.

And yet the justification of means can never be completely separated from the justification of ends. For instance, according to Hardt and Negri, biopolitics is the configuration that best represents peace as a universal ideal: "although the practice of Empire is continually bathed in blood, the concept of Empire is always dedicated to peace—a perpetual and universal peace outside of history."[22] Hardt and Negri suggest that the violence of practice and the peace of the universal are not as easily separated as either a Kantian cosmopolitanism or a Schmittian decisionism would have liked to assume. The instrumentalism of violence and the ideal toward which it aspires or that it denies are in fact imbricated. It is the condition of universal peace that is itself "bathed in blood." If what follows Bush's discomfort is a cycle of violence, if "the rest is history," still that instrumentalism requires an image of universality so justification can come into play. The U.S. administration appealed to other sovereign nations in the name of humanity as well as to institutions, such as the United Nations, whose function is enshrined as the defense of universal human rights, in order to garner support for its "war on terror." This does not simply mean, as Leo Strauss has argued, that universalism, especially in the form of rights, is ineliminable.[23] More accurately, it entails that the separation of the instrumental and its end, of history and transcendence, of the pragmatic and the universal—ultimately, of violence and peace—is in fact impossible. For instance, Derrida has shown in *The Politics of Friendship* that the entirety of Schmitt's political theory is plagued by the aporetic relation between the enemy as an actual enemy against whom violence can legitimately be directed and the enemy as an idealized, universal figure that guarantees the sphere of the political.[24] Further, only a "humanist sentimentality" would see the opposite of war as something absolutely good.[25] As Nick Mansfield has argued, war requires the other—violence and peace are dialectically interdependent.[26] Or, to put the same point in more general terms, the subject of political violence and the universality of a sovereign determination of order, peace, and stability are codetermined—a fact presupposed by their separation in the first place, even though this is always repressed in the various legal determinations of sovereignty.[27]

Given, however, that the separation between law as the regulation of the means of violence and justice as the universal order, peace, and stability presupposes their prior codetermination, the essence of justification—namely, the immediate connection between law and justice—is undermined because it emerges as tautological. Here arises the third aspect of justification. It little matters if law and justice are not separable, as is required for the justification of means to be distinguished from the justification of ends. What matters rather is for means and ends to be perceived to be separate so that justification can subsequently reunite them. Differently put, the crucial aspect is the *cosupponibility*—as I called it in the Preamble—of the different modalities of justification. To return to the image of the presidential cringe: it little matters if the violence that arises from discomfort is properly justified; instead, what matters is for this justification to be credible. "At the end of reason," as Wittgenstein observes, "comes *persuasion*."[28] The giving of reasons for the legitimation of sovereignty is never complete, but rather always relies on a rhetorical turn that supports sovereign power. The sovereign discomfort is the undermining of the prevalent narrative that justifies certain means in relation to certain ends. As Jacques Derrida puts it in his interview with Borradori, the perception of "September 11" as a major event was the effect of the end of the Cold War. Barely a decade after the collapse of the USSR, the one power that was thought to preside over and police all other sovereign states was exposed as powerless to stop attacks within its territory. Thus what collapsed that morning was "the system of interpretation, the axiomatic, logic, rhetoric, concepts, and evaluations that are supposed to allow one to *comprehend* and to explain" the geopolitical situation in general but also "precisely something like 'September 11.'"[29] The sovereign discomfort was the symptom of this panicked encounter with the collapse of meaning—the shuttering of the comforting illusion that the über-sovereign power of the United States had a monopoly on sovereign violence.

This shuttering is a traumatic event and religion; the assertion of universal values, is, as Nietzsche so well recognized, precisely consolation through the creation of meaning. In the saying, "the rest is history," we can now hear the original Greek meaning of history—that is, a story. The sovereign discomfort needs a new story to justify its restoration to comfort. By presupposing a separation between law and justice, justification constructs a narrative that makes the immediate link between law and justice credible. The extralegal space of the exception, the limit outside codifiable law where law as such and the universality of order, peace, and stability coincide—the space where the justification of means merges with the justification of ends—is narrative. Ultimately, the justification that arises out of a particular set of circumstances that place the sovereign in a position of discomfort is nothing but the spawning of a story that describes the transition from discomfort to comfort. This is a fable without which law loses its credibility. That is what Spinoza calls the "imagination" in his *Ethics* and in his *Tractatus Theologico-Politicus*. The role of narrative is crucial. By becoming the conduit for the parallel and mutual justification of means and ends, of violence and peace—ultimately of politics and religion, of political theology—narrative makes possible the absoluteness of sovereignty.

Michel Foucault expresses sovereignty's absoluteness thus: "What characterizes the end of sovereignty . . . is in sum nothing other than the submission to sovereignty. This means that the end of sovereignty is circular: this means that the end of sovereignty is the exercise of sovereignty."[30] Nothing escapes sovereignty. When its ends coincide with the means it exercises, it is absolute. All social, political, economic—biopolitics claims even personal—relations are reduced to the immediate connection between law and justice. Sovereignty assumes a field of absolutely policeable relations—or, more accurately, sovereignty is the absolute field where every relation can potentially be policed. Nothing escapes sovereignty, not because ends and means do actually coincide or because law and justice are indeed immediately connected, but rather because narrative imposes the understanding of means in the quotidian and of ends in the transcendent levels. Or, rather, nothing appears to escape sovereignty while the narrative of justification remains believable—so long as critique and judgment are repressed.

DEJUSTIFICATION, OR THE HISTORICIZATION OF THE TRINITY OF JUSTIFICATION

And yet it is precisely its absoluteness that also exposes sovereignty to judgment. As intimated earlier, judgment has two elements, the first being dejustification. To engage with the appearance of an invincible, absolute justification, its logic needs to become visible. That logic can be represented as a triangle—or what can be called the trinity of justification.

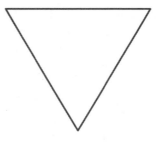

Justification of
means (violence)

Justification of ends
(order, peace, stability)

Exceptional justification
(narrative)

The particularity of violence and the universality of order, peace, and stability are united by that which can never be codified—an unpredictable narrative, the fabulations of the exception. Everything that tries to escape the borders of the triangle causes a sovereign discomfort. The restoration of "comfort" requires violent means (e.g., a "war on terror"), the justification of an end (e.g., the defense of Western liberal democracy and the spread of democracy in the Middle East), and the creation of an exceptional narrative (e.g., the panic not only that the enemy is everywhere and therefore emergency measures are required, but also that the enemy is less than human, a killing animal that needs to be indefinitely detained outside the territorial borders of the state). In the triangulation of these different forms of justification, sovereignty achieves a logical absoluteness that is complete and inescapable.

A dejustification of the trinity of justification has to start by exposing the absoluteness of sovereignty as appearance. Its logic is not inviolable, but subject to transformation—it is historical. This requires the renunciation of the resignation implied in the saying that "the rest is history." Instead of such an alibi for justification, what is required is a militant commitment to recognizing that what is historical in the logic of sovereignty is the way it dissimulates the initial separation between law and justice. As already intimated, this is necessary for their subsequent reunification as the process of the sovereign justification. A historicization of justification—an initial judgment on justification—starts from the observation that the tautological presupposition both of a codeterminacy and a separation of law and justice can assume three distinguishable forms. These three forms of sovereignty's absoluteness can be distinguished depending on which side of the triangle of justification is privileged. This distinction, as I argued in the Preamble, allows for a typology of sovereign power and will be examined in detail throughout the book, so I will outline here only its major features.

As I will be arguing in Chapter 2, ancient sovereignty privileges the justification of ends. For instance, in the *City of God*, Augustine defines the political in terms of the war between two cities. The first one, the pagan city, is dominated by the passions that give rise to discord and enmity. The second, the city of God, renounces the passions in order to strive for a kingdom of peace on earth. This peace is the final end toward which every action, every political means—including violence and justified war—should aim at. Peace becomes the universal value that dictates action. With modern sovereignty, I will argue in Chapters 3 and 4, the emphasis shifts to the justification of means. As Machiavelli puts it in *The Prince*, it little matters whether the sovereign is virtuous if that results in losing his grip on power. Instead of a justified end, Machiavelli advocates the justification of means. The sovereign should be like a lion in the sense of accumulating power and exercising force, but also like a fox in the sense that he can make his subjects believe in his capacity to lead and in the value of his leadership to the city. In biopolitics, as Foucault first described it in his lectures *Society Must be Defended* that I will be looking at in Chapter 5, the emphasis shifts again, this time to the exception. What characterizes biopolitics is that sovereign power disperses throughout the entire fabric of life. Instead of directly protecting the power of the executive, biopolitics is characterized by a heightening of policing power, whereby every action is subject to regulation and hence control.

By starting from a different side of the triangle, ancient, modern, and biopolitical sovereignties represent—that is, justify—their absoluteness in different ways. For ancient sovereignty there is a separation of law and justice because the city of God can never be properly realized on this earth. Justice has its source in the divine, whereas the city of God on earth can only approximate this justice through its laws. This schema is reversed in modern sovereignty. Here justice is separate from the law by analogy to the separation between the sovereign who embodies justice—he has a body politic, as it will be discussed in detail in Chapter 3—and the subject that is subjected to the law. The sovereign is justified to exercise his power with whatever means at his disposal in order to perpetuate his reign because the source of legality—the justice of his laws—emanates from his person. For modern sovereignty justice means legitimacy. Biopolitics has often been described as a perpetual state of exception. The exception becomes the rule, proffers Agamben.[31] The reason is said to be that there is a shift from the distinction between law and justice to the use of regulation to control life. However, as Foucault shows in *Society Must be Defended*, this shift to regulation is not due to a waning of the influence of either law or justice, but rather because the exception has the capacity to merge the justification of means and ends. Biopolitics signifies a resurgence of both ancient and modern sovereignty.[32] To mask the paradoxical incompatibility between the justification of ends and the justification of means, it resorts to a proliferation of regulations. In other words, regulation is the perfection of the tautological structure and hence of the absoluteness of sovereign justification.

The frantic attempts by the Bush administration to recuperate the American sovereignty's authority that was undermined at the moment of the sovereign discomfort provides a propitious illustration of how exceptional justification reunites the justifications of means and the justification of ends. The justification of ends can be recognized in the appeals to universal values in order to justify the "war on terror." Instead of representing itself merely as a policeman of the relations between sovereign nations, the United States presented itself as the guardian of values such as freedom, order, and democracy. Its expression in policy terms was the so-called "Bush Doctrine," according to which the deposition of the Iraqi dictatorial regime was said to instigate the spread of democracy in the entire Middle East.[33] Perhaps the culmination of this resurgence of ancient sovereignty was the depiction of Saddam Hussein as evil, as the "beast of Baghdad." Such a justification would have been unacceptable to the international community and its representative organizations, such as the United Nations and the Security Council. The reason is that international relations are governed by the logic of modern sovereignty. To address this, the U.S. administration developed the doctrine of preemptive strike, which essentially consists in an interpretation of the right of self-defense—that is, the right of the sovereign to perpetuate their power with whatever means available. Iraq's supposed possession of weapons of mass destruction was the empirical "evidence" that justified the means—that is, the exercise of

violence against the sovereign state of Iraq. These two justifications, however, were systematically conflated through the invocation of danger that
the worst had still not taken place.[34] The undemocratic Middle East was
said to be a harbor of "terror," and the greatest threat of all—the threat that
was utilized to provoke the greatest anxiety—was that the terrorists would
obtain weapons of mass destruction such as nuclear weapons. Through
this delirium of anxiety, the U.S. administration not only sought to become the de facto guardian of eternal values and to guard all sovereign
states from the rogue states that were denominated the "axis of evil"; in
addition, the U.S. administration sought to secure these two different
justifications by imposing its interpretation on its own people. The unprecedented erosion of civil liberties that were enshrined into law was characterized by the bypassing of the legal sphere. The agents of the sovereign
could exercise their interpretative powers to arrest and interrogate people
even before they had committed any crime, simply on the suspicion—that
is, the interpretation—that they might do so. Guantanamo Bay was perhaps the most visible articulation of this justification through the imposition of a narrative, but its effects impacted the lives of every citizen who
could potentially be subject to such an exceptional interpretation.

An important inference can be drawn here. As already stated, regulation is the perfection of the sovereign absoluteness. This regulatory process
reveals itself as a self-serving interpretation. In other words, the absoluteness of sovereignty is the dispensation of a sovereign narrative whose exceptionality is created by separating and reuniting law and justice. The
recognition of this tautology is, however, not enough for judgment to operate, since it would still remain on the empirical level. That every example of
justification is circular is, on the one hand, easy to prove, but on the other,
it proves nothing beyond the particular example discussed at every turn.
What is also required for judgment to come into play is an understanding
of the logic of sovereignty, which can only take place through a typology of
justification that is possible through sovereignty's historicization. Having a
conception of the way justification operates in ancient, modern, and biopolitical sovereignty affords one the power to distinguish different tactics
used to justify sovereignty. This process of recognition is a form of judgment because ultimately the tactics of justification amount to absolute
sovereignty only so long as the justification is muddled, only so long as the
means are surreptitiously conflated with the ends within a perpetuation

of exceptional narratives. There is a slippage between the different acts of justification. And this entails that three modalities of justification do not indicate merely a history of ideas about ancient, modern, and postmodern sovereignty. More importantly, the typology of sovereignty is constitutive of the justificatory narrative of sovereignty because it rehearses the tautological relation between means and ends. Sovereign justification relies on the cosupponibility of the three modalities of justification. Dejustification is the putting into question of the separability of, as well as the propriety of reuniting, different conceptions of sovereignty in particular acts of justification. Therefore, sovereignty is absolute only because it relies on a historical typology that allows its narratives to become illusory. History becomes the story that sovereignty tells in order to absolutize itself.

Dejustification expresses—and herein lies its judging function—the artificiality of this circularity, the way it is created out of specific historical precedents. Or, to put this the other way around, dejustification shows that the presumed absoluteness of sovereignty is in matter of fact a construct of power attempting to impose its own law, a dispensation of the means at its disposal, a pure and simple enactment of power that dissimulates as a form of justice. In Foucault's terms sovereignty is not absolute, but rather the nexus of knowledge and power as it is solidified in institutions whose purpose is the control of bodies. Irrespective of whether the power is classical, disciplinary, or biopolitical, the structure still remains artificial. Thus dejustification shows that sovereignty is not an absolute expressed in contingent, historical circumstances, but rather that the seemingly absolute structure of sovereignty is in fact reliant upon a molding of particular, historical circumstances into exceptional narratives.

Dejustification shows that sovereignty appears absolute only because of particular expressions of its tautological structure. Sovereignty can make itself the end of its means of power only so long as it has initially separated means and ends, law and justice—even though that separation has been carried out only in order to provide a justification for their immediate reunification. So dejustification is the demonstration that justification is artificial, not natural, and that the exceptional narratives in the service of the logic of sovereignty are actually predictable—precisely because they can be historicized.[35] Demonstrating the artificiality of exceptional narratives amounts to a demonstration that there is nothing exceptional in the sovereign narrative of exceptionality. This is a direct challenge to the absoluteness of sovereignty that requires exceptionality—that articulation of narrative that unites the justification of means and ends. By undermining exceptionality, dejustification deconstructs sovereignty's claims to absoluteness. The absoluteness of sovereignty is a fiction, a fabulation of trinitarian justification.

DEMOCRATIC JUDGMENT, OR THE EXIGENCY OF PARTICIPATION

Dejustification makes possible the inference that there is a *logic* of sovereign justification that never completely relies on either of the three sides of the triangle, but rather on justification as such—on the triangle as a whole. In each instance of justification the trinity of justification forms itself into a complete and coherent—that is, credible—story. This story, which sovereignty spins in accordance with particular circumstances, permeates the thought of the relation between law and justice. Consequently, as Bartelson correctly infers, "the history of sovereignty ought to be studied not in isolation or within a narrow temporal frame of inferential and theoretical connections, but in terms of its multiple relations with other concepts within larger discursive wholes, these not necessarily being confined to political ones."[36] Sovereignty cannot be confined to institutions or government. Sovereignty pertains to any enactment of its tautological logic. This self-referential process permeates all political relations, "public" and "private." It indicates the primacy of an economy—that is, a relationality—that forms the basis of the establishment and maintenance of institutions and interactions, as Georges Bataille has argued.[37] It also counters the usual claim that sovereignty commences only with the rise of modern sovereignty, the secular separation of temporal and religious authorities sometime in the sixteenth or seventeenth centuries.[38] Rather, it can be expressed anywhere there is an economy of justificatory relations. For instance, in *Rogues* Derrida designates "ipseity" as the main characteristic of sovereignty. "Ipseity" is, in the terms used here, the self-referentiality of the tautology of sovereignty in the sense that it presupposes a complete subject, while at the same time creating the concept of the subject.[39]

It is crucial to be attentive to the significant political question that arises at the point where sovereignty is recognized to pertain to all political relations and not simply to the politics of government and institutions. Dejustification shows that the historical narrative of sovereignty is a fabulation, a self-serving artifice. In other words, the absoluteness of sovereignty is the expression of a logic that stands above history—it is formal and ahistorical. Here the possibility of a disengagement from this circular logic of sovereignty arises as a formidable problem. How can one conceive of a structure of power that does not exhibit that circularity? Or, to put this differently, is there a politics other than the justificatory politics of sovereignty? Believing that all that needs to be done would be to eliminate the exceptional narrative that reunites means and ends does not solve the problem. Simply saying that an exclusion of sovereign justification is what is needed just recapitulates the process of exclusion and separation that precisely characterizes the logic of sovereignty. Such a belief in the overcoming of sovereignty presupposes and reaffirms the immediate connection between law and justice that characterizes justification and that is made possible by exceptional narratives. But if it is impossible to eliminate and hence exclude justification, then the logic of sovereignty appears as omnipotent and omnipresent. So is there no outside to sovereign power? Answering this question in the affirmative does not necessarily lead to resignation. For instance, Hardt and Negri argue that empire is the most developed form of sovereign power precisely because it explicitly has no outside. Nonetheless, Hardt and Negri insist on the possibility that the multitude can reshape that sovereignty from the inside.

The absoluteness of sovereignty can be rearticulated as a democratic politics.[40] As already intimated, the absoluteness of sovereignty arises out of the process of separation and reunification or exclusion and inclusion that characterizes the relation between law and justice, the means to and ends of power, as well as their fabulation within historical narratives. The contention here is that the second aspect of judgment consists in transforming the separations and exclusions that characterize the absoluteness of sovereignty into positive, agonistic relations that characterize democracy. Democracy is distinct from sovereignty because it radically reformulates separation and exclusion. Whereas sovereignty masks the conflict between law and justice through the justifications created by exceptional narratives, this conflict is brought to the fore through the agonism allowed by democracy. In other words, an agonistic politics identifies the democratic at the points of rupture between law and justice. Further, by working so as to sustain that rupture, a democratic politics affirms its distinction from sovereignty whose logic always reunites law and justice. By altering the way that exclusion operates within the logic of power, a democratic politics offers an alternative understanding of the relation between violence and intersubjectivity. This relation is now transformed into an incessant contestation that is the condition of the possibility of the democratic. It is never reducible to the violent means required by sovereignty.

The way that violence and intersubjectivity are related indicates the necessity to have a form of judgment other than dejustification—a democratic judgment. Whereas dejustification deconstructs the reasons offered for the separation and subsequent reunification of law and justice, the question of democracy arises not by asking how this separation and exclusion effects bodies, but rather how it effects interaction as such. Foucault's project shows the limits of dejustification. Foucault rejected outright the supposition that power can be *sui generis* and insisted instead that power is articulated through its effects on bodies, in particular by excluding those denominated as mad, abnormal, or, broadly speaking, policeable. Foucault shows how far dejustification can take the analysis of power, but he remains forever suspicious of the next step that I would like to take here—namely, an articulation of democratic politics departing from the transformation of the relations that seek to exclude the other. Or, differently put, I will try to show that the democratic is more primary in the sense that sovereignty is an effect of democracy.

The rise of democracy is intimately related to the radical reformulation of the question of exclusion or separation that underwrites the logic of sovereignty. The transition from the logic of sovereignty to democracy consists in abandoning the dialectic of exclusion and inclusion in favor of the notion of participation—that is, the maintenance of relations. This is recognized as a democratic imperative in the very first democratic constitution prepared by Solon. The *Athenian Constitution* describes the various institutions of democratic government, culminating with the Areopagus, the equivalent of a contemporary high court whose role was the protection of the constitution and its laws. At that very moment the author of the *Athenian Constitution* suddenly embarks on a brief, one-sentence diversion:

> And as he [Solon] saw that the polis was often in a condition of conflict [στασιάζουσαν], while some of its citizens through slackness were content to let things slide, he laid down a special law to deal with them, enacting that whoever when the city was in conflict [στασιαζούσης]

did not join forces with either party was to be disfranchised and not to be a member of the state [τῆς πόλεως μὴ μετέχειν].[41]

A superficial reading might infer that Aristotle instituted a law of exclusion: those who are lazy are to be expelled from the city. However, the infinitive "μὴ μετέχειν" (to be disfranchised) does not contain merely an injunction—that is, the content of a law, the assertion of the means. It does not merely mean that certain idlers must be excluded from the polis. In addition, it describes the condition of nonparticipation. When there is a conflict or *stasis* between two parties and when the city is threatened by the possibility that one party will prevail and exclude the other—that is, exclude the other party from participating in public disputes and in the administration of institutions—then everybody is obliged to take part in this dispute; everybody must participate in a conflict about exclusion. The reason is that, a *stasis*, a conflict that raises the specter of exclusion, directly challenges the democratic principle that the citizens have a voice in the politics of the city. The nonparticipant enacts in advance the sovereign gesture of exclusion through his own self-exclusion.[42] This moment of passivity presupposes the exclusion as distinct from the agonistic space of democracy—the space that requires conflict or *stasis* so that participation becomes possible. This explains why the author of the *Athenian Constitution* interjects this one sentence amidst the description of the institutions of Athens, and in fact immediately after the highest legal institution, the Aeropagus. The exigency of participation is not simply another law of the democratic constitution. Rather, it points to the infinitely contestable limit between law and justice as the principle of democracy. This is the principle of nonexclusion—the principle of participation—in the enactment of conflict.[43] Whereas sovereignty presupposes exclusion as the condition of the possibility of its absoluteness, democracy establishes, and is established by, the engagement of the other.[44]

This is not to say that a democratic disposition accepts the other absolutely. Instead, the other is engaged in an agonistic way that remains critical—remains agonistic. For instance, advancing a critique of the Bush administration's sovereign stance in the aftermath of September 11 places upon the proponent of democracy the imperative to critique the other side as well, when and because the other side reproduces a sovereign logic. The Islamic fundamentalists' antipathy toward the West and its institutions, including sovereignty in its liberal democratic form, relies nevertheless on a logic of sovereignty. For instance, as Olivier Roy has demonstrated, the desire to establish a global Islamic community is expressed through the establishment of religious laws such as dress codes or eating proscriptions. And this desire to return to a premodern theocratic state still contains within it a hidden political program, as is demonstrated, for instance, by the Iranian state.[45] The rhetoric of Islamic fundamentalism combines the theological and the political imperatives by creating an exceptional narrative that produces its other, the West, as its enemy. It *excludes* the other, and this brings into play a logic of sovereignty. The separation of the justification of means and ends, the exclusion of law from justice—ultimately, the separation between politics and religion—is always reproduced on bodies—the enemy—that are in their turn excluded. The logic of sovereignty and its justificatory processes operated clearly in both the Bush administration's "war on terror" and in the Islamic fundamentalist war against the "infidels" precisely because they both effect the creation of the enemy through exclusion.

Exclusion creates the enemy against whom violence is justified. In the logic of sovereignty as it is expressed in the trinity of justification, the enemy is the figure that makes possible, through the desire of his elimination, the creation of an ideal of order, peace, and stability. Further, the enemy gives content to this ideal just as law articulates in statute, in writing, the ends of justice. To arrive at a democratic politics the transformation of the process of exclusion can be understood as the transformation of the enemy into the other. Enmity is required by sovereignty, as Carl Schmitt well recognized in *The Concept of the Political*. Unless there is an enemy—that is, unless there is someone excluded from the way that a state configures the relation between law and justice—there can be no sovereignty, according to Schmitt. To make this inference Schmitt distinguished between the political and other spheres of activity such as social and economic activity. The reason was precisely so as to secure enmity as the foremost relation between people: "The concept of the state presupposes the concept of the political."[46] Prior to institutions of government, what is presupposed is that these institutions are not unique, but define other states that are different—that are excluded—from the way that law articulates justice. It is this exclusion that creates the enemy in a multiplicity of ways and historical registers.[47] And this also means that, according to sovereignty, the enemy is separated or excluded from the sense of universality that is indicated by order, peace, and stability. Conversely, the democratic judgment figures by transforming the enemy to the other with whom conflict as part of the democratic process is possible. Or, to put it the other way around, in democratic judgment, the other becomes the universal. The universality of the other here should be understood as the relation to the other that becomes the only available criterion of participation and hence as the only way that the democratic can be identified—that is, judged. As Solon's exigency of participation suggests, it is by engaging the other, it is by agonistically critiquing the other, that a democratic space can be created.

This returns us to the issue of change and the question of how it is possible to disengage from sovereignty's justificatory processes—an issue that is useful in clarifying the universality of the other. The question can now be formulated thus: Is it possible to regard the other as not an enemy, when the other perceives "us" as the enemy? This question does not pertain only to the relation between sovereign states, since within a state itself the government may be regarded as the enemy if it is repressing the citizens. Within a state a group of citizens itself that strives for certain changes could also be related to inimically. In other words, this is a question about the relations that are made possible by sovereignty. So long as the relation to the other is mediated by the assertion of competing senses of justice, so long as two parties are distinguished through their claims to competing senses of universality, enmity and the elision of the democratic are inevitable. But the question is whether it is possible that this relation of enmity that characterizes sovereignty can be countered by affirming participation with the enemy. How can one respond to enmity democratically? Or, more generally, how can democracy respond to sovereignty? This is where the universality of the other is crucial. Taking the other as the universal changes the terms of the relation between law and justice, as well as the relations between citizens. The immediacy that characterizes justification is now transferred to an agonism between law and justice. This affects the way that we understand both law and justice. The other as universal does not mean—as indicated above—that the other is immune from critique and accepted absolutely. Rather, universality figures as the resistance offered by the other in both separating and uniting law and justice. The other as universal also means that no justice is absolute, no justice is ever final, but rather justice is always part of—it participates in—the process of democratic conflict. The other as the universal means that the law can never presume to be absent, nor can it express immediately the content of a certain universal right or a universal justice. The other shows that the law and justice, as well as their conjunctions and disjunctions, are always a matter of agonistic relations. Democratic judgment affirms that relationality. Justification, on the contrary, presupposes exclusion.

The difficulty of understanding the other as universal, the exigency of participation as it was expressed in Solon's constitution, and by extension the dispensation of the democratic responsibility entails a difficult task, because there can never exist preestablished criteria for recognizing the other.[48] This allows a distinction from the exception. Sovereignty always requires the construction of an exceptional narrative that regulates the separation and reunification of law and justice. Conversely, the absence of preestablished rules in the relation with the other means that that relation itself, or a relation that calls for democratic judgment—*krisis* in Greek—is always in crisis. Or, more accurately still, it is that relation itself that takes as its condition of possibility the sustaining of participation entailed in democratic judgment. This is a crucial issue for a thinking of the democratic, as it will be argued in Chapter 4 with reference to Heinrich von Kleist's *Michael Kohlhaas*. Kleist's novella initially presents the clash between competing senses of justice. There is on the one hand the justice of the state that concerns itself with the perpetuation of order, and there is on the other hand the justice of the private, familial sphere that Kohlhaas feels justified to defend through his revolution. Between competing senses of right, enmity is the only possibility of (ir)relation. What remains unjustifiable at the end of the novella—in the sense that something is indicated that belongs to a register different than that of justification—is the contingency of the way that that relation is maintained. Intersubjective relations are presented as aleatory and hence as impossible to accommodate within preestablished rules. It is only through this emergence of the aleatory that the relation of otherness can be maintained. Or, to put it the other way around, it is only through the other as universal that singularity is possible.

Ultimately, then, democratic judgment consists in the exigency to sustain contingency. This maintains the space of the aleatory as the openness without which the encounter with the other in noninimical terms is impossible. Therefore the universality of the other that is the condition of the possibility of democracy must be sharply distinguished from the universality that operates in the logic of sovereignty—namely, order, peace, and stability.

Participation with the other means keeping relations open. This openness prevents any reconciliation between law and justice. Rather, their relation is always mediated by contingent factors. It is only by judging within this aleatory space that one can assume their singular democratic responsibility. Conversely, order, peace, and stability presuppose the effacement of contingency and hence the erasure of the possibility of singularity. Sovereignty creates an image of universality through the use of the means at its disposal and through the production of exceptional narratives in order to control, police, and regulate all relations of singularity. The democratic imperative—the democratic judgment—consists in the incessant struggle to keep open the possibility of singularity, to maintain the space of the aleatory. We will see in Chapter 5 how Coetzee's Michael K. learns the lesson of Kleist's Michael Kohlhaas, and instead of directly confronting sovereignty, as if the only response to enmity is further enmity, he rather arrives at a conception of political action as the defense of the accidental.

AN OTHER NARRATIVE: ON METHOD

At this point a question arises that has significant methodological implications. How is this democratic reformulation of the enemy that sovereignty requires related to dejustification that presents the logic of sovereignty? As already intimated, dejustification deconstructs the different forms of justification that have allowed sovereignty to separate means and ends, law and justice, only so as to be reunited through exceptional narratives. This circularity of separation and reunification not only constitutes the justification characteristic of sovereignty, but at the same time makes possible a distinction among different forms of sovereignty—ancient, modern, and postmodern. Such a distinction needs to be taken into account, since the deconstruction of justification is different in each instance, yet dejustification also shows that there is a consistency in the way that the logic of sovereignty operates across time and space. But for dejustification itself to be distinct from this expanded notion of sovereignty, an alternative space needs to be distinguished—a space that offers a different potential than sovereignty. The democratic judgment indicates such a space by insisting on participation instead of exclusion and by reformulating the enemy into the other with whom an incessant process of conflict and contestation takes place as the condition of the possibility of democracy. So, whereas dejustification deconstructs order, peace, and stability by showing that it is not really universal, but rather imbued in the exceptional narratives of sovereignty, the democratic judgment recognizes the other as the universal that is constitutive of retaining contingency and placing upon each one the responsibility to respond, not with recourse to preestablished criteria, but always in a singular way that sustains participation.

What, then, is the relation between the deconstruction of the particular articulations of justification and the affirmation of a space of infinite contestability? Or, differently put, what is the relation between dejustification and democratic judgment? The hypothesis of the present study is that the two forms of judgment are intimately related. It is impossible to have the one without implying the other. What holds them together is a narrative that resists exceptionality and challenges orthodoxies of power. To present the typology of sovereignty that that implies, this book is structured to have one chapter on ancient sovereignty, two on modern sovereignty—on absolute and popular sovereignty—and one chapter on biopolitics. The dejustification of the sovereign narratives is presented through the analysis of the manner in which the relation between means and ends is articulated. At the same time a parallel argument is conducted. This highlights the way that the opposition to sovereignty is in each case carried out so as to allow for the democratic exigency to conceive of justice as contestable. This parallel approach demonstrates that a deconstruction of sovereignty also necessitates a positive understanding of the democratic.

Finally, two points are implied in the approach that takes the construction of texts against exceptionality as the feature that both deconstructs sovereignty and leads toward a democratic politics. The first implication is that for both dejustification and the democratic judgment to work in parallel, an overcoming of sovereignty is not necessary. There are two reasons for this. The first reason is that it is impossible to describe a political regime—in the broadest sense—without reference to sovereignty. Since dejustification shows that there is a logic of sovereignty that permeates all forms of relations, and because that logic is a tautological one, then sovereignty comes into play every time one utters the first-person pronoun—an "I" or a "we."[49] It is impossible to eliminate completely the possibility of giving reasons for one's intentions, impossible to completely eradicate justification. Indeed, there is something infantile in the demand to found a politics without sovereignty, since such a politics can only ever be utopian.

But this is not the same as saying that it is not *our* responsibility, as sovereign subjects who must work with reason and justification, to also conceive of a space that is not subsumed by sovereignty—a different space, a space of the other. As Foucault famously says in *The Will to Knowledge*, "In political thought and analysis, we still have not cut off the head of the king." This should not be construed as a utopian plan, as is made clear a page later: "One remains attached to a certain image of power-law, of power-sovereignty. . . . It is this image that we must break free of, that is, of the theoretical privilege of law and sovereignty, if we wish to analyze power within the concrete and historical framework of its operation. We must construct an analytics of power that no longer takes law as a model and code."[50] Foucault is not proposing an alternative government or constitution when he is calling for a critique of sovereign power. Instead, Foucault is calling for the construction of a discourse of power that is not circumscribed by the analysis of legality and its claims to justification and legitimacy. Foucault calls for a new political thought that allows for a concrete analysis of the history of exclusion—of the history of the other.

But there is a further reason for the necessity of sovereignty that can be gleaned by turning to Jacques Derrida—namely, that sovereignty is an effect of democracy and hence not something that can easily be separated from it and expunged. Derrida echoes Foucault's main point when he addresses the separation of a free, democratic thinking that he calls "unconditional" from the operation of sovereignty: "The unconditionality of thought . . . may be identified wherever, in the name of freedom itself, it can put in question the principle of sovereignty, as a principle of power. Let us not pretend that this question is anything but formidable and abyssal. For thought thereby, the one that finds its place of freedom there, also finds itself, to be sure, *without power*. It is an unconditionality without sovereignty, which is to say at bottom a freedom without power." Derrida seems to be suggesting here that it is possible to separate unconditionality from sovereignty. However, the emphasis is not on the possibility of their separation—it is, rather, on their agonistic relation, as it is made clear from what Derrida goes on to say: "But without power does not mean 'without force.' And there, discreetly, furtively, another frontier is *perhaps passed through, at once inscribing itself and resisting the passage*, the barely visible frontier between the unconditionality of thought . . . and the sovereignty of power, of all powers, theologico-political power down to its national or democratic guises, economic-military power, the power of the media, and so forth. The affirmation I am speaking of remains a principle of resistance or of dissidence: *without power but without weakness. Without power but not without force, be it a certain force of weakness.* Far from retiring behind the certain frontiers of a field, a camp, an inoffensive campus protected by invisible authorities, this thought . . . must prepare, with all its force, a new strategy and a new politics, a new thinking of the political. And of political responsibility."[51] The distinction between unconditionality and sovereignty or, in the vocabulary employed in the present book, between democracy and sovereignty, between judgment and justification, is not one of exclusion. The frontier between them is "barely visible," says Derrida. Instead of separating them, what matters is the fact that their distinction necessitates "a principle of resistance or of dissidence." Unconditionality, democracy, and judgment manifest themselves on the site of their agonistic relation to sovereignty. As I argued at the end of the Preamble, it is crucial to recognize that the justification of violence that characterizes sovereignty is a product of its agonistic relation toward democracy and judgment. Justification is the defensive strategy employed to make sense of the operative presence of resistance and dissidence. In this sense the important aspect for a relational ontology of power is not to try to imagine a way that democracy abolishes sovereignty, but rather to describe the ways in which the relation between the two can unfold.[52]

This link between the construction of a political thinking that is not prey to the theoretical privileging of law and sovereignty—a democratic political thinking—and its repercussions for the analysis of historical facts leads to the second implication for the interdependence and parallel operation of dejustification and democratic judgment. This consists in a shift of emphasis from history to historiography. When history is understood as the "facts as they really happened," then it is impossible to avoid the resignation implied in the cliché "the rest is history," as shown earlier. But this "factual" history always assumes a set of axiomatic principles that are a matter of interpretation. The trick is how to develop this interpretation without lapsing into a blind assumption that the past is past and without relevance to the narrative that one is constructing—in other words, how to avoid collapsing the "facts" of history viewed as the means of historiography to a linear narrative that connects them with the end of the "truth" of "what really happened." This connection between "fact" and "truth" in history is a repetition of the sovereign logic that reunites means and ends, law and justice. Conversely, keeping the relation open—the sustaining of the parallel disjunction and conjunction of law and justice—is what Walter Benjamin referred to as "weak messianic power": "The past carries with it a secret index by which it is referred to redemption. Doesn't the breath of the air that pervaded earlier days caress us as well? . . . If so, then there is a secret agreement between past generations and the present one. Then our coming was expected on earth. Then, like every generation that preceded us, we have been endowed with a *weak* messianic power, a power on which the past has a claim."[53] From the perspective of this weak messianism the participatory exigency of democracy can be formulated in a different way. Democracy seeks to include not only those living in the present, but rather to construct a narrative, a historiography, that rearticulates the exclusions performed by sovereign justifications in such as a way as to redeem those excluded. The dead, the specters of the past, are also indispensable participants in this democratic process. But for this participation to be welcomed, a new philosophical thinking of power is called for. The present study is a contribution toward that incompletable exigency of participation.

2

THE VICISSITUDE OF PARTICIPATION

On Ancient Sovereignty

We saw in the first chapter that the democratic constitution prepared by Solon has a special provision, according to which "whoever when the city was in conflict did not join forces with either party was to be disfranchised and not to be a participant in the polis." I suggested then that this is not merely a law that forces citizens to participate in the public affairs, but rather an exigency that functions as the basis of legality—it points to a sense of justice. It is through this image of participation, then, that a closer examination of ancient sovereignty can be pursued.

As already argued, the main characteristic of ancient sovereignty is the privileging of the side of the end of justification. But a series of questions arise at this point. For instance, can the figure of order, peace, and stability be related to participation? And, if that is the case, then how can sovereignty be distinguished from democracy? For such a distinction to be possible, participation itself would have to receive different determinations.

WAR AND THE STATE: ON THE FOUNDATION AND
PERPETUATION OF THE POLIS IN THUCYDIDES

Is there a discourse of sovereignty in ancient Greece? To answer this question it is necessary to turn to Thucydides. The reason is not simply, as Leo Strauss has argued, that the historian is also attuned to political philosophy.[1] More importantly, Thucydides's *History of the Peloponnesian War* starts with an examination of the relation between war and the state that relies on the triangle of justification that, as already argued, characterizes the logic of sovereignty.[2]

What is the relation between war and the state according to Thucydides? In embarking upon his account of the Peloponnesian War (431–404 B.C.) that ravaged the Greek city states and ultimately led to the decline of Athens, Thucydides is compelled to answer this question. From Book I, paragraphs 2 to 21, Thucydides provides his version of the formation of the city states. These twenty paragraphs are burdened with a significant methodological tension, even paradox. Thucydides starts paragraph 2 by indicating that he is about to narrate something that is evident: "For it is plain that [Φαίνεται]" (I.ii.1). Paragraph 21, however, recapitulates by adopting a more cautious, even defensive tone. Referring to what has just been described, Thucydides insists that his version is better than that of the poets and the chroniclers because "the facts have been made out with sufficient accuracy, on the basis of the clearest [ἐκ τῶν ἐπιφανεστάτων] indications, considering that they have to do with early times [ὡς παλαιὰ]" (I.xxi.1). The defensive tone is clear in the shift of the certainty indicated by the *phainetai* of I.ii to the comparative *ek ton epifanestaton* of I.xxi. It is a direct result of the fact that what was initially claimed to be evident should have complied with the scientific method of history that Thucydides describes in the immediately succeeding paragraph (I.xxii), where it is explained that the account of the events is based either on his own direct perception or on evidence from other eyewitnesses. Instead, the description of the relation between war and state pertains to events so old that they transgress Thucydides's own criteria of evidence for scientific history, requiring instead a significant amount of conjecture. Thucydides exposes himself to such a methodological instability from the very beginning of his narrative because of the compulsion to describe the relation between war and the polis.

The reason that Thucydides needs an account of the relation between war and the state is that it offers an explanation of state formation and state perpetuation that would allow him to claim, first, that Athens was the greatest state ever created, and, second, that the dramatic and irrevocable decline of Athenian power by the end of Peloponnesian War justifies the claim that "for men who judge from actual facts, [the Peloponnesian War has] been more important than any [war] that went before" (I.xxi.2). Further, as a consequence of the rise and fall of the great polis of Athens in the greatest war of all time, Thucydides can say that his history will be of didactic value; it will be indispensable knowledge "for all time" (I.xxii.4). The question, then, of the relation between war and the state helps Thucydides express the heuristic principle of his narrative. This consists in the assumption that power is linked to knowledge. And this link points to the universal principle that underlies the entire Western tradition or, in Michel Foucault's words, "the idea that knowledge and truth cannot not belong to the register of order and peace."[3] But to arrive at this principle that underlies the didactic function of his own narrative, the narrative itself has already broken the rules of evidence that Thucydides himself sets in order to justify its adherence to historiography's epistemic claims. It is already an aberrance narrative, uncodifiable—it is an exception—because, or, even though, it is a narrative about the most important war ever fought. The whole of the *History*, then, is heuristically defined as an exceptional narrative—a narrative that does not conform to normal rules and that is written in unprecedented circumstances. Thucydides needs to provide the account of the relation between war and the state in times past in order to justify the exceptionality of his narrative.

Importantly, the account of the relation between war and the state requires an exceptional narrative. There is a circularity between the content of the account and its justification. To demonstrate this we need to present the detail of Thucydides extrapolation of the relation between war and the state. This takes two forms. First, it pertains to the state's foundation. Book I, paragraph 2 describes the situation prior to the formation of city states. According to this account the people in that bygone era were nomadic. They assumed that they could find sustenance anywhere, so they constantly changed their abode. In addition, the most fertile lands were always in a state of strife, since everyone wanted to live there. Only Attica, the region where Athens is, was free from such strife. Being a safe harbor of peace away from the perils of war was constitutive of the establishment of the great city of Athens: "the most influential [δυνατότατοι] men of the other parts of Hellas, when they were driven out of their own countries by war or sedition, resorted to Athens as being a firmly settled community, and, becoming citizens, from the very earliest times made the city still greater in the number of its inhabitants" (I.ii.6). The formation of the greatest city is not at all a matter of men of the same kin settling in one land. Instead, it is the most influential men—or, more accurately, the most powerful men (*dynatotatoi*), both in mind and body—that sought refuge from the widespread war to the security provided in the city of Athens. They made up the *demos*, the participants in Athenian democracy. The greatness of Athens is based on criteria of value instead of preestablished filiations. And moreover, these criteria of value are supported by the polis itself that provides safety and security. Athens is described as unique among all known political entities, Greek and foreign. For instance, "all the Hellenes used to carry arms . . . just as the Barbarians did. . . . But the Athenians were among the very first to lay aside their arms" (I.vi.1–2). The order, peace, and stability of Attica and the sense of safety that it provided to its citizens allowed for the great men of Hellas to gather there. Hence the first relation between war and the state consists in the foundation of city states in ancient Greece— and in particular of the greatest polis of all, Athens, by the virtuous ancestors who laid down their arms for the sake of peace.

The second aspect of the relation between war and state as it is described at the beginning of Thucydides's *History* consists in the perpetuation and expansion of the power of the city states. The perpetuation of their power was a concern of the Greek city states from the moment of their foundation. For instance, Thucydides describes how Minos, the king of Crete, established the fist navy, which functioned as a wall in the sea to protect his cities from piracy (I.iv). Later and in other parts of Greece, walls were built around the cities to protect them from attack and to allow their populations to thrive (I.vii). However, after peace and stability were established for a long time within the city states, the Greeks "began to send out colonies" (I.xii.4). There was a drive to expand that was articulated in the establishment of alliances. Ultimately, during this imperialist, expansionist stage, all the Greek city states were allied either with the Athenians or with the Spartans, the other strong power of the time, and it was this division that led to the destructive Peloponnesian War. The foundation of the state, then, necessitates the demarcation of an area through the creation of armed forces and fortifications in order to perpetuate the security and peace already established in the city state. This proliferation of armies, however, and the drive to find new markets and territories that would further strengthen the city state, necessitate war, at least as a possibility that dictates the defense and strengthening of the state. The protection of the established state is determined by the presence of hostile forces that threaten the state, and hence by the possibility of war.

The dual relation between war and the state that Thucydides describes preempts the distinction between internal and external sovereignty that is said to have been articulated clearly for the first time with the Treaties of Westphalia. There is an inner sovereignty in the sense that the state is responsible for providing the conditions of the peaceful operation of society—for instance, by providing policing so that its citizens are not compelled to carry arms for their own self-protection. And there is an external sense of sovereignty that consists in the recognition that every state has to provide for that sense of security for its citizens, or, more broadly, that every state has to do whatever is necessary for the perpetuation of its power—including expansion of its sphere of influence so as to allow for the strengthening of the state. This is not to suggest that there are no significant differences in the way that sovereignty is constructed in ancient and modern times. It is, rather, to indicate that, their differences notwithstanding, ancient and modern sovereignty are driven by the same logic that represents the foundation of the state in terms of the universal of order, peace, and stability and its perpetuation in terms of the use of any means at its disposal. Thus it would be precipitous to infer that the founding moment of the state that signifies the elimination of war and the continuation and strengthening of the state through the actual or potential use of violence present a paradoxical and contradictory relation between war and the state in Thucydides. In fact this paradoxical relation is constitutive of sovereignty. It is the rupture of ends and means of power. This separation is then obviated through the exceptional narrative of Thucydides's own history, which shows the unique, unprecedented circumstances that led to the creation of the two hostile alliances and their clash, which produced the greatest war of all time, the Peloponnesian War.

The end of the state needs to call upon peace, whereas its perpetuation and expansion need to call upon violence for an exceptional narrative to be possible. And yet, simultaneously, it is only that exceptional narrative that ameliorates and masks the contradictions between ends and means. We have already described this logic as the triangle of justification, which relies on the separation and reunification of means and ends through exceptionality.

Thucydides's history is structured according to this circular, tautological logic of sovereignty.

SELF-SUFFICIENCY: PERICLES'S "FUNERAL ORATION"

It would be easy to argue that Thucydides's account of state formation is not all that different from the seventeenth-century contractarian account. Like Hobbes, Thucydides might be understood to describe the pre-polis situation as a "state of nature," where everyone is an enemy to everyone else, and to suggest that the only escape from this is the establishment of the polis. Such a reading would be supported by Hobbes's own introduction to his translation of Thucydides's *History*, in which the Greek historian is presented as preempting the argument about state formation that Hobbes was still developing at that time.[4] However, there is a major difference between Thucydides and Hobbes that points to the distinction between ancient and modern sovereignty. The difference consists in that Hobbes's state of nature leads to a perpetual war because it is characterized by a complete lack of restrictions, by an absence of law and hence an overabundance of freedom—as we will see in more detail in the following chapter. Thucydides's account, on the contrary, describes the nomadism of the earlier times as a politics of kinship, and the transition to the polis and to democracy consists in gaining freedom. Athens became a great city not because there was a familial tradition, but rather because, as we already saw, the greatest men of the time assembled there. Thus the greatness of Athens consisted in overcoming the preordained blood relations and moving instead toward relations that pertain to human value—hence its democratic import.

This transition away from a politics of kinship and toward a democratic politics is articulated in the repetition of the principle of participation that, as it was described in Chapter 1, was Solon's blueprint for democratic engagement. The exact rewording of Solon's principle in the *History* reads: "For we alone [i.e., the Athenians] regard the man who does not participate [μηδὲν μετέχοντα] in public affairs, not as one who minds his own business, but as useless [ἀχρεῖον]" (II.xl.2). It is a distinctive feature of Athens and its citizens—something that characterizes them and nobody else—that they insist on participation. That which binds the citizens together is the principle of participation. In fact, as we will see in a moment, this principle is a cause for the greatness of the city. Before that, however, I would like to clarify one point. The pre-democratic politics of kinship is also related to ancient Greek religion. The figures of family ties, bloodshed, and forced migration—that is, the very figures that Thucydides utilized in order to describe the situation in Greece prior to the formation of the polis—are prevalently interknitted in Hesiod's *Theogony*. For instance, the newborn Zeus is separated from his mother and forced to hide in a cave in Greece in order to avoid being devoured by his father, Kronos.[5] The transition from a politics of kinship to a politics of democratic participation that I am describing here does not deny the import of Marcel Detienne's thesis that there is a proximity between politics and religion in Greece. This imbrication of politics and religion is attested, according to Detienne, by the actual proximity of political and religious institutions, as well as by the fact that the relations between the gods mirror the politics of the humans.[6] Rather, it is the nature of the political relation itself that changes with the shift from the lack of agency in determining one's kin to the active agency of democratic participation in the present. The sovereign logic that characterizes ancient Athens, as it is presented in Thucydides's *History*, relies on a privileging of the side of universality—the side of order, peace, and stability. However, what is unique in Athenian democracy is that this side is universal not in the sense that it is eternal or infinite. Instead, it is universal in the sense that it contains within itself the exigency to participate. Participation is not pregiven through kinship, but rather requires the engagement of the citizen. That's an exigency of the present moment, an imperative of finitude. Participation indicates a finite universal.

To delineate the finite universal distinctive of Athenian democracy, we need to turn to Pericles's famous "Funeral Oration" from Book II of Thucydides's *History*. The reason is not only that it is in this oration that we find the statement of the principle of participation quoted above—"we alone regard the man who does not participate in public affairs, not as one who minds his own business, but as useless." Moreover, the genre of the funeral oration is crucial in comprehending the Athenian democracy, as Nicole Loraux so convincingly has demonstrated—and Pericles's oration from Book II of *History* stands out as the most important of them all.[7] Pericles was the leader of Athens at its most imperial phase. He was a charismatic personality whose involvement in the construction of the image of "Athens" still reverberates today—for instance, in the identification of

Athens with the iconic Acropolis that he helped to build. The occasion of the oration was the official burial of the dead at the end of the first year of the Peloponnesian War. This oration took place in Keramikos, the cemetery at the foot of the Acropolis. The whole city would have been assembled to honor its dead soldiers. However, Pericles refrains from praising the dead and concentrates instead on a panegyric of the polis. The justification of this deviation from procedure is crucial in understanding the finite universal that characterizes Athenian democracy.

The oration opens in the following, seemingly innocuous manner: "Most of those who have spoken here in the past have commended that the lawgiver who added this oration to our ceremony, feeling that it is meet and right that it should be spoken at their burial over those who have fallen in war" (II.xxxv.1). Pericles acknowledges that the reason everyone has assembled at the cemetery is a law of the city, according to which there is an official ceremony at the onset of winter to celebrate the dead during the previous summer's hostilities. In addition, Pericles states that the majority of the speakers of the past, presumably tapping a general sentiment of the polis—a sentiment of the vast majority of Athenians—have opened their oration by praising the democratic politician who added the oration to the ceremony. After reminding his audience of these facts, Pericles asserts a contrast: "To me, however, it would seem sufficient [ἀρκοῦν], when men have proved themselves by valiant acts, by act only to make manifest the honours we render them" (II.xxxv.1). This contrast between the speeches of the past and the insufficiency of speech in the present occasion to honor the dead may be assumed to be a simple technique of *captatio benevolentiae*. However, much more than a faithful adherence to a rhetorical figure is at play here. The first two sentences of Pericles's oration function as a centripetal force that determines from the onset the center of the oration and that which will arise as the constitutive characteristic of the democratic polis—namely, self-sufficiency. Self-sufficiency will turn out to be characteristic of the finite universal indicative of Athenian democracy.

Self-sufficiency is inscribed in three distinct domains in Pericles's "Funeral Oration"—namely, narrative, the citizens, and the polis itself. These domains correspond to the three sides of the triangle of justification that was used in Chapter 1 to outline the logic of sovereignty. Self-sufficiency, or αὐτάρκεια in Greek, is determinative of the narrative structure, as is indicated by Pericles's assertion that mere words, the standard funeral oration legislated by the lawgiver, is *in*sufficient to do justice to those fallen in battle. The way the first two sentences are structured, however, only has the appearance of a *captatio benevolentiae*, which would have consisted in stating the speaker's inability to live up to the heroic deeds of the fallen soldiers. Instead, brazenly, the contrast suggests that Pericles here takes an action—namely, he breaks the law of the democratic constitution. That deviation from statute will consist in refraining from praising the dead and praising the polis instead. The breaking of the law to honor the dead by words is a speech act like a sovereign exception that stands above the law. Only such a speech act can be sufficient for the occasion. The entire oration is an exceptional narrative and hence flaunts a sovereign logic.

Pericles concludes the first paragraph with a gesture toward the ancestors that seeks to obfuscate the sovereign gesture with which the paragraph opened: "However, since our forefathers approved of this practice as right and proper, I also, following the law, must endeavor to the best of my ability to satisfy the wishes and beliefs of each of you" (II.xxxv.3). But this is followed only by a brief, almost forced salutary acknowledgment of the ancestors. In two sentences Pericles says that the ancestors bequeathed "to our time [μέχρι τοῦδε]" a free polis and that their immediate ancestors, "our fathers," contributed to the current (νῦν) greatness of the city (II. xxxvi.1–2). The ancestors are dispensed with summarily and by emphasizing only their contribution to the present glory of the polis. Everything in Pericles's oration is determined by the present tense—and we should keep this in mind when we turn to Augustine at the end of the chapter. To highlight further this present tense, Pericles introduces another contrast that is again reliant on the notion of self-sufficiency. "But we ourselves [αὐτοὶ ἡμεῖς] . . . have further strengthened the polis, making it most self-sufficient [αὐταρκεστάτην] in both peace and war" (II.xxxvi.3). After a brief acknowledgment of the ancestors that was so quick it appears almost like a digression, Pericles returns to the present citizens of Athens. The association is clear: "we ourselves" are the most self-sufficient—more self-sufficient than our predecessors—and it is on the basis of this self-sufficiency that Pericles has justified himself to break here, now, at that very moment, the law of his predecessor to deliver an oration about the dead, choosing instead to talk about the self-sufficiency that characterizes the present moment. I am not concerned here what the qualities of the citizens of Athens are, which Pericles is about to enumerate. What is more important is that these qualities are deemed to have created self-sufficiency to the contemporary population.

This self-sufficiency of the citizens also extends to the institutions of the polis. "We live under a form of government which does not emulate the institutions of our neighbors; on the contrary, we are ourselves a model which some follow, rather than imitators of other peoples" (II.xxxvii.1). The democracy established in Athens, suggests Pericles, is what makes the Athenians exemplary to other city states. The idea that self-sufficiency is ultimately a quality of the polis itself, rather than of its citizens as individuals, is explicitly asserted a few paragraphs later: "In a word, then, I say that our city as a whole is the school of Greece, and that, as it seems to me, each individual amongst us could in his own person, with the utmost grace and versatility, prove himself self-sufficient [αὔταρκες]" (II.xli.1). The citizens and the institutions of Athens are exemplary to all others because they have a polis as whole that makes possible the quality that proves greatness and requires emulation—namely, self-sufficiency. Ultimately, if the citizens are great, the reason is that the city is great—hence the exceptional decision to refrain from lauding the individual citizens who died in battle to defend Athens, and to offer instead a celebration of the polis itself. It does not suffice to praise the individuals. Only the praise of the city is sufficient.

Self-sufficiency, then, is inscribed in all three sides of the triangle of justification. It can be traced in the exceptional narrative that Pericles embarks upon by both announcing the law to honor the dead and by transgressing it in lauding the city instead. It can also be attributed to the citizens, who make the city self-sufficient and who are the creators as well as the beneficiaries of its institutions—the citizens produce the means of the polis's greatness, such as its law, as well as enjoy the fruit of their political engagement. Ultimately, however, it is the polis itself, as an end in itself, to which the attribute of self-sufficiency is appropriate. An important inference is possible at this stage. The inscription of self-sufficiency in all sides of the triangle of justification is Pericles's way of describing the absoluteness of Athenian sovereignty. Self-sufficiency unites narrative, means, and ends. But for this unification to be enacted, the three elements would also have to be separated. Here we encounter the distinctive feature of ancient sovereignty—namely, that it privileges the side of universality. The end, which consists in the self-sufficiency of the polis, is the object of Pericles's praise, because the greatness of the polis, its self-sufficiency, is the end of the sovereign logic outlined in the "Funeral Oration." The polis stands as more important than its citizens, and that's what justifies his exceptional narrative, which is meant to show the citizens' as a whole—not only the fallen soldiers'—contribution to this self-sufficiency.

An important problem arises as a result of the inference just drawn about the privileging of the polis as the side of universality of the sovereign logic. How is the universality of this ancient sovereignty related to what I called earlier the finite universality of democracy? That universal was called finite because it did not point to an infinite time, but rather to the active participation of the citizens in the conflicts of the polis. Let us recall the democratic imperative as it was expressed in the *History*: "For we alone [i.e. the Athenians] regard the man who does not participate [μηδὲν μετέχοντα] in public affairs, not as one who minds his own business, but as useless [ἀχρεῖον]" (II.xl.2). Now, two features are important here, which are in fact interrelated and which point to the finitude of the universal in its Greek articulation. The first consists in that the exigency of participation is inherently of the present moment. The citizens, in order to avoid being useless, have to engage in the disputes and conflicts that determine the political in the polis and that make Athens self-sufficient. This active engagement in the present is precisely what Pericles is performing in the speech act that cites the law of funeral rites only in order to decide on its exception. Participation is of the present, of the finite. Second, the conception of the finite universal is constructed in opposition to the past. I indicated earlier Pericles's quick, almost forced gesture toward the ancestors. But much more than a simple diminution of their role is at play here. More importantly, the democratic imperative to privilege the present moment is articulated through an agonism toward kinship. Athenian democracy enacts the agonism toward the politics of kingship.

But the question of the relation between the sovereign logic of self-sufficiency and democracy remains unanswered. As argued in the previous chapter, democracy is the other of sovereignty. So how can the praise of the democratic polis be reconciled with that praise being carried out in terms of the logic of sovereignty? How can self-sufficiency be distinguished from participation? We return here to the initial question of this chapter: How can the figure of participation distinguish sovereignty from democracy, thereby articulating their relation? This is a question that is not raised in Pericles's "Funeral Oration," but is, in fact, pivotal in Sophocles's *Antigone*.

"INVINCIBLE EROS" IN SOPHOCLES'S *ANTIGONE*: FOR THE LOVE OF DEMOCRACY

Antigone presents a complex relation between sovereignty and democracy because both Creon and Antigone can be understood as democratic and as antidemocratic.[8] Both the laws of the state, represented by Creon, and the laws of kinship, represented by Antigone, have the potential to function in a democratic and in an antidemocratic way. Therefore the question of the relation between democracy and sovereignty does not hinge on identifying either protagonist with one regime, but rather in showing how the two regimes are in an agonistic relation. This agonism is precipitated by the various determinations that participation can achieve—determinations that point to the sense of the tragic in ancient Greece as well as to a notion of irresolvable struggle as the site of a finite universal.

The play belongs to the Theban cycle. After Antigone's father, Oedipus, was deposed, Eteocles, his son, assumed the leadership of Thebes. To gain sovereignty the other brother, Polynices, assembled a foreign army and attacked Thebes. The siege ended when the two brothers encountered each other in the battlefield. Their fight resulted in the death of both, whereupon Creon, their uncle, became the leader of Thebes. The new ruler's first decree was to prohibit the burial of Polynices so as to dishonor his nephew who had attacked his own city, his own kin. Sophocles's play starts at this point. Antigone, dismayed at the breaking of the customary law to honor one's kin with a burial, disobeys Creon's decree by sprinkling dust over Polynices's cadaver.[9] Outraged, Creon orders a severe punishment against his niece: she is to be locked in a cave to starve to death. Notwithstanding the irony that Creon recapitulates Polynices's crime—attacking one's own kin—Creon eventually realizes that the whole city is opposed to his decision, and he relents. But his change of heart comes too late. Antigone has already hanged herself, Haemon, Creon's son and Antigone's fiancé, has taken his own life at the feet of his beloved, and upon hearing the news Creon's wife, Eurydice, has also committed suicide.

Antigone nuances the exigency of participation that we have already come across, first in Solon and then in Thucydides. The issue of participation arises explicitly in Creon's first speech. Creon frames his address to the elders of the chorus with the metaphorics of the polis as a ship. To recapitulate the actions preceding the present tragedy, Creon describes the city as a ship that has survived through a big storm: "[T]he gods have shaken the polis with a heavy shaking, but now they have set it right in safety again" (162–63).[10] The presentation of the background is followed by a long and significant discussion about participation.

> There is no way of getting to know a man's spirit and thought and judgment, until he has been seen to be versed in government and in the laws. Yes, to me anyone who while guiding the whole city fails to set his hand to the best counsels, but keeps his mouth shut by reason of some fear seems now and has always seemed the worst of men; and him who rates a dear one higher than his native land, him I put nowhere. I would never be silent ... when I saw ruin coming upon the citizens instead of safety, nor would I make a friend of the enemy of my country, knowing that this is the ship on which we sail and only when she prospers can we make our friends. (175–90)

I will return to the important metaphor of the city as ship later, when discussing the sense in which both Antigone and Creon are antidemocratic. I would like to explore first, however, the senses in which they are both democratic. Suffice it to say here that Creon, who is preparing to announce his decision to deny Polynices a burial, seeks justification for his decision through the figure of participation. Or, more precisely, the image of the good captain of the polis is framed by two senses in which participation collapses, either when one abstains from public affairs to mind one's own business or when one places one's kin over the city. These two failures of participation imply two positive senses of participation, provisionally understood as engagement in the public life and as an agonism against kinship respectively. Based on these two senses of participation we can ask the question: who is democratic, Antigone or Creon?[11]

Democracy figures in a complex, even paradoxical way in *Antigone*. The Romantics, in the aftermath of the French Revolution, celebrated the revolutionary maiden from Thebes because she stood up to the new leader's tyrannical decree. However, her opposition to sovereignty is not unproblematically democratic. In fact it is highly paradoxical. The reason is that democracy is understood in ancient Athens in terms of its agonism against kinship, as we have just seen in Creon's speech or earlier in Thucydides's *History*. Thus it would have been expected that Antigone would be deemed undemocratic because she represented customary divine laws. However, Antigone's resistance to Creon's perceived monarchical authority was sufficient reason for the Romantics to perceive her attitude as democratic. This unexpected alliance between democracy and kinship indicates, at the very least, that the relation between the participation principle of democracy and the logic of sovereignty is an unstable one. It can turn both ways. Tracing some of the most crucial twists and turns of this debate—from Hölderlin to Hegel, and from Judith Butler to Bonnie Honig—will contribute toward answering the question of who is more democratic, Antigone or Creon.

Hölderlin's translation of *Antigone* has attracted significant attention because it seeks to render in German the peculiarities of the Greek syntax and grammar.[12] Thus the language of the resultant text unsettles preconceived expectations of communication. Walter Benjamin famously decried this technique.[13] But besides the complex issue about the transmission of meaning and the translation of ideas that are embryonic in Hölderlin's translation, one aspect may be easily overlooked—namely, that the use of the idiosyncratic, even exceptional language in the translation as part of the attempt to glorify the revolutionary significance of Antigone's resistance to the sovereign reflects Hölderlin's own attempt to revolutionize the German language. It is precisely this revolutionary aspect that is at the center of Hölderlin's "Notes on Antigone."

In his "Notes" Hölderlin unambiguously states that the action of the play is directly dependent on revolution, or political conflict—the word Hölderlin uses is "Aufruhr," the German word that translates as "stasis," the state of conflict in the city that, according to Solon, everyone has to participate in. Hölderlin says: "The nature of the action in the *Antigone* is that in a revolt, where, insofar as it is a national matter, everything depends on the fact that everyone, being overwhelmed by the infinite reversal, and thoroughly moved, apprehends himself in the infinite form in which he is moved."[14] The action of the revolutionary conflict, however, not only is "national," but also pertains to the self-reflections of the individual involved. In other words, the conflict is not confined to a narrowly defined sphere of politics, but rather extends to the way that the individual's sense of self changes by participating in this upheaval: "For national reversal is the reversal of every mode of understanding and form."[15] Revolution is not confined to a change of the constitution or of government, but to a change of the modes of relating to the others and hence of understanding oneself. This is not to say that a revolution is an individualistic pursuit, as if a single genius could control the entire process. Hölderlin continues: "But a total reversal in these, like any total reversal without any check, is not gained to a man as a creature endowed with perception."[16] It is at this point that Hölderlin indicates a *Geistesgewalt*, a power of the spirit, or maybe also a spiritual violence, that is ultimately responsible for the conflict that extends across every level of self and community: "And in a national reversal, where the whole shape of things changes, and nature and necessity, which always remain, tend to a new shape, whether going over into wilderness or into a new form, in a change like this, all mere necessities are biased in favor of the change; whence in the eventuality of such change, even a neutral man (and not only one who is moved *against* the national form), can, by a spiritual violence of the time, be forced to be patriotic and present in an infinite form, in the religious, political and moral form of his fatherland."[17] Notice how this spiritual violence necessitates a reinscription of the moral and the religious in the sphere of the political. This provides the justification for the revolutionary aspect of Antigone. Her defense of the unwritten laws of kinship is the force that makes possible, over and above any individualistic pursuit, the revolutionary aspect. Change, as the mark of the democratic, is only possible by this reinscription of the religious and the moral within the sphere of the political—even though and because they are not the same as the political, they are not identical with the laws of the city, and hence they inscribe the other—they make possible the raising of the voice of alterity.[18]

For Hölderlin, then, the democratic exigency of participation is delineated as the openness to the other, even though that other may not be political—it may be moral or religious. This hearing of the other is that which allows for change and revolution. But such an unconditional openness to the other is not without perils.[19] For instance, the customary laws that Antigone is representing are characterized by their being handed down. They are unwritten laws. As such they are not up for debate. What would happen, then, when the customary laws of one people encounter those of another? Ultimately there is an impossibility of communication. There is no middle ground between two different religious dogmas or two opposing moral codes. Thus, whereas the encounter with the unwritten laws of custom may enrich, even revolutionize, as Hölderlin suggests, the written laws of a regime, still the encounter with another system of unwritten laws can only be resolved through violent means. In addition, it may be questionable to what extent a genuine revolutionizing of the written laws can be achieved through their encounter with the unwritten laws.[20] There can be no state within a state, as the proponents of temporal powers put it in early modernity to distinguish state power from the church. In other words, customary law has to be separated from written law for any notion of state to be possible. This is Hegel's position, outlined in the *Phenomenology of the Spirit* through an oblique reference to *Antigone* that is, at the same time, a response to his erstwhile friend, Hölderlin.

It should be noted at the outset that Hegel's own reference to *Antigone* takes place within the exceptional narrative of the dialectic. The dialectic is the struggle between particular and universal that is ultimately resolved through the absolute spirit that contains everything within it. But, unlike Hölderlin, who allowed for a spiritual violence, a *Geistesgewalt*, accommodating within it the conflict between the individual and society and between the national and moral laws, Hegel shows in his dialectic the gradual subsumption of inferior or more primitive elements in the road toward the absolute spirit. The reference to *Antigone* is situated at a crucial juncture of this dialectical struggle—namely, at the point where the customs and society that allow for the emergence of the individual encounter the ethical sphere that effects the transition to the state. The rise of the ethical and hence the founding of a state can only take place by recognizing that the laws of kinship are of a different order that must be overcome. The written and unwritten laws are incompatible. "Since it sees right only on one side and wrong on the other, that consciousness which belongs to the divine law sees in the other side only the violence of human caprice, while that which holds to human law sees in the other only the self-will and disobedience of the individual who insists on being his own authority."[21] Antigone, the "consciousness which belongs to the divine law," can only recognize caprice in Creon's decree that prohibits the burial of Polynices. In Carl Schmitt's terms the sovereign decision is exceptional precisely because it is unfounded.[22] For his part Creon, the consciousness that "holds to human law," sees only a selfish individuation in the resistance to the authority of the state. How can one decide which one of the two incompatible consciousnesses to prefer? Hegel provides the following justification: "For the commands of government have a universal, public meaning open to the light of day; the will of the other law, however, is locked up in the darkness as the will of an isolated individual which, as contradicting the first, is a wanton outrage."[23] In answer to the question, "Why is it that the voice of the other, the customary law of kinship, needs to be silenced?" Hegel answers, because it fails to hear alterity. The ethical sphere, the sphere that allows for the formation and perpetuation of the state, is superior because it provides "a universal, public meaning" open to public debate by giving reasons, by providing justifications.[24] Even if an end to the debate needs to occur on occasion and even if that ending is capricious, still all this takes place in "the light of day." Conversely, the "other law" is impervious to reason; it is "locked up in the darkness" and can only address the private needs and desires of an individual. Hegel, then, reformulates the principle of participation that now entails the ethical imperative to be heard by the other. Such a participation can only take place, according to Hegel, by renouncing the individualistic law of kinship and entering instead the public space for debate.[25]

Hölderlin sides with Antigone and Hegel with Creon because they delineate participation differently. For Hölderlin participation entails being open *to* the other. The hearing of the other voice has the potential to revolutionize. This was one of the senses of participation that we encountered in Creon's opening speech—participation as agonistically related to kinship. For Hegel participation entails the openness *of* the other. The other has to hear the voice and authority of reason so that the community is regulated by debates and laws that are exposed to the light of the day. This was the second sense of participation in Creon's speech—participation as public engagement. The difference, then, between Hölderlin and Hegel reflects the difference between the two senses of participation. It is the difference between hearing the other and being heard by the other. And yet, because of this difference, Hölderlin and Hegel's extrapolation of the democratic in *Antigone* share a common substance—namely, an adherence to a sovereign logic. The reason is that by creating an exceptional narrative— either the exceptional translation or the exceptional moment in the movement of the dialectic—and by limiting the way that participation is understood, both Hölderlin and Hegel provide a justification for the unification of violence with the universal. Their conclusions only appear different, but in fact they share the separation of written and unwritten laws as an axiomatic principle of their privileging only one sense of participation. It little matters if Hölderlin describes the universal in terms of the equilibrium that pertains with the reinscription of the moral and the religious in the state, or whether that equilibrium results from their elimination, as Hegel argues. The result in each case is the effectuation of a reunification of law and justice, of means and ends—just as Pericles's notion of self-sufficiency in the "Funeral Oration" seeks to unify enunciation, law, and justice. It is precisely this reunification that is resisted by Judith Butler and Bonnie Honig, who both insist in different ways that it is impossible to separate written and unwritten laws in the first place.

In *Antigone's Claim* Butler sides with the interpretation of Antigone's significance in terms of the revolutionary import of her stance. The starting point of her reading of the play, however, is that it is impossible to clearly separate kinship from the state. "Although Hegel claims that her deed is opposed to Creon's, *the two acts mirror rather than oppose one another*, suggesting that if the one represents kinship and the other the state, they can perform this representation only by each becoming implicated in the idiom of the other."[26] At the same time Butler resists Hölderlin's gesture of simply conflating written and unwritten laws in the name of a "total reversal." Instead she shows how kinship and the state contaminate each other because Antigone's own line of familial relations is contaminated, being the offspring of an incestuous union. Ultimately *Antigone's* revolutionary potential consists in the recognition that there are neither pure laws of kinship nor pure laws of the state. The two remain entangled. Or, to use the language from the previous section, democracy requires an agonistic relation with kinship.

Even though Bonnie Honig agrees on the agonism between democracy and kinship, she shifts the emphasis of the agonism. Whereas Butler insists that it is Antigone's aberrant progeny that produces this agonism, Honig argues that Sophocles presents Creon as a proponent of socially progressive and democratic reforms in the rituals of mourning. Honig argues that the play stages a binary between the rituals of Homeric mourning that are excessive and their moderation in classical Athens. "Thus, the play troubles the binary of Homeric versus democratic in which it also traffics and whose contention it restages."[27] From this perspective, "Creon metonymizes democracy substantively. His ban on lamentation and his repeated emphasis on the harms of individuality represent the fifth-century democratic view. . . . Creon's excess is what marks him as democratic."[28] Within the context of classical Athens, Honig suggests, the progressive position would have been assumed to be that of Creon, because he stands for a participation in modern forms of mourning.

Despite Butler's and Honig's quite brilliantly showing in different ways how it is impossible to separate completely written and unwritten laws, still they both retain a one-sided sense of participation. According to Butler's position, participation is seen from the perspective of the openness to the voice of the other—in this instance, the aberrant position of kinship represented by Antigone. According to Honig's position, participation is the engagement with the legal reforms as they were enacted by the polis, even though the legality can never stake a claim to completeness. For this reform to take place the reformist must also be heard by the other. So, despite seeking to elide the sovereign logic of Hölderlin's and Hegel's positions, Butler and Honig return to the same antinomy of participation. As we gleaned from Creon's speech, participation is defined through its dual imperative—to struggle with kinship and to engage in public affairs. However, the reception of Antigone shows that these two imperatives contradict one another. Remaining open to the other as kinship curtails the unrestricted engagement in public and vice versa. Democracy's end is in a double bind between the written and the unwritten laws that both need each other and yet, at the same time, cannot tolerate each other. Democracy is caught in the antinomic exigency between hearing the other and being heard by the other.

This antinomy of the two senses of participation that can be found in Creon's opening speech demonstrates that it is impossible to distinguish clearly democracy from sovereignty by focusing on only one of the senses of participation. To nuance further this antinomy, we need to return to Creon's initial address to the chorus, paying particular attention to the metaphor of the polis as a ship. It will be recalled that Creon described Thebes as a ship that had survived a storm and derived the two meanings of participation by showing that they led the ship of the polis to safety. The reason that the ship metaphor is crucial is not merely that later in the play Haemon returns to the same metaphor in a very important response to Creon, to which we will turn shortly. In addition, the metaphorics of the ship point to the way that participation leads to sovereignty instead of democracy. The ship metaphor, as it is used in Creon's speech in *Antigone*, has an antidemocratic thrust.

Such an antidemocratic thrust is quite common in the use of the state as ship metaphor, since the metaphor often revolves around the supposition that a strong and capable captain is needed to steer the ship away from peril.[29] In the long and complex history of the metaphor that presents the state as a ship, there is no better illustration of the way it has been mobilized toward an antidemocratic sentiment than Plato's *Republic*, paragraph 488.[30] Socrates here uses the ship metaphor to summarize his opposition to democracy—it is his decisive coup de grace to democracy as well as a topos of the description of democracy in ancient Greek philosophy, including Aristotle. Through a series of long and awkwardly connected clauses, Plato rhetorically renders the sense of unsettlement that he describes as taking place in a democracy. The aim is to argue that participation in the leadership of the polis cannot be extended to the multitude, but rather must be restricted to the few—the philosophers, according to Plato—who are equipped to make rational decisions. The polis/ship is ravaged by a motley of disastrous and individualistic interventions. Plato's ship metaphor presents an argument about the evasion of the antinomy between the two senses of participation in favor of restricting participation strictly to the best of the citizens. To describe democracy Socrates asks Ademantus to picture a shipmaster who is good-looking, "but who is slightly deaf and of similarly impaired vision, and whose knowledge of navigation is on a par with his sight and hearing." The sailors, because they have a weak leader, see it as their right to control the ship, even though they do not know how to navigate, and, "what is more, they affirm that navigation cannot be taught at all." While they try to persuade the shipmaster to hand them the helm, they fight between themselves. "[I]f they fail [to take the helm] and others get his ear, they put the others to death or cast them out from the ship, and then, after binding and stupefying the worthy shipmaster with mandragora or intoxication or otherwise, they take command of the ship, consume its stores and, drinking and feasting," lead the ship to ruin. During this chaotic self-indulgence, the only one who is celebrated is the "most cunning to lend a hand in persuading or constraining the shipmaster to let them rule." Concerned only about their self-satisfaction, they "have no suspicion that the true pilot must give his attention to the time of the year, the seasons, the sky, the winds, the stars, and all that pertains to his art."

All the while they disparage any "real pilot" as "a star-gazer, an idle bab-bler, a useless fellow." Socrates concludes that it does not even require proof "that the condition we have described is the exact counterpart of the rela-tion of the state to the true philosophers."[31] The antidemocratic fervor of this passage culminates in the solution offered by the strong captain, who will not tolerate haphazard participation in the steering of the ship. That captain is the philosopher-king, the sovereign of Plato's antidemocratic discourse. What this Platonic sovereign cannot tolerate is any admission of otherness to the government of the city. The problem with the other, the problem with the vulgar, unskilled, and selfish multitude, is that it wants to steer the ship without any knowledge of the technique of navigation. It is only concerned with its own profit and enjoyment. Moreover, precisely because the multitude is unskilled, any rational discussion with them is impossible. The indulgent sailors can only take the helm through trick-ing or overpowering each other and the pilot. They are unreasonable, stub-born, and recalcitrant.

It is possible to relate this Platonic resistance to otherness back to Creon's speech. The two limits of participation that Creon indicates—engagement in public and engagement without privileging friends and relatives—can be aligned with the exclusive sense of participation that is open only to the best men of the country. The suggestion then would be that Creon has steered the ship out of trouble and into the safety of the harbor because he is like the philosopher-king. A first possibility, then, to resolve the antin-omy between the two senses of participation would be to infer a delimited participation according to criteria of value or worth. According to this logic participation must exclude, because only the best captain can stir the ship to order, peace and stability. Creon paints a similar picture to the one on Plato's ship when he warns against *anarchia* (literally, lack of legitimate power): "But there is no worse evil than insubordination [ἀναρχίας]! This it is that ruins cities, this it is that destroys houses, this it is that shatters and puts to flight the warriors on its own side!" (672–75). Further, the descrip-tion of the self-interested multitude in the Platonic passage is echoed by Creon's accusation of avarice, leveled both against the guard who brings the news that someone has sprinkled dust over Polynices's cadaver and against Tiresias, the blind prophet who warns Creon against punishing Antigone. Finally Creon also concurs with the inflexibility of the multitude found in the passage from the *Republic*. Creon expresses this disdain for inflexibility during a tense exchange with Antigone. After accusing her uncle and sovereign to be a fool, the Chorus intervenes, addressing Creon: "It is clear! The nature of this girl is savage, like her father's, and she does not know how to bend before her troubles" (471–72). To this Creon responds: "Why, know that unbending wills are the most apt to fall, and the toughest iron, baked in the fire till it is hard, is most often, you will see, cracked and shattered!" (473–76) The intransigence prevents the proponent of kinship from hearing the legitimate authority, mirroring the sailor's self-indulgent conduct in Plato's use of the ship metaphor. It is this selfish inflexibility that characterizes the unchecked desire of those who are unfit to govern.

And yet this accusation of inflexibility is exactly what is leveled against Creon by his son, Haemon, shortly afterward. Haemon approaches his father cautiously. He does not plea for Antigone directly, and asserts that it is not in his power to contradict him. At this point he adds, however: "But for me it is possible to hear . . . how the polis is lamenting for this girl" (692–93). It is not merely the multitude with their selfish and unharnessed desires that are siding with Antigone. It is, rather, the polis—the community of people who are held together by participation. Plato restricted participation according to worth. Here, however, Haemon suggests that it is impossible to exclude from participation the *majority* of the polis. One will, no matter how rational or skilled it is, cannot ignore the will of the many. If the Platonic metaphor of the ship suggests that inflexibility is the attitude of those unworthy to navigate the polis/ship, Haemon responds here that inflexibility is also the attitude of a captain who does not listen to what the ship desires:

> You see how when rivers are swollen in winter those trees that yield to the flood retain their branches, but those that offer resistance perish, trunk and all. Just so whoever in command of a ship keeps the sheet taut, and never slackens it, is overturned and thereafter sails with his oarsmen's benches upside down. (712–17)

The tree that does not yield to the flood is like the toughest iron in the metaphor used earlier by Creon against Antigone. And, when it comes to the polis, the tree does not stand alone. Rather, the tree is like a boat in a storm, and its mast is going to shatter if the captain does not yield to the wind. Haemon warns his father that the polis of Thebes is not like a ship that enjoys the safety of the harbor, as Creon reassured the elders of the chorus in his opening speech. Rather, the polis/ship is still trapped in a storm because the will of the one, the decision of the sovereign, contradicts what the majority think.

We saw earlier that the two senses of participation—hearing the other and being heard by the other—can present both Antigone and Creon as democratic. The metaphor of the polis as a ship can mediate the antinomy between these two senses of participation, but it does not succeed in eliminating the antinomy as such. It merely displaces it. It is now reconfigured between the competence of the one who is best suited to make decisions for the polis and the right of the polis to decide by the weight of numbers, as a majority. At the same time, what arises out of this reformulated antinomy is the antidemocratic stance of both Antigone and Creon. The insistence on the sovereignty of their stance consists in their inability to discern that the will of the one is always implicated in the will of the many. As a consequence, both Creon and Antigone meet their fate standing alone, like the lone tree that does not yield to the flood, according to Haemon's metaphor. This figure of loneliness—the figure of the one who achieves absolute self-sufficiency, to recall Pericles's oration—is repeated several times in *Antigone*. "You would be a fine sovereign alone [μόνος] over a deserted [ἐρήμης] city!" (738–39), Haemon tells his father when he realizes that the sovereign is not interested in considering what the polis thinks about Antigone. And Creon, in his turn, condemns Antigone to be alone because of her unbending opposition to the will of the one who is assigned to govern. "Will you not lead her off as soon as possible, and when you have enclosed her in the encompassing tomb, as I have ordered, leave her alone, isolated [μόνην ἐρῆμον]" (885–88). And the Messenger who brings the news about the death of Eurydice, Creon's wife, following the suicide of his son, comments that, living alone in the palace, the king will be like an "animate corpse," and that all the glamour of the place is not worth even "the shadow of smoke" in comparison with the pleasures of life (1165–71). The loneliness of the one indicates the sovereign stance of both Antigone and Creon.

Antigone and Creon proved earlier to be *both democratic* according to different senses of the notion of participation. The democratic imperative was caught in the double bind between hearing the other and being heard by the other—being open to the other and the openness of the other. Antigone and Creon prove now to be *both also antidemocratic*. This sovereign stance is indicated by choice to privilege either the right of the skillful one to take the helm of the city or the will of the many representing what is true. The attempt to evade the antinomy of participation by delimiting the notion of participation only led to the sovereign inflexibility of both niece and uncle. This in turn consisted in a reinscription of antinomy in the problematic relation between democracy and sovereignty—an antinomy now articulated as the delimitation of participation according to skill or according to number. Antinomy, then, permeates the political discourse in *Antigone*, making it hard, if not impossible, to participate by taking sides.

This ineliminable antinomy following the question of democracy, this clash of laws (*nomoi*) as well as the excess of the laws, resonates with the name "Antigone," suggesting that it pertains to the core of the Sophoclean tragedy. Stathis Gourgouris provides a brilliant analysis of the protagonist's name that precisely relates this point: "The preposition *anti* means both 'in opposition to' and 'in compensation of'; *gone* belongs in a line of derivatives of *genos* (kin, lineage, descent) and means simultaneously offspring, generation, womb, seed, birth. On the basis of this etymological polyphony (the battle for meaning at the nucleus of the name itself), we can argue that Antigone embodies both an opposition of kinship to the polis (in compensation for its defeat by the *demos* reforms), as well as an opposition *to* kinship." The opposition between *genos* and *demos* corresponds to the opposition between the laws of kinship and the laws of the polis. And these laws are *anti*-thetical; they show how the polis forms a sense of participation in opposition to kinship. This means, however, that the polis presupposes *genos*, even though it is unable to accommodate it. Gourgouris continues: "But her name also embodies opposition at a generative level, an otherness at the core."[32] Maybe, then, the irresolvability of the antinomy between hearing the other and being heard by the other is in fact something positive because it allows a generative opposition—a contrast between two senses of participation that makes possible a democratic sense of justice. But this justice will no longer be something stable, defined in advance by either the laws of kinship or the laws of the state. Rather, justice can here be understood as the openness to the irresolvable relation of kinship and *demos*. Such an infinitely contestable coparticipation—such a finite universal, to recall the description of unceasing conflict from Thucydides—can generate a sense of agonistic justice. Consequently, the questions raised—Who is democratic, Antigone or Creon? Who is antidemocratic, Antigone or Creon?—should be understood as questions about the quality of their impossible relation. They are questions about the agon between competing senses of participation that constitute justice.

This suggests, however, a different notion of participation. It suggests a participating in the antinomy between the two senses of participation—hearing the other as well as being heard by the other—without seeking to resolve it in the Platonic manner that leads to the privileging of the one. An alternative notion of conflict is required in order to delineate such an alternative sense of just participating. The reason is that violence is inscribed in the antinomy between the two senses of participation in Creon's speech. For instance, both Creon's and Antigone's stance entails violence. Even though Creon eventually changes his mind, it is already too late. Antigone has already died, leading to the suicides of Haemon and Eurydice. In fact, as already argued, violence is part of the logic of sovereignty. Thus the agonistic justice suggested above requires a sense of the *agon*, of conflict, that does not resolve itself in the violence that characterizes the logic of sovereignty. Or, to put this another way, the logic of sovereignty justifies violence. The judgment against justification, on the other hand, is not only an opposition to violence, but also an affirmation of democracy.

Such an alternative formulation of the agon can start figuring by considering the most important reference to battle in the *Antigone*, the stasimon on *eros* that immediately follows the encounter between Creon and Haemon.[33] The first strophe says:

> Love invincible in battle, Love who falls upon men's property, you who spend the night upon the soft cheeks of a girl, and travel over the sea and through the huts of dwellers in the wild! None among the immortals can escape you, nor any mortal men, and he who has you is mad. (781–92)

There is a kind of love (*eros*) that, according to the stasimon, is invincible. This does not suggest merely a description of what takes place in the battles that occur because of love—that is, that eros is always victorious. Rather, more precisely, it suggests that eros is conceivable only as victorious. It is the vanquishing of the other that characterizes eros. This consists in being unable to resist profit when there is an eros for property, or to resist the beloved. It is the inability to resist that drives mad both mortals and immortals. The antistrophe expands:

> You wrench just men's minds from justice, doing them violence; it is you who stirred up this quarrel between men of the same blood. Victory goes to the visible desire that comes from the eyes of the beautiful bride, desire that stands beside the throne of the mighty sovereign powers [πάρεδρος ἐν ἀρχαῖς]; for irresistible in her sporting is the goddess Aphrodite. (793–800)

Such an invincible attitude destroys the justice of the written laws, leading the citizens to violence, and it also wrecks havoc in families, such as when brothers like Eteocles and Polynices raise arms against each other. This invincible love is adjacent to the throne of power—*paredros* literally means next to the seat of power. In other words, the invincibility of eros is a metonymy of the sovereign power and its insatiable desire to be self-sufficient. Instead of the Periclean self-sufficiency, however, the tragedy of the invincibility of eros entails that eros is fateful. There is no escaping its grip when one finds oneself on the side of power (*paredros*)—regardless of whether or not that is the side of politics or of kinship.

As opposed to this blind eros, which is adjacent to power, Haemon had already provided a suggestion about how to sidestep the violent conflict that it gives rise to. I quote it here again, adding one more crucial line:

> You see how when rivers are swollen in winter those trees that yield to the flood retain their branches, but those that offer resistance perish, trunk and all. Just so whoever in command of a ship keeps the sheet taut, and never slackens it, is overturned and thereafter sails with his oarsmen's benches upside down. No, retreat from your anger and allow yourself to change [μετάστασιν]. (712–18)

Heamon pleads with his father not to be like an unyielding tree in a flood—that is, not to assume the stance of invincibility. Instead, he asks him to slacken the sheets so that the ship does not capsize. This suggestion contradicts the Platonic metaphorics of the ship that revolve around the presence of skilled personnel who hold absolute authority. Instead of a justification of authority, here the good choice is to abstain from resistance—to adopt an attitude other than in the category of the irresistible that characterizes the invincibility of the violence of eros. A democratic judgment consists in this flexible, but agonistic attitude—the attitude that embraces the aporia between the two different sense of participation.

To understand what is involved in Haemon's suggestion—in the judgment that he is promoting—it is important to show how the Platonic metaphor of the ship is refigured. This different figuration of the ship metaphor recalls the use of similar imagery in Alcaeus:

> I fail to understand the direction [*stasis*] of the winds: one wave rolls in from this side, another from that, and we in the middle are carried along in company with our great black ship, much distressed in the great storm.[34]

The winds, like fate, are irresistible. The only possible solution is to renounce the illusion that one is justified to fight the winds directly—either because of his skill or because of a majority support. Rather, Alcaeus suggests that one should accept the contradictory—the anti-nomic—winds and that it would be best to allow the ship—or the polis—to be carried along by them. There is a point of suspension, a point of (dis)equilibrium, when one freely participates in this contradictory exigency. But the shift in the sense of conflict that Alcaeus's imagery suggests is also indicated by a resonance between Alcaeus's poem and the last sentence from Haemon's advice to Creon quoted above. The word *stasis* in the fragment indicates both the direction of the winds and, more generally, conflict—as it did in Solon's extrapolation of the exigency to participate every time there is *stasis* in the polis. The word for "changing one's mind" in Haemon's advice is *metastasis*, the same word as the Alcaeus poem with the prefix "meta." This prefix gives rise to the image of moving along, not remaining static in the inflexible intransigence that characterized the sovereign logic or the antidemocratic impulse in both Creon and Antigone. But in addition it suggests a readjustment of the conflict. It paints a picture of a stance that is no longer adjacent to the seat of power, as the antistrophe of the stasimon on eros put it, but rather a stance that is past that seat of power. Metastasis indicates an adjustment of the metaphorics of the invincible attitude in conflict. It enacts a displacement of the metonymy to the seat of sovereignty. This is the displacement from justification to judgment, from invincibility in battle to irresolvable agon.

This displacement of conflict consists in the acceptance of conflict. It is no longer a matter of winning the battle, however that battle is understood: between the two different senses of participation or between two different senses of the exclusion from participation, between written and unwritten laws, between state and kinship. This conflict is ineliminable. That's what also can make it fateful: both Antigone and Creon find themselves next to the seat of a power—to recall the metaphor from the stasimon on eros— and they are tragically compelled to side either with the state or with kinship. But this submission to fate also holds a chance: the understanding of justice as that adjustment or displacement—the *meta*stasis—that allows for a different notion of participation. This participation consists in the immersion in the agon that determines the antithetical imperative between law and custom. The point of the (dis)equilibrium between them is the figure of democracy offered by Greek thought.

It is this adherence to conflict at the present moment—the acceptance of the antinomies of the present—that also characterized Solon's exigency of participation. To quote the *Athenian Constitution* once again, according to Solon, "whoever when the city was in conflict did not join forces with either party was to be disfranchised and not to participate in the state."[35] This democratic conflict is the condition of the possibility of the political and hence of sovereignty. It is a conflict that has to be continuously enacted for the political to exist. Moreover, it is a conflict that is produced by participation, and in particular the different senses of participation that it makes possible, such as hearing the other and being heard by the other. At the same time, however, participating in the polis means that conflict is productive. There is, to put it somewhat paradoxically, a participating in the antinomies of participation. Classical Greek thinking names this conflictual participating justice.[36] Justice here is understood as a finite universal—as something that needs to be enacted in the present ever anew. This agonistic justice is democratic because its antinomic nature resists a steadfast identification or unification with any law. It dejustifies self-sufficiency. Further, by accepting the voice of the other, it also has no monopoly on narrative structures. Thus it is this conflictual nature of justice that ultimately allows for its distinction from the unifying logic of sovereignty. Justice as conflict can create narratives by judging how to infinitely sustain the participating in the vicissitudes of participation.

UNIVERSAL *AGAPE* IN CHRISTIAN SOVEREIGNTY: AUGUSTINE'S CITY OF GOD

The irresolvable conflict between politics and kinship marks the limit of Greek thought. This is not to suggest that the irresolvability of this conflict is a limitation. On the contrary, without it, as Solon's exigency suggests, participation and hence democracy would have been impossible. Further, Greek sovereignty presents the polis as a *finite* universal because the conflict is continuously enacted in the present. Eros takes place in the present. The transition from ancient Greek eros to Christian agape (*ἀγάπη*) presents an irreversible crossing of the limit of Greek thought and, at the same time, the logical culmination of ancient sovereignty. By turning love into an *infinite* universal, the end of sovereignty achieves an eternal quality. This entails that the universal conciliates the conflict between written and unwritten laws. Whereas infinity in Greek thought was inscribed in the present recasting of the conflictual relation between legality and kinship, Christian infinity signifies an eternal order, peace, and stability that will be realized in the future, after the end of time.

The eternalization of the universal consists in the elimination of the struggle or conflict that persisted between law and kinship. This overcoming of conflict that marked the limit of Greek thought can be summarized in a short sentence from the Apostle Paul: "love thy neighbour."[37] This reconciles a political imperative with a politics of kinship. The most significant reference to this principle can be found in the *Romans*. To denote love the Greek text uses the verb ἀγάπῶ, from which the substantive ἀγάπη is derived.[38] It is translated as follows in the King James Bible: "Owe no man any thing, but to love one another: for he that loveth another hath fulfilled the law. For this, Thou shalt not commit adultery, Thou shalt not kill, Thou shalt not steal, Thou shalt not bear false witness, Thou shalt not covet; and if [there be] any other commandment, it is briefly comprehended in this saying, namely, Thou shalt love thy neighbour as thyself. Love worketh no ill to his neighbour: therefore love [is] the fulfilling of the law" (*Romans* 13:8–10). Neighborly love becomes the principle of all law. It is "the fulfilling of the law" in the sense that it precedes all particular laws—don't commit adultery, don't kill and so on—and hence it is the founding principle of the state. This love, however, is also a love of kin, since it is analogous to the love of "thyself." This universal love that unifies state and kinship, or legality and morality, is encapsulated in the command "love thy neigh-bour." Paul's agape does not pertain to the category of the invincible because, unlike eros, it is conceived as empty of conflict. I do not want to diverge here into the detailed Christology that underlies this claim, whereby love is a divine attribute expressed through Jesus's sacrifice. I only want to add that "Christianity's stroke of genius," as Nietzsche called this Christology, had the effect of eliminating the conflict at the heart of the universal that characterized Greek thought and hence profoundly refor-mulating ancient sovereignty.[39] The main feature of this reformulation is a conciliation of political and moral concerns, premised on the conception of an eternal order, peace, and stability corresponding to eternal love. This explicit transformation of the end of justification to something universal manages to reconcile kinship and politics at a cost—namely, it robs the hu-man from any agency to determine that end. The end is universal precisely because it is transcendent—it is not manmade.[40] This conception attains its clearest expression in Augustine.[41]

Augustine conceives of a city that is explicitly described as overcoming the struggle between politics and kinship: "she [the city of God] summons citizens of all nations and every tongue, and brings together a society of pilgrims in which no attention is paid to any differences in the customs, laws, and institutions by which earthly peace is achieved or maintained" (XIX.17).[42] To appreciate Augustine's ingenious figuration of the concilia-tion between legality and morality, we cannot simply acknowledge that he overcomes the limit of Greek thought—the cessation of the just conflict and its transfiguration to universal love. Moreover, we need to ask, how is the limit understood in Augustine? What is the limit of the Christian con-ception of sovereignty that unifies law and kinship through universal love? This question revolves around a new conception of time, different from the Greek valuation of the present that allowed for democratic thought.

In Chapter XV of *The City of God*, Augustine draws the central distinc-tion of his politics—a distinction that relies on Augustine's reformulated temporality: "I divide the human race into two orders. The one consists of those who live according to man, and the other of those who live accord-ing to God. Speaking allegorically, I also call these two orders two Cities: that is, two societies of men, one of which is predestined to reign in eternity with God, and the other of which will undergo eternal punishment with the devil" (XV.1). For this distinction to be drawn, Augustine already has to have recourse to the eternity of time—a notion that, if it is not altogether foreign to Greek thought, then at least it plays no role in classical Greek politics. Augustine himself is aware that he is making a point about temporality: "I should now undertake to relate their history from the time when those first two human beings began to beget offspring down to the time when the begetting of offspring will cease" (XV.1). This distinction, which unifies politics and morality, relies on a conception of history. This history requires a conception of time with a determinate beginning and end.

The beginning of time, the beginning of history with "those first two humans," is the Fall.[43] As Augustine explains, "each man . . . is at first necessarily evil and fleshly, because he comes from Adam; but if, being reborn, he advances in Christ" (XV.1). The beginning of time, and hence the conception of the past, is given through the narrative of the original sin. The past time also determines the conception of the present. The present consists in man being "reborn" as a pilgrim. But this present pilgrimage is not amenable to eternity. This is clear in Augustine's further division within the notion of the city of God: "the earthly city [of God] has two aspects. Under the one, it displays its own presence; under the other, it serves by its presence to point toward the Heavenly City" (XV.3). This eternal city points to a future that is beyond time—the end of the time that the Fall inaugurated. Augustine, then, in fact distinguishes among three cities: the city of pagans, the city of God on earth—or, as I will refer to it, the fallen city of God—and the heavenly or eternal city of God. The temporal register, then, allows Augustine to distinguish among three cities, while this register constantly reiterates the interknitting of politics and kinship. This whole temporal structure needs to be outlined in more detail to show how it is ultimately constructed so as to eliminate judgment and to allow instead solely for justification. This examination of temporality can be carried out through an analysis of the three cities.

The Augustinian narrative rests on a fratricide, Cain's slaughter of Abel.[44] Augustine is at pains to distinguish this fratricide in *Genesis* from other fratricides, such as Romulus killing Remus before the founding of Rome (XV.5). Even though the establishment of a city is always premised on a founding moment of violence, still Augustine is striving to argue that there is a difference. To do so he has to arrive at an alternative interpretation of *Genesis*. After presenting a summary he quotes a passage that should explain Cain's motivation for the murder, and then immediately adds: "The obscurity of this passage has given rise to many different interpretations" (XV.7). Augustine does not indicate here the openness of interpretation. In fact, the opposite is the case. Augustine is indicating that he is about to offer an exceptional interpretation, an exceptional narrative that breaks with the preestablished interpretations. And the reason is precisely that a distinction needs to be drawn between fratricide as a marker of the founding violence of the political and Abel's slaughter. Unlike previous fratricides— presumably including the mutual fratricide of Eteocles and Polynices— Abel belonged to the city of God. Thus, through his exceptional narrative, Augustine can establish a typology of humans, the bad ones who are the descendants of Cain, and the good ones who are the descendants of Seth, the third brother who replaced the slain Abel (XV.8).

The city of pagans, as well as Cain, is characterized by an overvaluation of the present moment. The obsession with the present is a result of the predominance of passions. Augustine describes in detail Cain's envy, which led to his slaughter of Abel. However, the most sustained argument against the passions had already been carried out in Book XIV, which functions as the conclusion to Augustine's retelling of the narrative of the Fall. Augustine's castigation of passions—his passion against passions—is best illustrated through his argument against orgasm in Book XIV, Chapter 9. Augustine introduces the subject obliquely by saying that the word "lust" without any qualification conjures "the impure parts of the body." The significance of "lust" consists in that "lust triumphs not only over the whole body outwardly, but inwardly also." During intercourse, both mind and body fall prey to passions. And the worse part of this consists in a moment when mind and body are entirely overwhelmed: "When the emotion of the mind is united with the craving of the flesh, it convulses the whole man, so that there follows a pleasure greater than any other: a body pleasure so great that, *at that moment of time* when he achieves his climax, the alertness and, so to speak, vigilance of a man's mind is almost entirely overwhelmed" (emphasis added). This moment is the instant of orgasm. Augustine concludes: "And any friend of wisdom and holy joys . . . surely would prefer to beget children without lust of this kind." This frenzied opposition is not only against sex. The labored way in which Augustine references orgasm is significant. Orgasm points to a moment in the present time. Thus orgasm does not refer just to intercourse or any other passion, but also, and more importantly, to the purest of the passions, because it most explicitly indicates the predominance of the present. The orgasm is of the now.[45] Further, due to the fact that passions lead to violence, as Cain's example demonstrates, the city of pagans is a city in constant war: "The wicked, therefore, strive among themselves; and, likewise, the wicked strive against the good" (XV.5). The time of the present is a time of war.

The fallen city of God is defined by its opposition to the present—that is, as opposed to the city of pagans. Lyotard's assertion that *The Confessions* were written in the mode of an unfulfillable waiting equally applies to the city of God.[46] The temporality of the fallen city of God is given through its being indexed to an unreachable future. Thus the temporality of the city of God is given by the two temporal extremes, the beginning of history in the Fall and the end of history in the Final Judgment (cf. Book XX). The temporality of the past explains the detailed genealogy of the city of pagans and the fallen city of God that Augustine undertakes in Book XV as an attempt to "defend the historical truth of Scripture" (XV.8). Unlike Pericles, who, as shown, summarily referred only in two sentences to the ancestors and only insofar as they contributed to the present glory of Athens, Augustine spends the best part of Book XV in a painstaking description of the two cities' relations of kinship all the way back to the protoplasts. This illustrates that the transition to Christian sovereignty consists in a devaluation of the present that relies on the progeny of good and evil. Christian sovereignty revives a politics of kinship in order to determine its past limit. At the same time, the past does not guarantee that the pilgrims of the city of God will attain the Heavenly eternal city. Instead, the citizens of the earthly city of God are distinguished by their election to strive toward the eternal city. This election articulates itself in terms of a rejection both of the pagans and of the pilgrim's own inner passions. The quotation at the end of the previous paragraph about the enmity of the pagan city continues: "The wicked, therefore, strive among themselves; and, likewise, the wicked strive against the good *and the good against the wicked*" (XV.5, emphasis added). This is the conception of the external political sovereignty of the city of God. The internal political sovereignty is adumbrated in the sentence that immediately follows: "While they are making their way toward perfection, however, and have not yet attained it, there can be strife among them inasmuch as any good man can strive against another because of that part of him which he also strives against himself" (XV.5).[47] The fallen city of God is defined through its past kinship and its future direction, but its present is given solely as that perpetual struggle against the passions that can be articulated externally through the city of the pagans and internally as the inevitability of sin.

The pagan city and the fallen city of God are related through their mutual exclusion. They indicate two contradictory and incompatible impulses. This enmity determines a different conception of participation in Christian sovereignty. William Connolly offers a brilliant analysis of the politics of identity that permeates Augustinian politics. Connolly discusses the following passage from *The Confessions*: "For the confronting of the heretics makes the opinions of the Church more eminent, and the tenet which the sound doctrine maintaineth. For there must be also heresies, that they which are approved may be made manifest among the weak."[48] The function of the heretics in *The Confessions* is analogous to that of the pagans in *The City of God*. They indicate the necessity of the incessant war that the fallen city of God is forced to fight. The pagans and the heretics are the "political threat"[49] that allows for the articulation of the political means of Augustine's city of God—that is, it justifies violence. This is a necessity, not merely an accidental attribute. As Connolly puts it, "'There must be heresies' for Augustinianism to be."[50] This Augustinianism consists in an enforced participation in the earthly war between the pilgrims and the passions. No one can evade that struggle (cf. XIX.27)—there are no nonparticipants—because all, due to their ties of kinship to Adam and Eve, are sinners after the Fall. This contrasts with Solon's exigency of participation that allows, indeed requires, the presence of the nonparticipant to the conflicts within the polis. Historical time is defined in Augustine as the enforced participation in this conflict. The only choice within this inevitable participation is whether one is a pilgrim moving toward the eternal city or whether one is a pagan concerned only with the passions of the present.

The present state of enforced participation in the constant war against passions is counterbalanced with the promise of an eternal end to conflict in the Heavenly City. According to Augustine, the eternal or Heavenly City that will be attained by the pilgrims who fight the passions is characterized by a complete absence of enmity. "[T]his peace [in the Heavenly City] is a perfectly ordered and perfectly harmonious fellowship" (XIX.17). This is the image of the "final peace" to which "justice should be referred" (XIX.28). What is constitutive of this eternal peace that presents humanity with its end is a complete elimination of passions: "When we have reached that peace . . . [t]here will be no animal body to press down the soul by its corruption, but a spiritual body standing in need of nothing" (XIX.17). Now it should be recalled that this Heavenly City is not something that can be attained in history—that is, in the time that starts with the Fall. Instead, it is only possible after the end of time with the Last Judgment that Augustine discusses in the following book, Book XX. Thus the Last Judgment is the future limit of historical time. Historical time is, then, framed by the Fall in the past and the Last Judgment in the future. Within these limits there is only ever enmity; outside there is only ever eternal peace.

The positing of the double temporal limit—the Fall and the Last Judgment—has three important implications. It means, first, that eternal peace is separated from the realm of human production and creation. All political actions of the present are defined by a limit or *eschaton* in the past—namely, the Fall—and a limit in the future: the Last Judgment. Everything is directed toward this future limit, which itself, however, can never be reached through human action. Christian love is realized in the Heavenly City, which is, however, after historical time. It is something transcendent. The Heavenly City is never given in the present. As a consequence, the end of justification is only ever external to human relations. Humans can will to strive toward such an end, but as sinners in a fallen world they are incapable of achieving it through their own agency. The end of justification is produced for humans—the humans can never produce it themselves.

Second, the eternal love signified by the city of God is only ever a projection of those who are pilgrims. Such a projection discloses the eschatological temporality that grounds Augustinian politics. In other words, the end of justification is only ever produced for certain humans, those who are, according to Augustine, the pilgrims. But this universal love outside time and outside the sphere of human production justifies in history of violence against the pagans—that is, violence against anyone deemed not to be following the path of pilgrimage. Universal love justifies the universalization of war in the now. Agape is a death drive. Is there a need to recount here the medieval use of this logic to justify the Crusades or the Inquisition, or its most recent recasting as a "clash of civilizations"? Such a historiographical pursuit is significant, but it is more significant to realize the result of the devaluation of the present that is effectuated with the transition to Christian sovereignty—namely, the transition whereby *the end justifies the means*. The conciliation of state and kinship promises an eternal peace that perpetually justifies violence in the present.

This eschatology means also that the forced participation of human action is entirely lacking in the possibility of judgment. Judgment is a divine prerogative, and it points to the eschatological limit that organizes the temporality of the Augustinian politics because it allows for the distinctions between the three different cities. Yet, because the pilgrims are denied the power to make a legitimate judgment, they are endowed instead with the inherent justification to strive for that moment in the future. Through this justificatory power, the devaluation of one moment in the present—the moment of orgasm—in favor of one moment in the future—the Final Judgment—is not, however, only a different theory of time. Nor is it merely the assertion of an alternative justificatory discourse—the Christian conception of sovereignty. In addition, and most importantly, Augustine's eternal peace outside time and the perpetual violence it justifies in historical time allow for no possibility to conceive of anything outside Christian sovereignty. There is no possibility of democracy, because there is no possibility for nonparticipation and there is no possibility of judgment.

It would be premature, however, to conclude that Christian sovereignty successfully evades democracy. In the absence of faith in eschatology, through a suspicion of the temporal limits of the Fall and the Last Judgment, democracy as the reaffirmation of the present emerges as the real *eschaton* of Christian sovereignty. In its every step Christian sovereignty stumbles at this democratic limit. The passionate rejection of intercourse is the passionate rejection of any form of judgment as the precondition of the enforced participation in the war against passions in fallen time. If the present is not only determined by the death-drive of agape but also by eros, then judgment is possible. This means that participation and hence democracy are now reconfigured as the evasion of the binary of the pilgrim versus the captive of passions. Thus, far from achieving to erase participation, Christian sovereignty reinscribes *eros* in every triumphant proclamation of universal *agape*. Or, differently put, agape is a symptom of eros—a symptom that manifests itself by seeking to repress its cause.

3

THE PROPINQUITY OF NATURE

Absolute Sovereignty

The importance of Machiavelli's political theory, observes Michel Foucault, consists in raising the question, "How and under what conditions can a sovereign maintain his power?"[1] In the context of the early sixteenth century this question signifies a radical reworking of sovereignty. In ancient sovereignty the end justifies the means. This is reversed in modern sovereignty. The question of the perpetuation of the sovereign's power is premised on the idea that the means justify the end. As Hobbes puts it in the *Leviathan*, "whosoever has right to the End, has the right to the Means."[2] This reversal of the logical structure of ancient sovereignty by privileging the means instead of the end ultimately reverts to man the ability to make his own end. Or, more accurately, the state is no longer predetermined by certain ends that are or appear to be transcendent. Rather, the state is produced by the one man—the sovereign—who legitimately reigns over his subjects and controls the institutions of government. Ancient sovereignty is produced by the power of a transcendent end, whereas the modern sovereign produces his own power by creating the conditions to perpetuate his power.

The modern reversal of the logic to privilege the means in order to justify the end of sovereignty spawned complex transmutations—political no less than philosophical ones—that cannot possibly be discussed here. I will only concentrate on a few key moments. But it is important also to remember that despite the diversity, the problem encountered by modern sovereignty is how to align the sovereign's license to create power with the end of perpetuating his own power. This is not simply an empirical shortcoming of the sovereign—for instance, when his decisions might be ineffectual. More crucially, it is about the original sovereign motivation to effect the end. *Hamlet* presents this problem: if sovereignty is ipso facto justified, if the sovereign is by definition all powerful, then how can the sovereign decide on what means to exercise? Or, more generally, if any action is justified, is there any longer the motivation to make decisions? A discussion of *Hamlet* in the final section of the present chapter will show how this difficulty undermined the formulation of modern sovereignty as absolute. Prior to that, it is necessary to examine the salient points of the transition to modern sovereignty.

THE SUBJECT OF PSYCHOLOGY AND THE LAW: MACHIAVELLI AND BODIN

In the sixteenth century the upstaging of ancient sovereignty is a pivotal concern. The shift of emphasis from the end—the universal order, peace, and stability promised in the eternal city of God—to the means that indicate nothing else than the dispensation of government has to deal initially with the central characteristic of ancient sovereignty—namely, the conciliation of kinship and the polis through agape. Kinship was transformed into psychology by Machiavelli and the city into a theory of the sovereign's standing above the law by Bodin. Modern sovereignty—the justification of the ends through the means—is premised on the genesis of the subject that submits itself simultaneously to the laws of nature (psychology) and to the laws of the state. The subject is created—it is "artificial," as Hobbes will put it. This artificiality entails that the subject is not pregiven through relations of kinship. The psychology and the legality of the subject are defining features of modern sovereignty. I will delineate some of the most important features of this creation of the modern subject with reference to two of the most important thinkers in the sixteenth century, Machiavelli and Bodin.

The question "how and under what conditions can a sovereign maintain his power?" could never have been asked by Augustine. The reason is that thus expressed, the question does not admit a politics reliant on the idea of an end of, or moral purpose for, history. Without the eschatology that makes a conception of the city of God devoid of any conflict whatsoever, morality is expunged from politics. Augustine insisted in *The City of God* that "no one will be good who was not originally bad."[3] This makes the aim of politics the promotion of the "good" by combating the "bad," effectuating a unification of politics and morality. What the humans do is determined by a moral core represented by the city of God that is beyond human action in the sense that it will never be realized on earth. Machiavelli replies in *The Prince* that there are no "good people" from a political perspective. This suggests that it is an illusion to assume that morality is political. Instead, what matters in politics is human psychology.[4] "But since my intention is to write something useful for anyone who understands it, it seemed more suitable for me to search after the *effectual* truth of the matter rather than its imagined one" (XV).[5] Machiavelli is explicit that he is addressing individuals like himself who are versed in the art of government. For such individuals, what matters is not an "imagined" ideal like the universal peace of a divine city. Rather, what matters is the "effectual truth"— that is, how it is possible to effect power and to perpetuate sovereignty. The truth is effected—it is created by the sovereign's actions. This shift of emphasis from an imagined ideal to an effectual truth is founded, significantly, on a psychological fact: namely, that people are not good.[6] "A man who wishes to profess goodness at all times will come to ruin among so many who are not good. Therefore, it is necessary for a prince who wishes to maintain himself to learn how *not to be good*, and use this knowledge or not use it according to necessity" (XV). Everyone is working for himself and a sovereign "who wishes to maintain himself" in power has to learn how to use this insight to his own advantage. The only principle is the elimination of illusory principles—the only end is that the end must be able to be achieved instrumentally. Or, to repeat, the means justify the end.

The whole of *The Prince* consists in advice on how the sovereign can utilize means at this disposal to maintain himself in power. Should he be generous or parsimonious? Merciful or cruel? Should a prince be honest? It would not be possible to examine Machiavelli's answer to all these—and similar—questions, but I will turn briefly to the question of honesty because it highlights the psychological aspect of the theory of sovereignty. Machiavelli's answer is a resounding "no." "Since men are a wicket lot and will not keep their promises to you, you likewise need not keep yours to them" (XVIII). The citizen that Machiavelli is contemplating is far from the "self-sufficient" Athenians of Pericles's "Funeral Oration." But the reason is that they have psychology in the sense that their behavior is predictable; it obeys the natural law that everyone is acting in a self-interested way. The human is not justifying his or her behavior with recourse to abstract principles. This psychology of the citizen, moreover, generates a corresponding psychology in the sovereign. "Since, then, a prince must know how to make use of the nature of the beast, he should choose from among the beasts the fox and the lion; for the lion cannot defend itself from traps, while the fox cannot protect itself from the wolves" (XVIII). It is not only the subjects that are "beasts," says Machiavelli, but the sovereign himself. And he has to choose the "beasts" that he is to resemble. They should be the lion and the fox. In other words, the psychology of the sovereign should exhibit both strength and cunning. These dispositions allow the sovereign to produce and sustain his power.

The issue of the sovereign's honesty, or, rather, the psychological disposition of the sovereign that is not bound by moral laws of honesty, leads to two further points. First, it reveals a narrative that is itself breaking the rules. This is the narrative of the exception that, as argued in Chapter 1, is operative in the logic of sovereignty. This breaking of rules is indicated, initially, by subverting the anthropomorphism of the lion and the fox. As has often been noted in the secondary literature, according to Cicero's *De Officiis*, the force of the lion and the cunning of the fox are negative characteristics of the sovereign.[7] They lead to injustice, and hence Cicero regards them as "most alien to a human being."[8] Machiavelli here is transgressing the rule of what justice consists in. In effect he turns upside down Cicero's advice. Second, Machiavelli's own text suggests that this narrative dishonesty should be analogous to the sovereign modus operandi: "How praiseworthy it is for a prince to keep his word and to live with integrity and not by cunning, everyone knows. Nevertheless, one sees from expertise in our times that the princes who have accomplished great deeds are those who have thought little about keeping faith and who have known how cunningly to manipulate men's minds; and in the end they have surpassed those who have laid their foundation upon sincerity" (XVIII). The irony of this passage is clear. Machiavelli suggests that if a sovereign is to keep with the advice that insists on some kind of transcendent value of goodness, then that would simply create a consensual approval of the morality of the prince—"how praiseworthy it is . . . everyone knows." However, this narrative, which unanimously lauds the worth of the prince, is inadequate in keeping him in power. The sovereign should not be concerned with creating a universal consensus about his moral value, but rather with creating a narrative that, regardless of whatever moral rules, allows him to be successful by maintaining himself in power. It is the prerogative of the sovereign to create exceptional narratives.

This exceptional power that Machiavelli grants the sovereign is already pointing to the second feature of the creation of the modern subject—namely, its being subjected to law. Significantly, this takes place through the standing of the sovereign above the law. In the *Six Books of the Commonwealth*, Bodin expresses this positioning of the sovereign by saying that sovereignty is an unconditional gift: "the people or the aristocracy of a commonwealth can purely and simply give someone absolute and perpetual power to dispose of all possession, person, and the entire state at his pleasure, and then to leave it to anyone he pleases, just as a proprietor can make a pure and simple gift of his goods for no other reason than his generosity. This is a true gift because it carries no further conditions, being complete and accomplished all at once, whereas gifts that carry obligations and conditions are not authentic gifts. And so sovereignty given to a prince subject to obligations and conditions is properly not sovereignty or absolute power."[9] Sovereignty as an unconditional gift essentially means that the sovereign is not bound by positive law. Or, as Schmitt memorably expressed it, "the sovereign is he who decides on the exception." The sovereign stands higher than written law; he is above the law. He is released or absolved from the law in the sense that he can produce laws at will.

This despotism of Bodin's theory of sovereignty has often been castigated.[10] And it is also often and all too quickly related to the principle of *legibus solutus* from Roman law.[11] But the relation between the law and the individual is actually different in Bodin.[12] The above quotation continues: "This [absolute power] does not apply if the conditions attached at the creation of a prince are of the law of God *or nature*. . . . This power is absolute and sovereign, for it has no other condition than what is commanded by the law of God *and of nature*."[13] The theory of absolute sovereignty developed by Bodin is also a theory of natural law. Bodin's sovereign does not rely on the theory of divine rights that is characteristic of *legibus solutus*.[14] This entails that sovereignty's standing above the law has an instrumental character. It does not point to the end or justice of the state. Rather, it points to the means whereby the order, peace, and stability of the state can be attained. Like Machiavelli, Bodin's question is one of the creation of the conditions of government: How is it possible for the sovereign to govern his subjects? For the sovereign to be in a position to exercise his power, that power must stand above written law, avers Bodin.

To illustrate the point about the instrumentality of the sovereign's standing above the law and the way that it is linked to the subjection of the citizen to the law, we must turn to Bodin's discussion of sovereign rights or prerogatives. "The first prerogative [*marque*] of a sovereign is to give law in general and in particular."[15] The sovereign can give the law because his own authority stands above the law. At this point Bodin considers an objection to this first prerogative. The objection consists in the potential conflict between the law of the state that the sovereign has instituted and customary laws. At this point Bodin has an opportunity to demonstrate how modern sovereignty bypasses the old binary between kinship and the state. Bodin initially argues that custom acquires its power gradually, and that even then its power is not binding, whereas law "appears suddenly," and its power is violent—one will incur penalties, for instance, when one breaks the law. However, unlike Greek thought, which perceives an ineliminable conflict between law and custom, and unlike Christian sovereignty, which seeks to completely reconcile this conflict, Bodin indicates that it is possible for law to include or subsume custom. This possibility is premised on the fact that the sovereign has the right to create law: "custom has no force but by sufferance, and only insofar as it pleases the sovereign prince, who can make it a law by giving it his ratification. Hence the entire force of civil law and custom lies in the power of the sovereign prince."[16] Custom *can* turn into civil law. Because the sovereign can "give law in general and in particular," a custom that has but little force can turn into a law that is truly powerful. Bodin is endeavoring here neither to sustain nor to reconcile the conflict between written and unwritten law, but rather to reformulate it in such a way as to place every subject's actions within the purview of the law that is produced by the sovereign. Even if an action is based on custom and hence not codified yet, still every action is codifiable so long as the sovereign decides to do so. And the sovereign may decide to turn custom into a law when a customary law can be expedient for the sovereign to maintain himself in power. This indicates the transformation of sovereignty in early modernity. The starting point of its logic is no longer about the justness of ends. Instead, justification pertains to the means. Civil law, unlike the divine rights of the king that it substituted, is instrumental. It justifies the creation of laws that enable the use of violence for the protection of the state, and it has the capacity to transport customary law to the realm of the means, too.

The transformation of sovereignty in the sixteenth century does not entail the disappearance of ancient sovereignty. Bodin writes: "Just as God, the great sovereign, cannot make a God equal to Himself because He is infinite and by logical necessity two infinities cannot exists, so we can say that the prince, whom we have taken as the image of God, cannot make a subject equal to himself without annihilation of his power."[17] This does not simply mean that the political sphere carries within it theological remnants. Nor does it simply mean that the old concept of God informs the definition of a new concept, the sovereign—or, as Carl Schmitt put it, "all significant concepts of the modern theory of the state are secularized theological concepts."[18] Instead, and more emphatically, I would like to suggest that the new, modern logic of sovereignty contains within it the possibility of reverting back to ancient sovereignty. As I indicated in the Preamble and in Chapter 1, and as I will be showing again in more detail later, this possibility has always accompanied the logic of sovereignty. There is a cosupponibility between ancient and modern sovereignty because both aim at a justification of violence.

So, with modernity, sovereignty is radically reformulated. Instead of an end that justifies its means, now sovereignty is justified to use any means at its disposal to achieve its end. This end may be articulated as the maintenance and perpetuation of sovereignty or as the establishment of order, peace, and stability—and, for Machiavelli and Bodin, these two ends are, if not the same, at least adjacent. The implication is that those who control the means can determine the end. The strongest in the state, the absolute sovereign, is justified in any action that protects his right to maintain himself in power. Or, in other words, *might is right*. Thrasymachus expressed this view in the *Republic* by saying that "justice is nothing but what is advantageous to the strongest."[19] Socrates was the victor of the Platonic dialogue by propagating instead the superior justice of the philosopher-king. In the sixteenth century philosophy recognizes the soundness of Thrasymachus's position, but only so long as it applies to the sovereign producing power—only so long as the means justify the end of power. Only the sovereign legitimately uses his might to create what is right. The sovereign is the one who has indefinite means at this disposal—the entire legal system and the violence that this generates—in order to maintain himself in power. We can recognize here the tautological structure of the logic of sovereignty. To put it in the terminology used in Chapter 1 to define the absoluteness of the logic of sovereignty, there is an initial separation between means and end only so they can be reunited later. The fact that the sovereign's might is right is justified because it leads to peace. But at the same time, there is no peace without absolute sovereignty, as we will see Hobbes arguing in a moment. The means lead to the end, but the end also determines the means.

Hobbes best articulates the circular logic of absolute sovereignty with recourse to fear. Hobbes constructs a narrative of exceptionality by referring to the state of nature as the perpetual civil war between people. As we will see in the following chapter, the recognition of its circularity forms the core of Rousseau's critical argument against absolute sovereignty.

FEAR THY NEIGHBOR AS THYSELF: HOBBES'S ARTIFICIALITIES

Michael Foucault has argued that the modern subject is a double that is split between the empirical and the transcendental.[20] This double corresponds to the two aspects of the human that we just discussed: namely, Machiavelli's insight about psychology—being subjected to the laws of nature—and Bodin's description of the individual's submission to the sovereign—being subjected to state laws. In the following century Thomas Hobbes combines Machiavelli and Bodin's positions to produce a theory of sovereignty that is consequent upon his extrapolation of subjectivity. Thereby, Hobbes constructs a political ontology that assumes that might is right. To grasp the antidemocratic fervor of Hobbes's philosophy, it is necessary to depart from his delineation of the subject.

The subject in Hobbes points both to natural and positive law. Hobbes opens the *Leviathan* by stating in the introduction this distinction. "NATURE . . . is by the *Art* of man, as in many other things, so in this also imitated, that it can make an Artificial Animal. For seeing life is but a motion of Limbs, the beginning whereof is in some principall part within; why may we not say, that all *Automata* . . . have an artificiall life?" (9).[21] Hobbes compares the human to an automaton. He means by this that there is a regularity of behavior. This consists in that the human's desires are analyzable or psychologizable. It is not life as such that is artificial, but rather the laws of nature that have been created by "art." The first part of the *Leviathan*, entitled "Of Man," consists in an analysis of this human psychology.

Simultaneously, human psychology forms the basis upon which sovereignty is created. The quotation continues: "*Art* goes yet further, imitating that Rationall and most excellent worke of Nature, *Man*. For by Art is created the great LEVIATHAN called a COMMON-WEALTH, or STATE, (in latine CIVITAS) which is but an Artificiall Man; though of greater stature and strength than the Naturall, for whose protection and defence it was intended; and in which, the *Soveraignty* is an Artificiall *Soul*, as giving life and motion to the whole body" (9). The commonwealth signifies the institution of the legal order to which every citizen is subjected. This system of laws is erected upon the natural laws, or, as Hobbes puts it, there is a relation of imitation between the laws of nature and the laws of the state. It is unclear what kind of relation this word "imitating" refers to. In fact, it would be possible to read Hobbes as paradoxically suggesting that the chronologically posterior—the state law—is more primary in this imitative relation, or even that there is a codependence between natural and state laws.[22] Suffice it to point out here that imitation produces the commonwealth whose purpose is the "protection and defence" of the natural man. At this point Hobbes has recourse to the figure of the state as a body—a metaphor derived from Plato's *Timaeus* that was prevalent in the Middle Ages.[23] The commonwealth signifies a transition from the natural to the artificial man—the so-called body politic that incorporates everyone who is within the territorial and legal purview of the state. But unlike the medieval use of the metaphor that represents the king as the head of the state/body, here Hobbes describes the sovereign as the soul that animates "the whole body." The suggestion is that without the sovereign, man would have remained an automaton. And this really means that he would have acted mechanically and would have never reached the end of "protection and defence."

Thus Hobbes creates a hierarchy. At the base is the natural man, who is called an "artificial animal" because he is subjected to the laws of nature that indicate the regularity of passions. Higher than the natural man is the subject, the "artificial man," who is subjected in addition to the laws of the state, having developed rationality and thereby a sense of prohibition. Higher still, released (*ab-solutus*) from the laws of nature and the state, is the sovereign, the "artificial soul" of the commonwealth. The fact that this hierarchy is *artificial* indicates the distance that separates Hobbes from Augustine.[24] Christian sovereignty can reconcile the state and kinship by privileging the end of justification because the entire narrative is eschatological, as already argued. The direction is always toward the city of God, which is divine; it is never artificial. Conversely, the fact that Hobbes's hierarchy is artificial evades eschatology, replacing it instead, as I will argue shortly, with causality. Instead of a transcendent eschaton, Hobbes insists on immanent relations.[25] Further, we will see how this artificial hierarchy transforms the Solonian notion of participation and in the final section of the present chapter how the positioning of the sovereign above the subject is the linchpin of the theory of the king's two bodies that is central in *Hamlet*'s political import.

The subjection to the laws of nature and the state creates a discourse of justification that conceives of the state as manmade. The aim of the creation of the subject is protection: "The only way to erect such a Common Power, as may be able to defend them from the invasion of Forraigners, and the injuries of one another, and thereby to secure them . . . is to conferre all their power and strength to one Man . . . and acknowledge himselfe to be Author of whatsoever he that so beareth their Person, shall Act, or cause to be Acted, in those things which concerne the Common Peace and Safetie; and therein to submit their Wills, every one to his Will, and their Judgments, to his Judgment" (120). For protection to be achieved, Hobbes contends, only the sovereign should be able to judge how order, peace, and stability are to be achieved. Order, peace, and stability are not determined by a power that transcends the realm of politics; rather, the end of the political is immanent within the exercise of sovereign power. In other words, the sovereign has absolute control of the means of power at his disposal. The creation of law by one man, the sovereign, concerns both the relations with other sovereign powers and the relations between citizens. We can easily recognize here the Westphalian principle of the distinction between external and internal sovereignty that is ultimately responsible for two institutions that enforce sovereign power, the military and the police. In the seventeenth century there is a consistent attempt to define borders, thereby solidifying the principle of territorial integrity upon which the idea of external sovereignty is based.[26] But this is accompanied at the time by the development also of the principle of internal sovereignty: within the borders of the state, the psychology of the citizen must be controlled—it must be policed. Even though policing as an activity is possible from the moment a moral value, let alone a law, is established, still the police did not become an institution until modernity. In the sixteenth century the first police forces started appearing in Europe. In the seventeenth century, as the police were becoming well organized, they were theoretically legitimated in Nicolas Delamare's *Traite de la Police*.[27] Policing, however, is premised on the subject—having an individual will that can be submitted to law.[28] The inference that Hobbes draws from this is that the subject renounces the ability to judge about the end of politics—the "Common Peace and Safetie." Or, differently put, the subject is created by the sovereign. The artificiality of the law that subjects the individual contains within it the possibility that policing itself becomes a self-justified and self-perpetuating activity that shapes human behavior. This possibility contained within modern sovereignty will be designated as a central feature of biopolitics in Chapter 5.[29]

The sovereign is the only figure in a position to make judgments about the end, just as God was the ultimate judge in Augustine. Even if this indicates the transformation of the end from something transcendent to something created or artificial, still the symmetry between God and sovereign betrays remnants of ancient sovereignty in modern sovereignty. This retention of remnants from ancient sovereignty is signified by the nomination of sovereign as the "Mortall God" (120) and as "Gods Lieutenant" (122). Being the ultimate judge within the territories of a state, the sovereign's decisions are absolutely justified. Thus the sovereign combines in his figure the use of means for the justification of ends, from which every other person in the state is excluded. This combination of subjection to psychology and law that produces justification forms the social contract, the covenant that creates the commonwealth. These "mutuall Covenants" determine both the sovereign and his subjects: "he that carryeth this Person [the body politic], is called SOVERAIGNE ... and every one besides, his SUBJECT" (120). The famous frontispiece of the *Leviathan* represents the subjection of every citizen in the body politic, thereby absolutely justifying the sovereign's control of both political and religious matters that pertain to the end of peace and safety.[30]

The construction of the subject as the cause of the social contract that justifies sovereignty is antidemocratic. This is not to say that democracy is not entertained as a possibility. Rather, democracy is represented as the psychological condition that precedes the formation of the commonwealth. As Carl Schmitt observes, "'democracy' prevails in the state of nature."[31] For Hobbes the question about the formation of the state depends upon a causal chain that leads from the state of nature to the ordered state headed by a sovereign. After explaining at the beginning that man is an artificial animal, Hobbes spends the following twelve chapters discussing the rise of emotions. The first part of the *Leviathan* is a psychological treatise. The hinge between this psychology and the formation of the social contract is the theory of the state of nature, examined in Chapter 13. This chapter opens with the following statement: "Nature hath made men so equall, in the faculties of body, and mind . . . as that one man can thereupon claim to himselfe any benefit, to which another may not pretend, as well as he" (86–87). The psychology of man developed previously culminates in the recognition that, from the perspective of nature, all men are equal. They are not equal because there is a regulation or a written law that determines their status. On the contrary, they are equal because of the absence of positive law. They are equal because everyone has ultimately equal physical and mental strength and therefore an equal claim to desire. Desire is still unconstrained by human law; desire is free. The result of unchecked desires is generalized warfare, "a civill Warre" or a "warre of every man against every man" (90). The reference to civil war indicates the transformation of the politics of kinship in ancient sovereignty to the psychology of the subject in modern sovereignty. Thus it is important to distinguish Hobbes's state of nature from Thucydides's description of the state of war in Greece prior to the formation of Athens. The different descriptions of generalized war highlight the antidemocratic discourse in Hobbes. As we saw in the previous chapter, the generalized fighting in Greece forced people to lead nomadic lives. According to the opening of Thucydides's *History*, this was a constraint on the people, the best of whom gathered in Athens and built a democracy so as to enjoy freedom. So, whereas both Thucydides and Hobbes describe a state where everyone is fighting with everyone else, the starting point is radically different. For Thucydides there is fighting because there is inequality and lack of freedom, while Hobbes identifies the opposite causes—namely, the presence of absolute freedom and equality. For Thucydides the remedy to civil war is democracy; for Hobbes democracy is civil war.[32] The antidemocratic orientation of Hobbes's discourse can also be highlighted through a comparison to Solon. According to Solon's exigency of participation that we encountered in the previous two chapters, the citizen has to take sides when there is internal conflict. Without that conflict or agonism, democratic participation is impossible. Conversely, for Hobbes, that democratic participation in conflict is precisely the civil war of the state of nature.

Due to its antidemocratic orientation, Hobbes's state of nature resembles Plato's ship with the drunken sailors who vie among themselves to satisfy their capricious, unjustified desires.[33] We saw in the previous chapter how Plato contrasted this pernicious freedom of democracy to the state led by the philosopher-king. Yet, even though both share an anxiety about the freedom characterizing democracy, still Hobbes's sovereign has an essential difference from Plato's philosopher-king. Plato is describing different political arrangements or constitutions, seeking to find which is the best one. Hobbes, on the contrary, is not contrasting constitutions, but, rather, departing from human psychology, he makes an argument about the *only* possible political arrangement for the attainment of peace and security. More precisely, Hobbes constructs a causal argument that departs from the laws of nature and that leads to the social contract.[34] This causal argument requires a hierarchy of passions. Such a hierarchy is possible because of a dialectic of hope and fear. The equality and freedom that distinguish the state of nature cause passions that consist in the desire to acquire something for oneself. These desires for something are signified as hope. "From this equality of ability, ariseth equality of hope in the attaining of our Ends" (87). Emotions provide the psychological means to achieve certain ends. The characteristic of passions of hope is that the end is always selfish. Thus the combination of equality and hope is destructive, according to Hobbes: "And therefore if any two men desire the same thing, which neverthelesse they cannot both enjoy, they become enemies; and in the way to their End . . . endeavour to destroy, or subdue one an other" (87). The effect is generalized warfare: "they are in that condition which is called Warre; and such a warre, as is of every man, against every man" (88). The results of this generalized warfare are devastating for society: "In such condition, there is no place for . . . Arts; no Letters; no Society; and which is worst of all, continuall feare, and danger of violent death; And the life of man, solitary, poore, nasty, brutish, and short" (89). These pernicious effects of hope cause the natural man to fear that his ultimate end, the preservation of his life, is unachievable. This "continuall feare . . . of violent death" effects the overcoming of the illusions of hope. "The Passions that encline man to Peace, are Feare of Death; Desire of such things as are necessary to commodious living; and a Hope by their Industry to obtain them" (90). Fear makes it possible to identify the true end of mankind—namely, order, peace, and stability. Without fear, the hope for one's self-preservation and prosperity is impossible. The Paulinian "love thy neighbour as thyself" is now transformed into a perpetual fear of your neighbor. It is through this fear of the neighbor that desire is renounced or at least curtailed: "Whatsoever you require that other should do to you, that do ye to them" (92). In other words, Hobbes proposes to "fear thy neighbor as thyself." It is only through the overcoming of the dominance of desire through fear that rationality can become operative, allowing for the institution of laws. Thus, according to Hobbes, there is only one way for psychology to support the end of politics: namely, to recognize that fear is the most important emotion in the human because fear is the efficient and sufficient condition for reason to overcome unchecked desire, leading to the social contract. Fear effects the transition to the "artificial man," the modern subject that is subjected both to the laws of nature and to the laws of the state.

Hobbes fundamentally mistrusts the natural man and his passions. This explains the title of his book: "I have set the nature of Man, (whose Pride and other Passions have compelled him to submit himselfe to Government;) together with the great Power of his Governour, whom I compared to *Leviathan*, taking that comparison out of the two last verses of the one and fortieth of *Job*; where God having set forth the great power of *Leviathan*, calleth him king of the Proud" (220–21). Being the "king of the Proud" means that Leviathan reigns all passions, eradicates false hopes and effects a transition to the rationality that characterizes the law of the commonwealth.[35] This psychology that regards passions with suspicion must not be confused, however, with the Augustinian passionate renunciation of passions. It will be recalled that the forced participation in the conflict between the city of God and the city of the pagans consisted in a struggle against the passions. This determined the time of the present in Augustine, which attained an eschatological dimension due to its framing by the two limits, the Fall and the Last Judgment. Hobbes's theory of the passions, however, is not amenable to eschatology. Stephen Collins underscores this point: "Hobbes's political order . . . posits a radical celebration of noneschatological existence."[36] Hobbes posits a link between ontology and politics that relies on a different temporality, as he makes explicit: "For WARRE, consisteth not in Battell onely, or the act of fighting; but in a tract of time, wherein the Will to contend by Battell is sufficiently known: and therefore the notion of *Time*, is to be considered in the nature of Warre" (88). The state of nature need not be in actual war all the time. Rather, it signifies the "tract of time" where war is possible.[37] "All other time is PEACE" (89). Instead of two cities, as in Augustine, Hobbes posits two temporalities, the time of war and the time of peace. In the former hope is the predominant psychological condition, whereas in the latter it is fear for one's life. This allows for a typology of psychological means that causally lead from the freedom of democracy to the submission to the sovereign. To the extent that psychology is determined neither by the past nor by the future, both these temporalities, the time of war and the time of peace, are of the present. Hobbes's political ontology relies on an analysis of immanence. As we will see in the last section of the present chapter, *pace* Hobbes, the democratic possibility of participating in the now remains alive because of his ontology of immanence.

It is important that Hobbes does *not* say that hope characterizes the state of nature and that fear is indicative of the commonwealth. We already saw that, according to Hobbes, the primary passion that inclines man to order, peace, and stability is fear of death; however, this is accompanied by the hope for "commodious living." In Hobbes's political ontology it is not psychology that effects the transition to the state. Instead, it is the creation of the legal framework. In the state of nature where there is war of "every man against every man . . . nothing can be Unjust" (90). Or, put differently, "where no Law, no Injustice" (90) exist, every hope is as legitimate as any other hope. Even though psychology is separated from law, still it is important for the discourse on natural law and human rights in the *Leviathan*. "The RIGHT OF NATURE . . . is the Liberty each man hath, to use his own power, as he will himselfe, for the preservation of his own Nature; that is to say, of his own Life" (91). The liberty that characterizes the state of nature allows the articulation of the right to use power for the protection of one's life. This sphere of rights, however, is sharply distinguished from the sphere of laws: "A LAW OF NATURE . . . is a Precept, or generall Rule, found out by Reason, by which a man is forbidden to do, that, which is destructive of his life" (91). What Hobbes calls "law of nature" is what I have been calling the law of the state. Instead of the psychology of the passions, law indicates the operation of reason. And reason emerges the moment a prohibition is established. In other words, law is the curtailment of unrestricted desire. Hobbes summarizes the distinction between right and law thus: "RIGHT, consisteth in liberty to do, or to forbeare; Whereas LAW, determineth, and bindeth to one of them: so that Law, and Right, differ as much, as Obligation, and Liberty" (91). He concludes the distinction by saying that "as long as this naturall Right of every man to every thing endureth, there can be no security to any man" (91). The primary desire of the state of nature—the primary natural right—is self-preservation, but this can only be realized outside the state of nature, by submitting to the law of the commonwealth. To realize this end, man has to transfer his right to the sovereign and this transferring is a legal obligation referred to by Hobbes as a "contract" or a "covenant" (94).

The social contract can be seen as a spatial arrangement. The motor power is the passions—in particular fear as the desire for self-preservation. Fear drives natural man—the "artificial animal," according to the opening of the *Leviathan*—away from nature, away from the sphere of right, liberty, and equality. Fear drives man away from a complete subjection to the laws of nature. One remove from nature is the subject, which is now subjected also to the laws of the state. In addition to passions, reason is present in the subject who can comprehend the prohibitions that curtail desire and allow his ascension from the "artificial animal" to the "artificial man." Higher yet than the subject is the sovereign, the "artificial soul" of the commonwealth. The sovereign is fearless, like the Leviathan. He is also not subject to the laws of the state, but rather stands above them. The sovereign is absolute because he is separated from the lower position of the hierarchy. He stands above the law in order to effectuate an end to the civil war of the state of nature caused by the self-interested passions of hope. The sovereign's standing above the law means that he has all the means at this disposal to achieve the end of order, peace, and stability. The means, his power, justify the end. But also the end is only achievable through this figure, the "soul" of the commonwealth, the absolute sovereign. His might makes him right, but that right that he acquires is premised on his superior power. Therefore, we see that the absoluteness of the logic of sovereignty—the separation and reunification of means and ends—is encapsulated here in the formula "might is right" that characterizes the absolute sovereignty in Hobbes's theory.

At this point a significant question in Hobbes's theory of the social contract arises. This question that points to the core of the logic of sovereignty is a direct result of the hierarchy from the most low, the natural man, to the most high, the "artificial soul" or sovereign. This spatial relation requires a significant distance between the sovereign and nature. This distance raises the question whether the sovereign is to be subject to the laws of nature. In other words, is the sovereignty completely separated from nature? Is he impervious to passions, ensconced above psychology?

THERE MUST BE MADMEN. . . . THE ABSOLUTENESS OF THE SOVEREIGN IN THE *LEVIATHAN*

The sovereign's distance from the laws of the state and the natural laws is best articulated through the political metaphor of the king's two bodies that was prevalent in medieval jurisprudence and that was analyzed by Ernst Kantorowicz in his 1957 seminal book, *The King's Two Bodies: A Study in Mediaeval Political Theology*. The two bodies of the king correspond to the two aspects of the subject, psychology and legality. As Kantorowicz has extrapolated it, the doctrine of the king's two bodies has two main characteristics. First, the legal body (or body politic) of the king is higher than his natural body, and second, the two remain inseparable. Kantorowicz quotes from Edmund Plowden: "this Body [politic] is utterly void of Infancy, and old Age, and other natural Defects and Imbecilities, which the Body natural is subject to, and for this Cause, what the King does in his Body politic, cannot be invalidated or frustrated by any Disability in his natural Body."[38] The king has no natural defects. His standing above the state law means that he can never be subjected to the law of nature. He is immune from any natural defects such as "imbecilities." The hierarchy between the two bodies is expressed thus by Plowden: "His Body politic, which is annexed to his Body natural, takes away the Imbecility of his Body natural, and draws the Body natural, which is the lesser, and all the Effects thereof to itself, which is the greater."[39] Thus, to put it in Hobbes's terms, the sovereign or "artificial soul" includes the "artificial animal" and the "artificial man," but rises higher than them. Kantorowicz analyzes the implications of this doctrine by turning first to Shakespeare, whom he regards as an exponent of the metaphor of the king's two bodies.[40]

Kantorowicz's case study is *Richard II*, but, as we will see shortly, *Hamlet* is also an excellent illustration of the doctrine.[41]

Although the doctrine of the king's two bodies may justify the separation of the sovereign from the subject and even provide a legitimation for his authority, it still does not adequately explain how it is possible to separate the king from passions. How can the sovereign not be subject to psychology? Whereas Kantorowicz does not provide an adequate answer to this question, Hobbes does, at least implicitly. In fact the answer is contained in the quotation from *Job* that explains the title of the book: "Hitherto I have set the nature of Man . . . together with the great Power of his Governour, whom I compared to *Leviathan*, taking that comparison out of the two last verses of the one and fortieth of *Job*; where God having set forth the great power of *Leviathan*, calleth him king of the Proud" (220–21). We saw earlier how pride in this context refers to the passions that dominate natural man, who has to transfer his rights to the sovereign in order to enter the social contract and to subject himself to the laws of the state that guarantee order, peace, and stability. The two verses that Hobbes quotes immediately after the previous citation are: "*There is nothing*, saith he, *on earth, to be compared with him. He is made so as not to be afraid. Hee seeth every high thing below him; and is the King of all pride*" (221, emphasis in the original). The Leviathan is the "king of all pride"; that is, he is the authority over the passions and psychology because he "is made so as not to be afraid." The lack of fear is constitutive of the sovereign. Hobbes immediately qualifies the statement, saying that being mortal, the sovereign can actually be subjected to fear, which results in the dissolution of the commonwealth, as Hobbes analyzes from Chapter 29 onward. In other words, Hobbes assumes the sovereign's standing above the law—the maintenance of his rule—and his standing above fear as parallel functions or, even more emphatically, as functions that imply one another. When the sovereign becomes subject to fear, he loses his legitimacy; he reverts to being a subject.

To make sense of Hobbes's assumption that the lack of fear is connected to the sovereign's standing above the law, it is crucial to recall the argument about the psychology of the human that he expounded in the first part of the *Leviathan* and that culminated in the theory of the state of nature. It will be recalled that we discovered two crucial characteristics. First, there is a law of passions—there is a psychology—because the passions give rise to a causal chain. The passion of hoping to attain something results in civil war; the civil war effects fear for one's life; and the fear gives rise to the transference of rights. Second, this causal chain is premised on a hierarchy of passions. There are, on the one hand, the passions referred to as hope and that consist in the externalization of a desire—the hope *for* A, or B, or C. And, there are, on the other hand, the passions of fear, which are higher for two reasons: they express the most fundamental right of self-preservation; and fear for one's life effects the transition from the sheer dominance of passions to the operation of reason. The social contract is possible because reason can instruct the subject to obey the law, which signals the move from the liberty of rights to the proscriptions of obligation. Thus the sovereign's fearlessness indicates that the sovereign does not undergo the entire causal chain of passions. Because of his lack of fear the sovereign does not renounce his rights and hence does not become subject to the law. Without fear there is no submission to proscriptions or prohibitions. The hierarchy of emotions due to the causality that leads from hope to fear reflects the hierarchy of the human within the political order. The psychological and the legal hierarchies mirror each other.

The mirroring of these hierarchies may provide an explanation of the connection between the fearlessness of the sovereign and his standing above the law. But this is still not an adequate account of how fearlessness is possible in the first place. How is it possible to say that the sovereign is subject to the laws of nature and yet not subject to fear? To justify this exception, Hobbes provides an account of how one can possibly feel hope without ever feeling fear—or, at least, fear as the emotion that leads to the operation of reason and hence to the institution of legality. A number of figures are mobilized for this purpose, such as the savage whose political organizations rely on "naturall lust" (89)—that is, on a form of hope for attaining something pleasing rather than on the fear that is necessary for the covenant to be obligatory (97). Yet Hobbes's standard expression for the figure that does not, or rather cannot, enter the social contract, is "Children, Fooles, and Mad-men."[42] Thus, for instance, Hobbes contends that the "Foole hath sayd in his heart, there is no such thing as Justice" (101). As we saw at the end of the previous section, there is neither justice nor injustice in the state of nature, where there is "naturall lust" instead of the covenant. And as soon as Hobbes describes the transition to the social contract, he gives an account of cases in which a contract is invalid: "Children,

Fooles, and Mad-men that have no use of Reason, may be Personated by Guardians" (113). These figures cannot enter the social contract because they are not conscious of inhibitions. They can only recognize their rights, but they are incapable of submitting to obligations. Hobbes summarizes his conclusions thus: "Over naturall fooles, children, or mad-men there is no Law, no more than over brute beasts; nor are they capable of the title of just, or unjust; because they had never power to make any covenant, or to understand the consequences thereof; and consequently never took upon them to authorise the actions of any Soveraign, as they must do that make to themselves a Common-wealth" (187). "Children, Fooles, and Mad-men" are like "brute beasts" because they do not go through the causal chain of emotions that leads from hope to fear and thence to rationality. They are "naturall" instead of "artificial" because they do not renounce hope and hence they do not recognize fear. There are certainly different reasons that all these figures do not fulfill the psychological laws—for instance, the infant may be capable to do so upon maturing. Yet the result is the same—namely, exclusion from the laws of the state.

The use of the figures of the savage, the foole, the infant, and the madman allows Hobbes to provide an account of how the causality of passions—human psychology—can stop short of fear, but this again further displaces the problem of how it is possible that the sovereign is not subject to the natural laws of psychology. The reason is that these figures now appear perilously close to the definition of the sovereign. The madman is, like the sovereign, outside both natural and state law. Thus, in order to clearly distinguish the sovereign from the madman, Hobbes requires a further criterion. This is provided through the figure of the rebel: "And for the other Instance of attaining Soveraignty by Rebellion . . . the attempt thereof is against reason. Justice therefore, that is to say, Keeping of Covenant, is a Rule of Reason, by which we are forbidden to do any thing destructive to our life; and consequently a Law of Nature" (103). The rebel is added to the list of those who are excluded from the social contract because they act "against reason."[43] But the rebel is explicitly contrasted to the sovereign. Rebellion escapes the purview of justice that characterizes the covenant because the rebel's actions are against the self-preservation of the commonwealth. The rebel is not entitled to make political judgments. Conversely, it is the sovereign, by deciding on the exception, to recall Schmitt's formula, that preserves the commonwealth. It is only the sovereign who is justified to stand above the law. The lack of concern for the preservation of the polity renders the rebel purely self-interested, slave to his self-gratifying passions. He is too proximate to nature. Like the madman, the rebel's decisions are merely expressions of his desires, whose end is self-interested. Conversely, it is only the sovereign, according to Hobbes, who has the power to decide for the good of the community. The reason is that he is distant enough from nature not to be under the sway of false hopes or distracting fears. We can recognize here the significance of the spatial arrangement of Hobbes's hierarchical structure. The hierarchy of passions mirrors the hierarchy of legality not simply because the sovereign is not subject to natural laws, but rather because his fearlessness makes him stand above the causal chain of passions. He is above the state law because he is above natural law. The sovereign is distant from nature.

Legitimacy and justification are the prerogatives of the one who is released (*ab-solutus*) from law. The sovereign's distance from nature, however, can only be established by designating those who are excluded from the laws due to their proximity to nature. The upshot of this exclusion creates, and is created by, the narrative of exceptionality. The rebel, the madman and the other figures that are placed below the law are excluded from the polity because they act destructively toward the commonwealth. The most high position of the sovereign is required in order to protect the subject from those who remain unsubjectable, the natural men who cannot turn into subjects, into "artificial men."[44] And yet, without those who threaten the commonwealth—without the possibility of an emergency inscribed in the various figures who remain unsubjectable—the need for a sovereign whom everyone fears and yet who is himself fearless would have evaporated. Hobbes's sovereign is absolute in the precise sense that there is a radical separation, an unbridgeable gap, between the sovereign and the madman. The mirroring hierarchies of passion and legality produce the enemy. The rebel and the madman are the other, the enemy to Hobbes's sovereign, just as hope is the other, the enemy to fear. Augustine needed the pagan and the heretic in order to divide the human types into two categories, the pilgrim and the captive. As William Connolly put it, "'There must be heresies' for Augustinianism to be."[45] These excluded figures are needed for identity to be constructed. Identity is conferred in a different manner in Hobbes. Instead of an eschatology that is premised on the division of the human into two types, Hobbes identifies as the other or the enemy those who act out of their equal power, those who remain wedded to liberty, those who are incapable of renouncing the democracy signified by the state of nature. Yet, in both cases, exclusion is the precondition for the conferring of identity. There must be madmen for Hobbesian sovereignty to exist.

The entire hierarchy, from the "artificial animal" to the "artificial man" to the "artificial soul," is premised on the possibility that something escapes this hierarchy. There is the realm of the artificial that is linked to the creation of modern politics, and at the same time there is the "natural man" who escapes artificiality, who remains "bare life," in Giorgio Agamben's formulation or, in Eric Santner's preferred expression, "creaturely life."[46] This point is very important because it constitutes, according to Agamben, the defining feature of biopolitical sovereignty—its being inside and outside the law: "The state of nature and the state of exception are nothing but two sides of a single topological process in which what was presupposed as external (the state of nature) new reappears . . . in the inside (as state of exception), and the sovereign power is this very impossibility of distinguishing between outside and inside, nature and exception, *physis* and *nomos*."[47] Thus, according to Agamben, it is the fact that "there must be madmen" that determines not only the extrapolation of sovereignty in the seventeenth century, but rather sovereign power even today. Those excluded are those who are subjected to violence, then and now. They are thus reincluded by being subjected to the violence of the sovereign. There is a codetermination between the sovereign who stands above the law and all the figures who are placed below the law. The reason is that without the excluded, violence could not be justified. This parallel exclusion and inclusion that characterize Agamben's paradox of sovereignty can be called a logic of exclusory inclusion.[48] And yet, as I have argued in more detail elsewhere, even though Agamben wants to conduct a critique of sovereign power and biopolitics, still he conducts that critique by presupposing the hierarchy.[49] The paradox of sovereignty—the sovereign's standing both inside and outside the law—is possible in Agamben's discourse only because there is a separation of *physis* and *nomos*. In the terms used here, sovereignty is only possible because of the "artificial man," the subject, who is split between the law of nature and the law of the state.

A critique of sovereignty that presupposes sovereignty's logic of exclusory inclusion will only ever be able to assert that "there must be madmen for sovereignty to exist." What it would be unable to recognize, however, is the importance of the initial democratic paradigm that defines the state of nature. The madmen for Hobbes are the democrats, those who aspire to equality of power and to freedom. Thus *there must be democrats for the Hobbesian sovereignty and for the modern subject to exist.* If sovereign power is the impossibility of distinguishing between *physis* and *nomos*, in Agamben's sense, then that impossibility is premised on something that escapes from and is presupposed by that topological distinction. It is an excess and, following Hobbes's own description of the state of nature, we can call it a state of equality and freedom, and we can give it a specific name: democracy. Or, differently put, democracy does not arise out of the impossibility between natural and state law that determines sovereignty. Rather, it needs a set of relations that dismantle the spatial or topological relations between the sovereign, the subject, and the madman.

Hamlet's melancholia, it will be argued, indicates power's propinquity to nature, which, by definition, is not amenable to the hierarchy. Hamlet shows that the sovereign and the madman were never separate by an unbridgeable gap, by an abyss of power. Rather, by the very fact that the sovereign is the most mighty one in the state, he approximates the natural man. The absolute might of the one mirrors the man in the state of nature, since the natural man is also one, "poore, nasty, brutish" (89)—that is, one who relies on might. But this propinquity is not amenable to the hierarchies that structure the logic of "might is right." Melancholia is not amenable to the causality of the laws of nature and the state in order to produce absolute sovereignty. Hence *Hamlet* performs a forceful critique of the logic of exclusory inclusion that characterizes the separation of the sovereign and the madman, or psychology from state law.[50]

MELANCHOLIA AS DEJUSTIFICATION: *HAMLET'S* ANTI-ABSOLUTISM

The political aspect of *Hamlet* can be recognized initially in Claudius's fratricide of King Hamlet, the prince's father.[51] "O, my offense is rank," admits Claudius to himself, "it smells to heaven, / It hath the primal eldest curse upon it, / A brother's murder" (3.3.36–38).[52] We have already encountered this fratricide numerous times: in the civil war that ravaged Greece prior to the formation of Athens according to Thucydides, in the mutual killing of Eteocles and Polynices in *Antigone*, and in Augustine's use of Cain's slaying of Abel to construct the narrative about the two cities. Even Hobbes's state of nature as a civil war is a form of fratricide. Despite their differences, in all these cases the figure of fratricide is used to indicate justifications of violence. In Act 1 of the play the murdered king appears as a ghost to Hamlet and entreats his son to avenge his murder. This justified violence against his brother is also linked to the issue of who is the legitimate sovereign of Denmark. As a result the predominant questions in the political interpretations concern Hamlet's entitlement to the throne of Denmark, or to what extent Shakespeare was trying to make a comment about succession in Britain through the allegory of the young Dane prince.[53] I do not want to delve into these lines of inquiry, except to point out that they are usually completely separate from a different set of questions that has been very influential in the scholarship.

This other set of questions concentrates on Hamlet's melancholia. This line of inquiry tends to read melancholia as a psychological predicament that is not related, or at least is not essential, to the political questions raised above. The main instigator of the interpretations of Hamlet's melancholia is not, in fact, a scholarly work, but rather Goethe's influential *Wilhelm Meister's Apprenticeship* (1795–96). The eponymous protagonist of this *bildungsroman* becomes fascinated with *Hamlet* and even stages a performance of the play, leading to a series of influential observations. And none is more influential than the comments in Book IV, Chapter XII, where Wilhelm compares Hamlet to an oak tree in a vase: "An oak tree planted in a precious pot which should have held delicate flowers in its bosom. The roots spread out, the pot is shattered."[54] According to Wilhelm, Hamlet is misplaced. This misplacement, however, is articulated as the discontinuity between the personal and the political: "And when the ghost has vanished, what do we see standing before us? A young hero thirsting for vengeance? A prince by birth, happy to be charged with unseating the usurper of his throne? Not at all! Amazement and sadness descend on this lonely spirit."[55] Hamlet's melancholia and chronic indecision make him incommensurable, according to Goethe, with the heroic figure of a prince that aspires to the throne. Goethe continues: "A fine, pure, noble and highly moral person, but devoid of that emotional strength that characterizes a hero, goes to pieces beneath a burden that it can neither support nor cast off. Every obligation is sacred to him, but this one is too heavy."[56] Hamlet's moral nature makes him melancholic because he cannot act like a hero and hence cannot act in such a way as to aspire to the throne. The reason is that he finds "the present too hard." Thus, in Goethe's influential interpretation, Hamlet's psychological constitution precludes him from participating in politics.[57] Hamlet is denied the possibility to engage in the now—the possibility that constituted the precondition of democracy according to Solon's exigency of participation that we discussed earlier.

Contrary to these established lines of inquiry, I suggest that it is possible to find the essential political import of *Hamlet* only through the figure of melancholia. Hamlet's inability to act against Claudius, his pervasive indecisiveness, challenges the psychology of the human that is, as already intimated, an intrinsic part of absolute of sovereignty. Goethe fails to recognize that the misplacement of Hamlet—the placing of a tree in a jar—contains a radical political message. According to Franco Moretti, "Elizabethan and Jacobean tragedy . . . disentitled the absolute monarch to all ethical and rational legitimation."[58] It is this sense of disentitlement to be above the laws that I termed "dejustification" in Chapter 1. As I argued there, dejustification deconstructs the way in which the sovereign justification is expressed. In our case, the logic of absolute sovereignty is articulated through the creation of the subject that is premised on the hierarchy that posits two exclusions to the law, those below the law who are perceived to pose a threat to the state, and the sovereign who stands above the law, distant from nature. As it was argued earlier, this hierarchical topology can be understood with reference to the doctrine of the king's two bodies. There are clear references to this doctrine in *Hamlet*. Having killed Polonius, Hamlet is asked where the cadaver is. He responds: "The body is with the King, but the King is not with the body" (4.2.26–27). The dead body is indeed with the king as the body politic that represents the entire state—and in this sense Hamlet is metonymically saying that Polonius's body is in Denmark. But the body is not in the vicinity of Claudius, the body natural of the sovereign. The disentitlement or dejustification of sovereignty occurs when this hierarchy that characterizes sovereignty and is indicated by the king's two bodies is placed alongside Hamlet's melancholia. This juxtaposition is not arbitrary. A feature of Hamlet's brooding thoughts is the contemplation of this hierarchical structure. A scene later, when Claudius himself asks Hamlet where Polonius's body is, Hamlet responds: "Not where he eats, but where 'a is eaten. A certain convocation of politic worms are e'en at him. Your worm is your only emperor for diet. We fat all creatures else to fat us, and we fat ourselves for maggots. Your fat king and your lean beggar is but variable service—two dishes, but to one table. That's the end" (4.3.19–25).[59] The worms are "politic" precisely because they bridge the gap—they eradicate the distance or "ab-solution"—between the most high, the sovereign, and the most low, those excluded from participation in the social contract, such as the beggar.[60] What is the impact of these melancholic thoughts on the way that sovereignty is understood to stand above the laws of nature? How can melancholia fit within the causal chain of the psychology of emotions propounded by Hobbes?

The simple answer to the question is that melancholia just does not fit. In this sense melancholia and the figure of Hamlet destabilize the hierarchies of sovereign power observed by Hobbes—*Hamlet* becomes a critique of the exposition of absolutism in the *Leviathan*, even though it was written half a century earlier. But to show how this is enacted in Shakespeare, we have to show the way that the subject in *Hamlet* is constructed as an "artificial man," as the figure that stands between the sovereign and the madman. From this perspective the most revealing scene in *Hamlet* is Act 2, Scene 1. There Polonius, the courtier and father of Ophelia, gives instructions to his servant, Reynaldo, about how to find out whether his son, Laertes, has been behaving himself in Paris. In terms of plot development this is a useless scene. Neither does it function as an interlude to the action, since it comes too early in the play. In fact it seems entirely out of place immediately after the dramatic scene of the encounter with the ghost.[61] But this is the most revealing political moment, because it indicates the positioning of the subject between the two extremities—the sovereign and the madman—and hence allows for a presentation of absolute sovereignty. In the previous scene, Act 1, Scene 5, Hamlet decides, upon hearing from the ghost that Claudius poisoned his father, that he should usurp power from Claudius. At that point Hamlet devises a plan that leads him up to the throne and that consists in his pretending to be a madman, or, as he tells his friend Horatio, "To put an antic disposition on" (1.5.171). Hamlet here positions himself as a sovereign in waiting, and hence as someone who is already above the law, or at least as moving up toward that position that is higher than all others. From this perspective Polonius's instructions to Reynaldo make perfect sense. The best method of finding out whether Laertes has been proper in Paris is to bait Laertes's acquaintances to talk about his son. As Polonius puts it, "But breathe his faults so quaintly / That they may seem the taints of liberty" (2.1.31–32) so that, "By indirections find directions out" (2.1.66). In other words, Laertes and his friends are subjects because they are subject to the law—they can act appropriately or inappropriately—and their behavior is predictable, analyzable, and psychologizable. This is the middle position in the hierarchy, the position of the citizen or subject. The next scene of the same act opens with the perception that Hamlet is suffering from madness. As Claudius puts it, "Hamlet's transformation; so call it, / Sith nor the exterior nor the inward man / Resembles that it was" (2.2.5–7). This madness may be temporary, a result of his love for Ophelia, as Polonius reassures the king and the queen (2.2.95–108), but it is madness, nevertheless. This completes the descending movement through the hierarchy, leading to the lowest position of the madman.

So in Act 1 we find an ascending movement that culminates in the expressed plan that Hamlet devises to avenge his father's death and for himself to ascend to the throne. This is followed by the descending movement in Act 2 that defines the middle position of the subject as well as the lowest position of the madman. Act 2 concludes with Hamlet devising the plan to put on stage the murder of the king by Claudius in order to discover whether the ghost was telling the truth: "I have herd that guilty creatures sitting at a play / Have by the very cunning of the scene / Been struck so to the soul that presently / they have proclaimed their malefactions" (2.2.576–79). In other words, like Polonius, Hamlet is seeking "by indirections to find directions out," except that now this recourse to psychology does not pertain to the subject, but rather to the sovereign. In fact, it is a trick that moves the sovereign to the lower position of the subject. Hamlet puts on stage Claudius's fratricide in order to instill fear in the sovereign. The king will be brought to the middle position, that of the subject, when he betrays by his reaction the murder of the previous king. So Shakespeare presents in the first two acts all the positions of the hierarchy that make absolute sovereignty possible. In these first two acts there is a certain regularity in the presentation of the hierarchy, in the sense that the movement between the different levels is one-directional: in Act 1 there is the ascending direction, and in Act 2 the descending one that encompasses even the sovereign.

In the following act, Act 3, the famous stage within the stage dramatically escalates and complicates this up-and-down movement within the hierarchies of power. Unlike the previous two acts, where the movement is one-directional—either ascending in Act 1 or descending in Act 2—here the movement is multi-directional. Thus, for instance, there is an actor, who is a subject, acting a sovereign, and therefore indicating an upward direction. But this is designed by Hamlet to bring the actual king down— and this does not mean simply that Claudius is to become subject to psychology, but if ascertained to be guilty of the king's murder, also to be deemed illegitimate, a rebel and hence subject to execution. So the stage presents simultaneously all the different positions that are required by absolute sovereignty. At the same time the inclusion of Hamlet on this stage radically challenges absolute sovereignty. Hamlet is included, but his positioning is not fixed; rather, it is fluid and changing, not amenable to hierarchies. Hamlet is both like an actor in the sense that he wants to move up (to install himself in the throne), but at the same time moves downward, since he is acting out the "foole" while reclining on Ophelia's lap. The stage within the stage mirrors Hamlet's position. It is an unstable position. A position that is impossible to "pin down." It is a position that *does not exist*, in the sense that it is a representation, an acting out of the hierarchies of power. And yet, at the same time, it is a position that functions as *the condition of the possibility of existence*, in the sense that all other positions within the hierarchy—the sovereign, the subject, and the madman—are defined through this excess. Hamlet's position includes all other positions, but without being reducible to either of them. Hamlet is the structural impossibility that makes the structure of absolute sovereignty possible. To put it another way, Hamlet destructures the hierarchies that the exception presupposes—or, more accurately, Hamlet destructures the possibility that hierarchy as such can form a basis for articulating sovereign power. Hamlet is a supplementary anomaly to the system—an exception to the exception. As such Hamlet presents a position that cannot be accommodated in the topological arrangement that justified the sovereign's absoluteness. Hamlet dejustifies absolute sovereignty.

If the various movements of the play enact a critique of the absolute separation of the king from the madman, at the same time Hamlet's melancholia performs a parallel critique of the aspect of absoluteness that arises out of the sovereign's nonsubjection to psychology—namely, his distance from nature. By accentuating this critique of psychology, melancholia becomes decidedly political. Hamlet contemplates human nature with detachment:

> I have of late—but wherefore I know not—lost all my mirth, forgone all custom of exercises; and indeed it goes so heavily with my disposition that this goodly frame, the earth, seems to me a sterile promontory, this most excellent canopy, the air, look you, this brave o'erhanging firmament, this majestical roof fretted with golden fire, why, it appears no other thing to me than a foul and pestilent congregation of vapours. What a piece of work is a man![62] how noble in reason! how infinite in faculty! in form and moving how express and admirable! in action how like an angel! in apprehension how like a god! the beauty of the world! the paragon of animals! And yet, to me, what is this quintessence of dust? man delights not me: no, nor woman neither. (2.2.291–304)

The destabilization and misplacement of the hierarchies that make absolute sovereignty possible are reflected in the designation of man, the newly created subject, as the "quintessence of dust." In the Elizabethan cosmology this is an oxymoron. Quintessence refers to the highest sphere, whereas dust refers to the lowest, most base sphere. Even if both of these aspects are part of the human, they are still separate aspects, and it is highly oxymoronic to synthesize them in a single expression.[63] The Hobbesian and Agambeian logic of exclusory inclusion both require the exclusion—that is, the absolute separation—between the sovereign and the madman—or between quintessence and dust. *Hamlet* indicates an excess that bridges the gap between the sovereign and the madman—or, more accurately, the play shows that an absolute separation between the sovereign and the creature never actually existed and is in fact impossible.[64] In this sense the figure of Hamlet—as *both* the prince who at least potentially stands above the law *and* the madman who by definition is placed below the law—puts forward a radical critique of the logic of exclusory inclusion. Hamlet offers that critique by showing that the absolute separation between king and madman/rebel—and it is the absoluteness of this separation that makes this conception of sovereignty *absolute*—in fact presupposes a melancholic prince who is neither sovereign nor madman/rebel. Significantly, the neither/nor here is not exclusory, but rather productive. It produces an excess, a supplement to sovereign power that destructs its absoluteness.

At this point arises the question of how to understand the resistance to sovereignty, the dejustification of the absoluteness of sovereignty, enacted through Hamlet's melancholia. In other words, is there a revolutionary demand in his stance? A comparison with Antigone shows two very different attitudes to sovereignty. Antigone sprinkles dust on her brother's cadaver as an act of defiance toward the sovereign. On the contrary, Hamlet's image of the human as the "quintessence of dust" prevents him from assuming action. Antigone is decisive. She stands up in front of Creon and the elders of the chorus, proclaiming her right to conform to the law of kinship. Her actions and words are a direct affront to the sovereign. By contrast, Hamlet never confronts Claudius directly. At the stage within the state, in Act 3, Hamlet is a spectator, not an active participant. And shortly after, when he finds Claudius alone and he has the chance to avenge his father and usurp the throne, Hamlet invents excuses to refrain from action. Even in dying, Antigone acts. She does not wait for starvation to kill her, but rather decisively precipitates her own death. Haemon's suicide at the feet of his beloved allows us to imagine a maiden who remains beautiful even after death. Hamlet's own death-wish in Act 5, when he decides to duel with Laertes, who is a master in fencing, is stripped of any allure or beauty. At one point the Queen, his own mother, observes that Hamlet is "fat, and scant of breath" (5.2.273). Antigone presents as full of purpose. Hamlet is devoid of purpose. Even the election of Fortinbras as king of Denmark, Hamlet's dying wish (5.2.341–42), shows no purpose; since the election was an accident, it was pure chance that Fortinbras was crossing Denmark at that moment, after his campaign against the Poles. So how can one possibly argue that there is a political, even revolutionary demand in Hamlet, when his stance is so passive, so lacking in purpose, so lacking an end?

It is precisely this lack of end, characteristic of melancholia, that subverts absolute sovereignty in a way that would have been impossible with ancient sovereignty. As already argued, ancient sovereignty consists in an articulation of ends, and the tragic conflict between Antigone and Creon is the irreconcilability of their respective ends. Modern sovereignty, conversely, concentrates on the articulation of means. Modern sovereignty consists in the justification of the end through the means. Melancholia, however, is a feeling without a specific object.[65] This disturbs the causality of emotions that Hobbes delineated. It will be recalled that, according to the first part of the *Leviathan*, there is a causal chain of emotions. The starting point is the passions of hope that consist in desiring an object—hoping *for* A, B, or C. The equality of hope, however, causes war, which in turn causes fear, which causes the rational recognition that desire must be curtailed. Melancholia resembles fearlessness, but it is different in the sense that there is no sense of inhibition, since there was no object desired to start with. And it also resembles hope with the difference again that the hoped-for object is lacking. If Hamlet hopes for something, then that is for the presence of hope itself. Melancholia is desire of desire. As desire, it is propinquous to nature and hence approximates the position of the madman. As pure passion, melancholia is, as Walter Benjamin has put it, "the most genuinely creaturely of the contemplative impulses."[66] At the same time, however, Benjamin also observes that the "prince is the paradigm of the melancholy man."[67] Melancholia is also distinctive of the sovereign because of his excessive power. The "indecisiveness of the tyrant" indicates the difficulty of making decisions when one is absolutely justified.[68] If the modern sovereign has all the means at his disposal, if he is absolutely in control of the law as well as the institutions that implement his decision, then it is easy to lose sight of the end. Paradoxically, the stronger the sovereign, the most absolute his power, the more total control of the means he has, the less he is able to identify his goal. Thus the conception that might is right leads to the *reductio ad absurdum* of absolute sovereignty. Melancholia shows that the moment the power of the sovereign is truly absolute, then the end of power evaporates and the sovereign loses his capacity to decide. Melancholia destroys the modern sovereign's ability to produce an alignment of the means and ends of power—including the ability to create the conditions for sovereignty's own maintenance of power.

The *reductio ad absurdum* of absolute sovereignty is very different from the paradox of sovereignty as it was articulated by Agamben. You will recall that, according to Agamben, the paradox consists in the fact that the sovereign is both inside and outside the law. The inability of the sovereign to decide, the radical passivity of his melancholia, is a result of his ambivalent position in relation to the law, but it is not the same as that position. As we demonstrated, Hamlet, who occupies that position of indecision, is an excess or supplement to the relation between the sovereign and the madman. In fact, Hamlet escapes the logic of sovereignty because his melancholia does merely show that excess or supplement is propinquous to the nature. It also shows nature's infusion of sovereignty. Melancholia is the attraction of nature. But, to put this in Hobbes's terms, melancholia is the desire of equality and freedom. It was this equality and freedom that characterized the state of nature in Hobbes. Now they return as the only possible way to give substance to the desire of desire that characterizes the melancholia of the prince. The desire of desire is the melancholia felt by the most powerful and constitutes in fact a desire against his power, a desire for equality and freedom. Melancholia is a passion that is neither hope nor fear, and thus an exception to the law. But it is an exception that brings the two laws of nature and the state in close proximity to each other. Melancholia is the propinquity of nature that, paradoxically, is intensified the more mighty the sovereign becomes. Thus melancholia appears as democracy's reinscription in the realm of absolute sovereignty.

The last point can be made much more emphatically. The propinquity of nature displaces the hierarchy that operates the logic of exclusory inclusion in Hobbes. It underwrites the fact that there must be democracy as the precondition of absolute sovereignty—or that the precondition of the separation between sovereignty and nature in fact presupposes the operative presence of democracy. This does not simply mean that the psychological and the legal hierarchies in Hobbes mirror each other and that the mirroring is reproduced between the figures of the sovereign and the madman. It also means that the absoluteness of a series of separations and reunifications that produce the absoluteness of sovereignty—law and justice, means and ends, power and peace—presuppose a space excessive of the topology of sovereign power. That excess eradicates any claim to absolutes because it establishes the propinquity of nature—of equality and freedom, of democracy—to that which cannot tolerate them, the sovereign. This excessive proximity subverts the hierarchies of absolute sovereignty and thereby de-justifies its claim to use the means at its disposal for its end—that is, sovereignty's own perpetuation of power.

We saw at the beginning of the chapter that, in modern sovereignty, the means justify the end. But the end is invariably implicated in the means. As Foucault argued, the question of modern sovereignty is how the sovereign can maintain himself in power. Might is right. The absolute sovereignty in Hobbes's *Leviathan* is premised on a psychology of the passions that consists in an overcoming of the state of nature that is described as a space of equality and liberty. Thus Hobbes's social contract is the negation of the democratic. But democracy persists where is it least expected, in the very figure of the absolute sovereign who, paradoxically, the most mighty he is, the closer he reverts to the natural state from which is supposed to be separated. This propinquity of nature dejustifies the legitimacy and claims to justification of absolute sovereignty. It shows that the one man—the sovereign—who seeks to determine the order of the state is plagued by the indeterminacy of what he desire to produce. But democracy still does not achieve a positive description. This can only happen by taking away all the power from the one. Rousseau's general will attempts to do exactly that.

4

REVOLUTION AND THE POWER OF LIVING

Popular Sovereignty

The previous chapter opened with Foucault's observation that the question animating sovereignty in Machiavelli is, "How and under what conditions can a sovereign maintain his power?" In the evolution from absolute to popular, the question of modern sovereignty remains largely the same. It is still a problem about how the means of power justify its ends. Power is still understood as actively created through human agency. At the same time, the question is posed in a slightly, yet significantly, altered form: How and under what conditions can *sovereignty* maintain its power? The transition from "the sovereign" to "sovereignty" does not solely signify the generation of theories, both republican and representative democratic, about the people's participation in the means of power. Nor does it merely introduce the division of the sovereign's power into the executive, the legislative, and the judiciary.[1] These two aspects designate the opposition to the previous conceptualizations of sovereignty as absolute. They mark the transition from access to the means of power being confined to one person or assembly of men to the means of power being extended, under certain conditions, to the people. In other words, the legal theory of participation reflects the socioeconomic changes of the time, such as the shift of power to the Third Estate. But the more important aspect of this question in the context of a conceptualization of sovereignty pursued here is the problem of who controls change in popular sovereignty. If the means of power enable the sovereign to create the laws and the institutions that support and are supported by the legal system, then extending the sovereign prerogative to the people expeditiously complicates the conceptualization of change. This ultimately leads to the problematic of revolution. Since the people hold sovereign power through their representatives, the people retain the right to change not only their government, but also the very structure of the state's governance. Thus Machiavelli's question is now mobilized to tackle the problem of how the means of power are related to change, giving rise to a discourse on revolution.[2]

"THE SOVEREIGN IS ALWAYS WHAT IT SHOULD BE": ROUSSEAU'S PERPETUAL REVOLUTION

The question of the revolution cuts through Jean-Jacques Rousseau's political theory and animates his republicanism.[3] "Simply by virtue of its existence, the sovereign is always what it should be" (58), writes Rousseau in his *Social Contract*.[4] For Rousseau, sovereignty is exercised by the general will; a few pages later he refines the previous assertion: "the general will is always in the right, and always tends to the public welfare" (66). The "public welfare" as the end of politics is possible because the general will, as sovereignty, has as its disposal the means of power. The problem of the exercise of power also pertains to the foundation of power. Rousseau can argue that change is indispensable for the foundation of the state because change is constitutive of legitimacy: "In order, then, for an arbitrary government to be legitimate, it would be necessary for the people, at every new generation, to have the power to accept it or reject it; but in that case the government would no longer be arbitrary" (50). A government is "arbitrary," according to Rousseau, when it is impervious to change. Conversely, a government becomes legitimate and its power is justified when it remains open to change—and that includes the change even of its foundations.

We can recognize in Rousseau's insistence on change a trenchant opposition to absolute sovereignty. As it was discussed in the previous chapter, absolute sovereignty operates on the principle that might is right. The one who holds the means of power, be that a single person or assembly of men, is justified to determine what the end of power is. As it was indicated in the previous chapter, this points to the absoluteness of the logic of sovereignty—namely, to the fact that the means are coimplicated with the ends. The end of the most mighty entity's power is premised on the fact that there is such a single entity that holds power and hence controls change. Rousseau is acutely aware of this circular logic, and the *Social Contract* seeks to enervate the power of the one and to vitiate the principle that might is right. "Is it not plain," asks Rousseau rhetorically, "that there is a vicious circle in basing the right of life and death on the right to enslave, and the right to enslave on the right of life and death?" (52). The sovereign can stand above the law to protect the state, even by exercising the "right of life and death," only because his legitimacy is premised on the subject's transference of its rights to the sovereign. But, avers Rousseau, this also means that by transferring its rights, including the right to self-preservation, the subject posits the authority that stands above the law. The sovereign right to exercise the death penalty and the subject's lack of freedom are the opposite sides of the same coin—a coin that the logic of justification continuously flips around to suit its ends.[5] As opposed to Hobbes's position that a transference of right constitutes the foundation of the social contract, Rousseau argues that no such transference of right to the sovereign is necessary—in fact, an authority is legitimate only in the absence of such a transference: "the word 'right' adds nothing to force; it has no meaning at all here" (48), states Rousseau, from which he infers: "Let us agree then that might is not right, and that we are obliged to obey only legitimate powers" (49). In other words, if power is legitimate only when it is open to change, then the subject is "obliged to obey" only that popular sovereignty that allows for the refoundation of the state—that allows for revolution.

The difficulty, however, is that the thinking of revolution bestows upon sovereignty also a certain circularity, as Hannah Arendt so clearly recognized in *On Revolution*. If there is a right to "rebellion and revolution,"[6] then that right must be articulated not merely as a new foundation, but rather as a perpetual refoundation.[7] Or, in Arendt's words, "if foundation was the aim and the end of revolution, then the revolutionary spirit was not merely the spirit of beginning something new but of starting something permanent and enduring; a lasting institution, embodying this spirit and encouraging it to new achievements, would be self-defeating. From which it unfortunately seems to follow that nothing threatens the very achievement of revolution more dangerously and more acutely than the spirit which brought it about."[8] In other words, so long as the end of sovereignty cannot be reduced to maintaining the one in power, so long as might is not right, then no single constitution or foundation can be regarded as permanent or justified in such a way as to be impervious to change. A beginning is not really new unless it implies that it remains open to the "revolutionary spirit" that allows for its refoundation. Or, differently put, "constitution-making . . . [is] the foremost and the noblest of all revolutionary deeds."[9] The making of the constitution entails the license for its remaking. It follows that the means of change and the aim of changing are coimplicated. The circularity that characterizes the logic of sovereignty is not eliminated, but rather forms the basis of the "revolutionary spirit." This circularity constitutes the essence of the figure of sovereignty as perpetual revolution that both Rousseau and Arendt espouse.

The circularity of the figure of perpetual revolution does not mean, however, that Rousseau's or Arendt's conceptions of sovereignty are essentially the same as Hobbes's. There is one fundamental difference that separates the two ways that the logic of sovereignty is articulated. Whereas for absolute sovereignty might is right because the means and the ends of sovereignty coincide in a single entity, the sovereign who is the lawmaker, for popular sovereignty, the end is not commensurable with an entity, but rather with an ideal. In the case of both Rousseau and Arendt that ideal is freedom. In Arendt's formulation, "the central idea of revolution . . . is the foundation of freedom, that is, the foundation of a body politic which guarantees the space where freedom can appear."[10] This ideal of freedom is linked to the revolutionary spirit that refounds the polity because "political freedom . . . means the right 'to be a participator in government,' or it means nothing."[11] According to Rousseau's famous opening of the *Social Contract*, "Man was born free, and everywhere he is in chains" (45). The political project is to regain this freedom. With this idealized freedom Rousseau hopes to break the vicious circle between the sovereign right of life and death and the subject's enslavement. Thus it this ideal itself, as a source of the current political imperative and as the metier of participation, that generates the circularity of sovereignty as perpetual revolution.

To fully grasp the implications of this perpetual revolution, it is necessary to contrast Rousseau's conception of the state of nature to that of Hobbes. The reason is that Rousseau reformulates the theory of the state of nature in order to explain the way that the ideal is understood differently in absolute and in popular sovereignty. He writes in the second *Discourse*,

"[Absolute sovereignty] is the final stage of inequality, the extreme point that closes the circle and links up with the point from which we set out. Here, all individuals become equal again because they are nothing, here subjects have no law save the will of the master, nor the master any rule save that of his passions, and here the notions of the good and principles of justice once more evaporate. Here, everything is brought back solely to the law of the strongest."[12] Whereas man in the state of nature is born free, the state of nature can return in an altered form that is none other than absolute sovereignty. This stage exhibits freedom and equality between each person only because they are all uniformly unequal in relation to the "master," the strongest one in the society—that is, the absolute sovereign who produces the means and the end of power. The first paragraph of the *Social Contract* continues after the reference to the modern man being in chains: "If I were to consider force alone, and the effects that it produces, I should say: for so long as a nation is constrained to obey, and does so, it does well; as soon as it is able to throw off its servitude, and does so, it does better; for since it regains freedom by the same right that was exercised when its freedom was seized, either the nation was justified in taking freedom back, or else those who took it away were unjustified in doing so" (45–46). The end of Rousseau's social contract is to "*regain*" the lost freedom of the state of nature. The ideal of freedom has a distant source that grounds Rousseau's political discourse. Thus the idea of freedom cannot be produced by the actions of a single individual, since it taps the past of a community. The republican discourse that starts by indicating the intention to throw off the chains of servitude reformulates the theory of the state of nature in order to show that the sovereign cannot produce an end of government. Rather, the productive function of sovereignty is only ever a public affair.

A closer comparison between Rousseau's and Hobbes's theories of the state of nature is needed to provide a clearer delineation of the fundamental difference between the two philosophers. Rousseau contradicts every major point of Hobbes's description of the state of nature. The first paragraph of Book I, Chapter II contains *in nuce* all the major differences. It starts by asserting that the "most ancient of all societies, and the only one that is natural, is the family" (46). Unlike Hobbes, there is society in nature— man's life is not "solitary, poore, nasty, brutish, and short." Rousseau continues: "Even in this case, the bond between children and father persists only so long as they have need of him for their conservation" (46). On the one hand, the general premise of the organization of the state of nature is the same for Hobbes and Rousseau—namely, that it is about the means, it is about power. But, whereas for Hobbes this concerns the power of the individual to hope for the attainment of personal goals, for Rousseau the family is the means of the self-preservation of its members. According to Hobbes, the realization that self-preservation is an end leads to the recognition that it can only be achieved through the social contract. Here self-preservation is already in play in the state of nature. The reason is that, whereas Hobbes was intent to emphasize the radical equality and liberty of humans in the state of nature, Rousseau is concerned to underscore the inequality of strength in the state of nature. Thus it is the father, as the strongest member of the family, who shoulders the responsibility of protecting the weaker children. "As soon as this need ceases, the natural bond is dissolved. The children are released from the obedience they owe to their father, the father is released from the duty of care to the children, and all become equally independent" (46). When the children achieve strength, like their father, then they are entitled to relinquish the expedient bond that constitutes the family. "If they continue to remain living together, it is not by nature but voluntarily, and the family itself is maintained only through convention" (46). In the absence of a reason, when the family is no longer a means to the goal of self-preservation, then cohabitation might continue by voluntary choice. We are a long way here from Antigone, who regarded the bonds of kinship as sacred. The family, as the prototype of the modern conception of sovereignty, is regarded by Rousseau as a means. But we are also a long away from Hobbes, who substituted the laws of kinship with the psychological laws that led, with causal certainty, from the solitary individual to the member of the social contract subjected to the laws of the state. There are no scientific chains of psychological causality in Rousseau, who also sees no essential discrepancy between attaining the end of self-preservation and the parallel exercise of other habitual attitudes by convention.

The differences between Rousseau and Hobbes can be summarized in the way that the madman figures in their extrapolations of the social contract. As it was argued previously, there must be madmen for Hobbes's hierarchy of the commonwealth to be possible. The madman is excluded from the commonwealth because his lack of rationality does not allow him to transfer his rights to the sovereign in order to enter the social contract. Conversely, it is precisely this transferring of rights that constitutes madness for Rousseau: "To say that a man gives himself for nothing is an absurd and incomprehensible statement; such an action is illegitimate and void, simply because anyone who does it is not in his right mind. To say the same about an entire people is to imagine a nation of madmen, and madness does not make rights" (50). So, instead of the "madness" that consists in transferring one's right to the sovereign, Rousseau needs an alternative marker for the transition to the social contract.

This alternative transition from the state of nature to the social contract is characterized as the "complete transfer of each associate, with all his rights, to the whole community" (55), and it leads to what was characterized earlier as the figure of the perpetual revolution in Rousseau. In Chapter VI of the *Social Contract* Rousseau introduces for the first time the notion of the general will: "the social pact . . . may be reduced to the following terms. Each of us puts his person and all his power in common under the supreme direction of the general will; and we as a body receive each member as an indivisible part of the whole" (55). The general will represents that transfer of association accompanied by one's rights that characterizes the transition to the social contract.[13] The figure of the perpetual revolution is introduced in the context of the general will as the fraternity of citizens: "it is contrary to the nature of the body politic [i.e., of all those who have transferred their association] that the sovereign should impose on itself a law that it cannot infringe . . . whence it will be seen that there is no kind of fundamental law, and cannot be any, not even the social contract, which is binding on the people as a body" (57). By becoming part of the general will, the citizen is like a small sovereign. Each is an "indivisible part" of the general will. And since the general will signifies the popular sovereignty that stands above the law, there is no law that is absolutely binding to each "indivisible part" of the general will. Hence, to quote again, "by virtue of its existence, the sovereign is always what it should be" (58) and "the general will is always in the right" (66). And it is because of this that "at every new generation" (50) the people can decide anew about the terms of the social contract.

I indicated earlier that the figure of the perpetual revolution in Rousseau recreates the circularity of the logic of sovereignty. This circularity in Rousseau can be posed in different ways. Bonnie Honig is acutely aware of this issue, which she discusses in terms of democratic theory: "The paradox of politics names a fundamental problem of democracy in which power must rest with the people but the people are never so fully who they need to be . . . that they can be counted upon to exercise their power democratically."[14] And a page later: "The irresolvable paradox of politics commits us to a view of the people, democratic actors and subjects, as also always a multitude. . . . The assumed antagonism between democracy and emergency is to some extent undone from this angle of vision."[15] So, for Honig, the circularity of the paradox of politics has the potential to lead to a genuine democratic articulation. Honig identifies the paradox of politics in Rousseau at precisely the moment that was called above the perpetual revolution. "In order for there to be a people well formed enough for good lawmaking, there must be good law, for how else will the people be well formed? The problem is: Where would that good law come from absent an already well-formed, virtuous people?"[16] In other words, if the general will is always right, is that because the people are already part of a social contract that allows them to form proper political judgments—in which case they no longer need to review the social contract "at every new generation" (50)? Or, alternatively, if the general will is hampered by the wrong constitution, then there is no guarantee that its refoundation of the social contract will not be a failure, precisely because the laws have provided wrong guidance. Honig shows how this paradox is fundamental to William Connolly's thinking of the political in Rousseau, as well as how both Seyla Benhabib and Jürgen Habermas try in different ways to evade this paradox. After showing that the paradox of politics cannot be eliminated in Rousseau's writings, Honig concludes: "If the paradox of politics is real and enduring, then a democratic politics would do well to replace its faith in a pure general will with an acceptance of its impurity and an embrace of the perpetuity of political contestation made necessary by that impurity. In such a setting, democracy's necessary conditions (e.g., the reproduction of a supposed general will) may be found to offend some of its own commitments (to freedom and self-rule) in ways that call for (a certain model of) democracy's self-overcoming (i.e., in quest of a different democracy)."[17] In other words, Honig keeps faith with the possibility of using this circularity productively to assure its commitment to freedom and respect for the other. An agonistic notion of democracy should not be eliminating the other by placing it in the position of the enemy, but rather seeking to embrace values such as freedom that make it possible to welcome the other. Even though I agree with Honig's insistence on the ineliminable operative function of the paradox of politics for a thinking, as well as practice, of the democratic, still I do not believe that Rousseau manages to aspire to this agonistic model of democracy—in fact, he seeks to refute it irrevocably. The circularity of Rousseau's perpetual revolution reinstates a logic of sovereignty instead of a democratic politics.

Immediately after introducing the concept of the general will, in Chapter VII of Part I, entitled "The Sovereign," Rousseau states that "the act of association," that is, the act that founds the social contract, "involves a reciprocal commitment between public and private persons" (56). The public and the private constitute "two different capacities" (57) in the subject. The public refers to the manner in which the individual is an indivisible member of the general will and thus acts according to the common good. In addition, "it is solely on the basis of this common interest that society must be governed" (63). Therefore, the imperative of government—the question of how to maintain sovereignty in power—arises solely in relation to the body politic and its pursuit of the common interest. In this sense the common interest is higher than any private interest: "Why is that the general will is always in the right, and why is the happiness of each the constant wish of all, unless it is because there is no one who does not apply the word *each* to himself, and is not thinking of himself when he votes for all?" (68). The happiness of each indivisible member of the general will, including oneself, is identical with the happiness of the entire brotherhood that constitutes the general will. Love for one is love for all, and vice versa. The perpetual revolution is possible—the refounding of the social contract can take place—only so long as this body politic is higher than the other "capacity" identified with the private body.

In the same chapter on "The Sovereign" in Part I of the *Social Contract*, after having described how the general will is always right when it pursues the common good, Rousseau considers the individual acting against the common interest. In that case, observes Rousseau, the social contract is in danger of becoming an "empty formula," and hence the individual must be "forced to be free" (58). Adherence to the ideal that structures the original commitment to the social contract is not a matter of choice. One does not choose to be free. Instead, coercion is justified in ensuring that the community is not derailed from the pursuit of freedom. In Part II, Chapter III, Rousseau states that "when properly informed" (66), the majority of the people always act with the common interest in mind, rather than for personal gain. This ultimately, however, requires a consensus that is opposed to "partial associations" (66), saying that "there should be no partial society within the state" (67). We do not only recognize here Honig's "paradox of politics," since who can judge in advance whether the majority or the minority are acting out of the appropriate motives? We can also recognize here Rousseau's opposition to Solon's exigency of participation. According to Solon, it is precisely "partial association" or *stasis* that makes democratic engagement possible. Democracy operates by taking sides. Privileging instead Lycurgus (67) and the Spartan model of submission to the general good, Rousseau has no difficulty stating that "it is not so much the number of persons voting, but rather the common interest that unites them" (69) that matters for the social contract. This leads in turn to a justification of violence: "the sovereign authority has jurisdiction exclusively over the body of the nation" (69).

For Rousseau this jurisdiction over the private body ultimately means that sovereignty retains the right of life and death. We saw earlier how Rousseau's reformulation of the state of nature led to an understanding of sovereignty as determining the end of power through the public. This was made possible because, according to Rousseau's theory of the state of nature, humans are not enemies by nature: "[Humans] are not naturally enemies" and it is "the relationship of things, not of men, that constitutes a state of war" (51). This enables a differentiation from Hobbes's state of nature, which is described as a generalized civil war. But when Rousseau's conception of enmity, which differentiates the starting point of his political theory, is coupled with the distinction between private interest and public good, the figure of the enemy is reintroduced in a way that betrays an essential similarity with Hobbes. In Part II, in order to reinforce the priority of the public body over the individual, Rousseau states that the end of the social contract is "the preservation of the contracting parties. He who wills an end wills the means to that end" (71). Thus the general will has the means of power at its disposal, but this also allows for an immediate connection with the end of the state. And this immediate connection is forged by the renunciation of the individual for the sake of the state. The "life" of one who enters the social contract is "a conditional gift of the state" (71). Unlike absolute sovereignty, no one can single-handedly determine or produce the end of the state; rather, the end is a public concern. At this point Rousseau discusses the death penalty in the following terms:

every wrongdoer, in attacking the rights of society by his crimes, becomes a rebel and a traitor to his country. By violating its laws he ceases to belong to it, and is even making war on it. The preservation of the state becomes incompatible with his own; one of the two must perish; and when a criminal is put to death, it is as an enemy rather than as a citizen. His trial and the sentence are the proofs and the declaration that he has broken the social treaty and is consequently no longer a member of the state. But since he has acknowledged his membership, if only by his place of residence, he must be removed from it, by exile inasmuch as he has infringed the contract, or by death inasmuch as he is a public enemy. An enemy of this kind is not an abstract entity personified, but a man, and in such a case the right of war is to kill the vanquished. (71–72)

Here the wrongdoer or the criminal who is subject to the death penalty is identified as an enemy. Enmity is not a relation between things when the issue is the internal order, peace, and stability of the state. The internal enemy is not an "abstract entity" like the external enemy, but a "man," because he privileges his personal interest, his private body, over his body politic. Avoiding becoming an enemy is only possible by privileging the common good. One who "breaks the social treaty" is no longer a "member of the state." Like Hobbes's madman and rebel, Rousseau's wrongdoer also falls below the law, justifying the force of the law being directed against him.[18]

The right of life and death, as it is expressed in Rousseau's *Social Contract*, recreates the relations of the king's two bodies within the division between the public and the private.[19] It will be recalled that there are two principles for the doctrine of the king's two bodies: first, that their relation is indivisible, and second, that the body politic is higher than the body natural. We have discovered both of these principles in operation in Rousseau's discourse. The transference of association splits the body into two "capacities," one personal and the other public. These two capacities are indivisible from the perspective of the general will, the body politic. But the natural body is inferior to the body politic, so much so that it is only a "conditional gift of the state." When someone acts in such a way as to make himself a "public enemy," then the gift of the natural body can be withdrawn by the body politic. The death penalty can be justified. Even though the traditional articulation of the king's two bodies confines the body natural and the body politic to a single person, Rousseau's general will recreates this division within the social contract through the split between the private and the public body.[20] And the effect in both cases is the same: stratification, a hierarchy of actions and motives—or, more succinctly, the creation of the enemy. The retention of the right of life and death revitalizes the vicious circle of sovereign justification that Rousseau had criticized and had hoped to overcome with the figure of idealized freedom. This circularity of sovereignty, once again, fails to lead to a politics of freedom, asserting instead of politics of death, a thanatopolitics.

In an illuminating reading of the *Social Contract*, Louis Althusser points out the discrepancy between the individual and the community—or what I called above the private and the public—as the unstable center of Rousseau's political theory. Althusser explains that the entire contractarian tradition relies on a juridical notion of the contract, whereby there are two recipient parties that enter an agreement of exchange. In Rousseau's case the contract is between each individual and the community that stands for the general will. However, observes Althusser, "the 'peculiarity' of the *Social Contract* is that it is an exchange agreement concluded between two RPs [recipient parties] (like any other contract), but one in which the second RP does not preexist the contract since it is its product. The 'solution' represented by the contract is thus preinscribed in one of the very conditions of the contract, the RP_2, since this RP_2 is not preexistent to the contract."[21] In other words, how is it even possible to talk about a contract, when the second contracting party, the community, is the very "object" and "end" of the contract?[22] Althusser shows how Rousseau denegates or represses this discrepancy, which nevertheless permeates his entire theory. Althusser is correct that the entire tradition that relies on the social contract had never before described it in terms that produced the second contracting party. Nevertheless, Rousseau's invention may not appear as aberrant if we take the medieval doctrine of the king's two bodies as its precedent. The body of the king is individual, and yet at the same time produces the entire body politic. I am not suggesting here that Rousseau explicitly made use of the doctrine of the king's two bodies. Rather, the fierce violence that he justifies against the "wrongdoer" may indeed be a symptom not only of the wrongdoer's exhibition of self-interest (*amor propre*), but, moreover, of offending against the mystical union that both the

Social Contract and the king's two bodies metaphorize. Or, differently put, the justification of the death penalty is a symptom of the repression that the separation between the individual and the community, between the private and the public, presupposes. This is the repression of the unspoken—and uncodified—fact that they can never be reunified in a theory of popular sovereign based on a self-refuting contract. Perhaps the social contract for Rousseau is precisely the communal agreement to forget or denegate the noncontractual basis of the social contract. The acts of the "wrongdoer" or internal enemy are an affront to this communal forgetting.

The enemy is the one who "breaks the social treaty." This breaking of the legal order signifies the realm of the uncodifiable, which points to a state of emergency and the generation of a narrative of exceptionality. As it was argued in Chapter 1, this is the element that creates the circularity in the logic of sovereignty by unifying the means and the end of power. At the same time it is precisely through a notion of the break that the idea of the perpetual revolution was grounded. According to Rousseau, each generation has the right to revisit and, if necessary, revise the social contract, because the general will is always right. The absoluteness of the logic of sovereignty is the palimpsest of the circularity of the perpetual revolution. So long as the general will's right of life and death is obscured, then Rousseau's general could lead to the agonistic democracy that the paradox of politics capacitates, according to Bonnie Honig. But the moment that the right of life and death is reasserted, Rousseau's logic of sovereignty precludes the possibility of democracy, because it operates through the logic of justification.

THE OTHER OF OBEDIENCE: SPINOZA'S DEJUSTIFICATION OF SOVEREIGNTY

The logic of justification, as it was explicated in Chapter 1, relies on a circularity between means and ends. The law is conceived as the means to the just end of order, peace, and stability. Spinoza's contribution to the development of the idea of sovereignty consists in eliminating the end. In the Preface to Part IV of the *Ethics*, entitled, "Of Human Bondage, or The Strength of the Emotions," Spinoza outright rejects the idea that "God, or Nature" can be understood as having a telos: "just as he [God] does not exist for an end, so he does not act for an end" (321).[23] Spinoza constructs the elimination of an end through the disjunction between state and natural laws.[24] The transition from the divine rights of the kings to the creation of the modern subject requires a separation between the laws of the state and the laws of nature.[25] Thus the subject, by its subjection to the two sets of laws, constitutes the realm of the means that allows for a conception of the end of the state. Spinoza can refrain from identifying an end by rejecting any end to the two sets of laws.[26] Thus the two laws are never separated in Spinoza. Rather, their disjunction results in a productive engaging between state and natural law.[27]

The rejection of an end has far-reaching implications for Spinoza's extrapolation of the political. First, the elimination of an end entails dejustification. Second, this allows for a theory of the democratic. I will deal in the present section with Spinoza's construction of dejustification, and I will present in the following section the essential aspects of Spinoza's conception of democracy. If an end is no longer conceivable, or, more emphatically, if the end is revealed to be an illusion, then it is no longer possible to show a separation and reunification of means and ends, hence the justificatory logic of sovereignty is derailed. This pertains specifically to how reason enters in an agonistic relation with written law.[28] But to be able to make this argument, Spinoza needs to show that written laws produce that agonism, regardless of whether they are religious or state laws. Intimations of this argument can be found throughout Spinoza's works, but the most explicit articulation occurs in chapters 14 and 15 in the *Tractatus Theologico-Politicus*.

The first thirteen chapters of the *Tractatus* deal with the biblical account of the exodus of the Jews from Egypt and the establishment of their state under Moses's leadership. This discussion shows that the purpose of law is nothing other than the following of the law. As Spinoza puts it in Chapter 14, which summarizes and concludes the discussion of the Old Testament, "the aim of Scripture is simply to teach obedience" (515). But saying that the aim of the law is solely the following of the law means nothing more than that the law is necessary. The law has no true content as such—the law is empty.[29] As Spinoza stresses repeatedly, the written law is a means that can be adapted to suit specific circumstances. Specific laws are merely "means to promote obedience" (515). The modality of necessity can be ascribed to the law only when the law is emptied of all content. It is never what the law says that is necessary. It only ever the law as lawfulness, the law as that which must be followed, that is necessary.

The modality of necessity of the written law, the lawfulness of the law, is the condition of the possibility of the social contract. Spinoza's account of the exodus in the first part of the *Tractatus* constitutes his account of the formation of the state. "Moses's aim was . . . to bind them [i.e., the Jewish people] by covenant" (515). The aim of the lawgiver is nothing transcendent. The creation of the Jewish state is never described as the fulfilling of a universal. Instead, the covenant is the effect of following the law. Or, differently put, the covenant and the necessity of obedience are means for the creation of commonalty. As Gatens and Lloyd put it, "*utility* is a central component in Spinoza's account of how and why human beings come to develop more and more institutionally structured forms of collective life."[30] The modality of necessity that pertains to the written law produces a community. In other words, if religion and faith indicate obedience, the state also requires obedience in order to form a legal entity. This double function of obedience—its religious and political aspects—is indicated by Spinoza as the principle of the love for one's neighbor: "the entire Law consists in this alone, to love one's neighbor. . . . Scripture does not require us to believe anything beyond what is necessary for the fulfilling of the said commandment" (515). This love for one's neighbor should not be confused with Paul's *agape*. According to Paul, as shown in Chapter 2, every law can be understood in terms of the love for one's neighbor. In other words, every content of the law can be reduced to this principle. Paulinian agape forges a connection between law and a transcendent justice. Conversely, for Spinoza, neighborly love indicates simply the effect of the two forms, religious and state, of the written law—namely, the effect of obedience: "he who . . . loves his neighbour as himself is truly obedient" (515). And, "Worship of God and obedience to him consists solely in . . . love toward one's neighbour" (518). The love for one's neighbor is linked to the modality of necessity. This modality can assume a variety of articulations. The law is written so as community can be possible. What is ultimately necessary—and that is the single necessity in Spinoza's conception of written law—is the fact that written law requires the other. Without the neighbor, there is no written law. One cannot obey when one is absolutely alone. In other words, unlike Paul, neighborly love indicates for Spinoza the persistence of immanence. We will see in a moment how this novel conception of neighborly love, arising out of the link between the emptiness of the law and the necessity of obedience, radically reformulates the way that enmity is understood. But first we need to show the modality that is agonistically related to the necessity of written law.

If the lawfulness of the written law, both as religious and state law, is empty and its function consists in its being obeyed, then the question arises as to how it can receive any content. Or, differently put, how can one account for the variety of different written laws? To respond to questions such as these, Spinoza juxtaposes contingency to necessity. The first move is to insist that the obedience that arises from the modality of necessity does not require passive faith, but, on the contrary, active engagement: "only by works can we judge anyone to be a believer or an unbeliever" (516). The realm of the political requires participation, as Solon had already highlighted. Spinoza also describes an exigency of participation in the present moment by insisting that the necessity of the law rejects blind faith in favor of engagement determined by the circumstances of any given situation. Thus the necessity of the law is the *means to responding* to the contingent facts.[31] As a result, Spinoza is dismissive of the scholastic adherence to "letters that are dead" (521): "Nor, again, does it matter for faith whether one believes that God is omnipresent in essence or in potency, whether he directs everything from free will or from the necessity of his nature, whether he lays down laws as a ruler or teaches them as being eternal truths, whether man obeys God from free will or from the necessity of the divine decree, whether the rewarding of the good and the punishing of the wicked is natural or supernatural" (518). These debates about religious law are secondary to how that law makes action possible. And this means that law should allow people to assume responsibility by responding to the contingent circumstances: "every man is in duty bound to adapt these religious dogmas to his own understanding and to interpret them for himself in whatever way makes him feel that he can then more readily accept them with full confidence and conviction" (518). Duty is not understood here as the mere following of preestablished rules or laws, nor the following of rules or laws that aspire to universality. Instead, duty is delineated as a response to the particular conditions of one's existence.[32] To account for the creation of laws, Spinoza couples the modality of necessity with the modality of contingency. Thus he argues that laws are not created through adherence to transcendent principles or values. Instead, the necessity of the law is given content by accepting the law's immanence. And immanence places a responsibility upon those who are subject to the law. The subject is no longer merely subjected to the law, but rather it is "duty bound" to respond to—and if needed transform—the law by considering the present, contingent circumstances.

The coupling of the modalities of necessity and contingency makes singularity possible. Singularity designates the responsibility that necessity places on the individual to respond to the given circumstances. The recognition of singularity is designated by Spinoza as the operation of reason and is identified with philosophy. This sets up an agonism between philosophy and religion within the realm of written law: "The domain of reason . . . is truth and wisdom, the domain of theology is piety and obedience" (523). This agonism undoes the possibility of an end to the written laws. The elimination of the end can be shown by pointing out two inferences that follow from the coupling of necessity and contingency that produces singularity. First, the agonism between religion and philosophy enables the interrogation of the inscription of content to the pure necessity of the law: "I am utterly astonished that men can bring themselves to make reason, the greatest of all gifts and a light divine, subservient to letters that are dead, and . . . that it should be considered no crime to denigrate the mind, the true handwriting of God's word, declaring it to be corrupt, blind and lost, whereas it is considered to be a heinous crime to entertain such thoughts of the letter, a mere shadow of God's word" (521). The written law, the "letter," makes obedience possible, but that obedience is not premised on truth. Truth arises only when the written law vibrates within the singularity of the moment, and this is only possible through the use of reason. Laws are "dead letters," and the only "true handwriting of God's word" is the use of reason. Only when reason is used in the *now* can one go beyond the "mere shadow of God's word." Spinoza is here invoking God in order to argue against adherence to religious dogma. Spinoza's God becomes the symbol of nonadherence to religious commands.[33] Thus the agonism between religion and philosophy or obedience and reason shows that singularity contains at its core an element of instability. This instability, produced by the impossibility to reconcile necessity and contingency, is incompatible with the end as a universal that denotes the order, peace, and stability that characterize the logic of sovereignty.

Second, the creation of singularity contains a defense of revolutionary activity. The previous remarks about the dead letter of the law are introduced by the following rhetorical question: "who can give mental acceptance to something against which his reason rebels [*reclamat*]?" (521/199) The verb "reclamare" that Spinoza uses here indicates the action of raising one's voice in protest. This action is attributed to reason's resistance to the dead letter—that is, the pure necessity—of the law. But the two modalities—necessity and contingency—are not separated. Instead, according to Spinoza, the rebel is necessary: "faith requires not so much true dogmas as pious dogmas, that is, such as move the heart to obedience; and this is so even if many of those beliefs contain not a shadow of truth, provided that he who adheres to them knows not that they are false. If he knew that they were false, he would necessarily be a rebel [*rebellis necessario esset*], for how could it be that one who seeks to love justice and obey God should worship as divine what he knows to be alien to the divine nature?" (516–7/193)[34] The modality of necessity is linked to the modality of contingency, not only through the intervention of reason that generates truth and provides content to the dead letter of the laws. In addition, philosophy is also necessary as the rebellion against obedience when the laws are against reason. So, even though there is an instability that prevents the reconciliation of necessity and contingency, still religion and philosophy or obedience and reason can never be completely separated. They are always connected through the figure of rebellion. Thus rebellion becomes the figure of the absence of an end to the relation between necessity and contingency in such a way that it allows for the operative presence of reason and truth.

The agonism and ineliminable connection between necessity and contingency that characterize the written laws and that are expressed in the relation between religion and philosophy do not only explain why Spinoza entitled his treatise "politico-theological."[35] In addition, and more importantly for the argument pursued here, the inscription of singularity within written law overturns Hobbes's conception of the internal enemy. It will be recalled that Hobbes requires the other to the social contract in order to establish the hierarchies of absolute sovereignty. As it was put in the previous chapter, there must be madmen who are excluded below the law for the absolute sovereign to exist. In other words, the law, according to Hobbes, is constituted by a foundational exclusion that justifies violence. As opposed to this conception, Spinoza constructs the agonism and connection between religion and philosophy in such a way as to prevent exclusion. Obedience and reason are distinct, but they are not separated: "By theology I mean . . . the way of achieving obedience. . . . Theology thus understood . . . will be found to agree with reason. And if you look to its purpose and end, it will be found to be in no respect opposed to reason" (523). Religion and philosophy are not opposed, or do not exclude each other, because it is perfectly rational to recognize that the political requires obedience. There cannot be laws of the state without obedience. Indeed, Spinoza designates as madness such an idea. "It would be folly to refuse to accept . . . that which is . . . of considerable advantage to the state" (525). Neither obedience is subservient to reason, nor reason to obedience. Neither excludes the other. Madness for Spinoza does not designate the space excluded from the law, as Hobbes argued. Rather, madness designates the complete submission to the law—and such a complete submission requires an exclusion, as Hobbes aptly demonstrated. Conversely, Spinoza insists that it is madness to exclude, because the critical aspect of obedience is that "all men without exception can obey" (526). Everyone is subject to necessity; no one is outside the law—there is no outlaw in Spinoza's ontology of the political. The enemy is not someone who falls below the law and who thereby becomes the subject of sovereign violence. Spinoza is opposed to thanatopolitics.

At this point one could argue that the circularity that is a defining feature of the absoluteness of the logic of sovereignty and that we identified in Hobbes is also part of Spinoza's extrapolation of written law. In particular Spinoza argues that necessity empties law of content and that contingency enables reason to find truths that give it content. But, then—it could be objected—does this not simply mean that obedience requires reason at the same time that reason is inconceivable without obedience? Spinoza acknowledges this circularity in the following terms: "However, since reason cannot demonstrate the truth or falsity of this fundamental principle of theology, that men may be saved simply by obedience, we may also be asked why it is that we believe it if we accept this principle without reason, blindly, then we too are acting foolishly without judgment; if on the other hand we assert that this fundamental principle can be proved by reason, then theology becomes a part of philosophy, and inseparable from it" (524). Spinoza observes that for this circularity to be operative, either obedience is taken as more important than reason or reason is assumed to be more primary than obedience. As it was shown in Chapter 1, the circularity that characterizes the absoluteness of the logic of sovereignty requires that one side is privileged. The same point was made earlier in relation to Hobbes. For might to be right, the sovereign must have all the means at this disposal to be able to determine how the end can fulfill the universal of order, peace, and stability. The means are privileged, but only so as to be reunited with the end. In other words, the means can be coordinated with the end through this circularity. Conversely, the distinction, but nonseparation of obedience and reason in Spinoza entails that there is no transcendent end that can determine such a separation and reunification. The agonistic relation between religion and philosophy and between the modalities of necessity and contingency describes precisely this lack of end. Neither religion nor philosophy is privileged. Spinoza responds to the imaginary objector: "To this I reply that I maintain absolutely that this fundamental dogma of theology cannot be investigated by the natural light of reason, or at least that nobody has been successful in proving it, and that therefore it was essential that there should be revelation" (524). With the lack of an end, it is no longer possible to justify sovereignty—revelation as the foundation of obedience and the state cannot be justified through rational means. The circularity of sovereignty is deconstructed by restricting the written law to the agonistic relation between the modalities of necessity and contingency. This lack of justification—or, rather, the dejustification of sovereignty—has already been indicated as the necessity of rebellion as well as the rejection of the outlaw or any position of exclusion from the social contract in Spinoza's philosophy. "No body politic can exist without being subject to the latent threat of civil war," as Étienne Balibar puts it. This threat of the internal enemy and the necessary rebel is the "cause of causes" of the political.[36]

Spinoza's dejustification of the logic of sovereignty shows that the political must avoid constructing the outlaw or the internal enemy and must instead welcome the necessary rebel, who can challenge the laws by applying reason to the contingent circumstances. Thus Spinoza can provide an account of written law through the modalities of necessity and contingency. This is a significant difference from the tradition that seeks justification in order to provide legitimacy to sovereignty. Such a legalistic tradition always understands power as the means of the state. This justifies, for instance, the exercise of violence, since violence is a means of governance—a means justified by law for the maintaining of the existing legal order. Conversely, by confining written law to necessity and contingency and thereby eliminating the possibility of justifying an end to legality, Spinoza's position is not amenable to the logic of sovereignty. More emphatically, the figure of the necessary rebel dejustifies the exercise of violence on the part of the modern sovereign. The agonism between necessity and contingency is never-ending—and this means that there is no end or aim such as to support the legitimation of power. Written law is a site of contestation for Spinoza, not a basis of justification. Thus the agonism between necessity and contingency allows politics to remain open to change. The law is transformable. Rebellion is not an attack on the state, but rather an effect of the historical contingency of any written law coupled with the reminder that no law can justify itself. The other of obedience is the condition of the possibility of written law.

In addition, the other of obedience also necessitates a welcoming of the other—the internal enemy, the necessary rebel—and in such a way as to lead to a conception of the democratic. But Spinoza's description of democracy requires a different modality—namely possibility. And the modality of possibility is not given through written law, but rather through the law of nature.

THE REGIME OF BROKEN PROMISES:
THE POSSIBILITY OF DEMOCRACY

Spinoza's agonism between the modalities of necessity and contingency and their expression in the incessant struggle between obedience and reason or between religion/the state and philosophy dejustifies sovereign power. To put this dejustification from the perspective of power, Spinoza's position entails that it is a category mistake to confine power in the realm of the written law—both state and religious. Instead of the modalities of necessity and contingency, power pertains to the modality of possibility. And the modality of possibility, according to Spinoza, is associated with natural law. The displacement of power from the realm of written law ultimately makes it possible for Spinoza to provide his account of democracy. Spinoza seeks to describe democracy in terms of the relation between right and power that is constitutive of his state of nature. His theory of right is developed in Chapter 16 of the *Tractatus Theologico-Politicus*. Spinoza's theory of right, however, will remain obscure so long as written law is not properly distinguished from the law of nature.[37] As Spinoza puts it in Chapter 16 of the *Tractatus*, "a state of nature must not be confused with a state of religion; we must conceive it as being without religion and without law, and consequently without sin and without wrong" (534). Even though the lack of written law in the state of nature resembles Hobbes's description, Spinoza is making a different point. According to Proposition 29 of Part I of the *Ethics*, "nothing in nature is contingent" (234). For Hobbes the creation of the legal order amounts to the transference of one's right. For Spinoza the legal order is given through the agonism between necessity and contingency. This is not to say that there is no necessity in the laws of nature. The same proposition of the *Ethics* continues: "but all things are from the necessity of the divine nature determined to exist and to act in a definite way." The necessity of the laws of nature is not determined by a relation to contingency. Instead, it is determined in relation to the modality of possibility. Right is related to power. And this relation constitutes for Spinoza the realm of natural law and the modality of possibility or power.[38]

It is precisely the same relation between right and power that defines the sovereign, according to Spinoza. Thus it is through a discussion of natural law that it is possible to delineate the distinction between democracy and sovereignty in Spinoza. The question that arises at this point and that will allow us to delimit Spinoza's conception of democracy is to what extent and in what way is his determination of natural law—the relation between right and power—able to evade the circularity that reinscribed justification in Rousseau's discourse. The comparison between Spinoza and Rousseau is crucial for an understanding of how right produces democracy, since both philosophers deny the Hobbesian description of the transition to the social contract as the transference of the subject's rights to the sovereign. We saw that Rousseau castigates such a complete transference as madness and proposes instead a transference of association that creates the body politic or general will. It will be recalled that, according to Rousseau, the general will is always right—there is a perpetual revolution, as we called it earlier—in the sense that it has all the means at its disposal to determine how liberty, as the end of the social contract, is to be realized. This includes the right of life and death, or the exercise of the death penalty upon any "wrongdoer," in Rousseau's expression, who puts private gain over common interest. Spinoza also argues against a complete transference of right. "Nobody can so completely transfer to another all his right, and consequently his power, as to cease to be a human being, nor will there ever be a sovereign that can do all it pleases" (536). In other words, might is not right. Spinoza adds: "the individual reserves to itself a considerable part of his right, which therefore depends on nobody's decision but his own" (536). Decision-making power and judgment are retained by the individual. Spinoza uses the manner in which right is transferred to distinguish between different regimes: "in a democratic state nobody transfers his natural right to another so completely that thereafter he is not to be consulted; he transfers it to the majority of the entire community of which he is part" (531). The more power the individual has—the more natural law is allowed to operate—the more democratic are the state and its written laws. But the way that right is transferred to the community recalls Rousseau's general will and gives rise to a series of questions: Does this community that Spinoza refers to here function in an analogous way to Rousseau's general will? How can Spinoza avoid the circularity of the logic of sovereignty that still plagued Rousseau? Again, we will discover that the answer is related to the absence of an end in Spinoza's conception of the community. In other words, whereas Rousseau determined that the end of the general will was the regaining of natural freedom, Spinoza refrains from providing an abstract ideal as an end that can be inferred from his theory of natural law. Thus Spinoza provides a different account of freedom that is no longer conceived of as an ideal end.

The entire Chapter 16 of the *Tractatus* is structured in such a way as to argue against the possibility of ascribing an end to power by providing an account of the freedom of judgment. The modality of possibility and the natural right of the individual do not point to an end. Significantly, Spinoza seeks to determine a sense of freedom that is not ideal. Spinoza opens Chapter 16 by observing that he had hitherto concerned himself with the distinction between religion and philosophy—or, in our terms, the relations between the modalities of necessity and contingency that pertain to written law. It is now time, says Spinoza, to move to the question of the "limits of freedom" (526), which in fact involves a discussion of rights. He immediately associates rights with natural law and with power—rights are understood through the modality of possibility. "For example, fish are determined by nature to swim, and the big ones to eat the smaller ones" (526–27). So, from the perspective of natural law, "Nature's right is coextensive with her power" (527). This correlation of natural law and the modality of possibility is crucial because it applies to every individual: "But since the universal power of Nature as a whole is nothing but the power of all individual things taken together, it follows that each individual thing has the sovereign right to do all that it can do; i.e., the right of the individual is coextensive with its determinate power" (527). Everybody's natural right is determined solely by what they can do.[39] Just as from the perspective of the written law everyone is included because everyone is capable of obedience, so also from the perspective of natural law everyone is included because everyone has a "determinate power." This applies to the sovereign himself: "the rights of sovereigns are determined by their power" (567). Sovereignty is determined through the modality of possibility. Determining sovereignty through possibility entails that the sovereign has the same ontological status as any other person. Moreover, Spinoza extends this natural law, which is provided by the modality of possibility, to all animate and inanimate things. "And here I do not acknowledge any distinction between men and other individuals of Nature, nor between men endowed with reason and others to whom true reason is unknown, nor between fools, madmen and the sane. Whatever an individual thing does by the laws of its own nature, it does with sovereign right, inasmuch as it acts as determined by Nature, and can do no other" (527). Everyone is part of the relation between right and power that characterizes the law of nature. From the sovereign to "fools, madmen and the sane," no one can claim any special privilege of access to right and to power. This contradicts the legalistic understanding that defines sovereignty in terms of its standing above the laws of the state. Matheron correctly observes that in fact Spinoza is not a contractarian: "Political society is not created by a contract."[40] This means that, since right is not transferred to any entity that is different from any subject, no one can claim the authority to determine an end. No one has a right to life and death. If there is an end to the modality of possibility, then that end can be nothing else than the determination of what one can do, or the exercise of what is possible to each individual. But such an "end" is not reduced to any authority, but is rather exercised—or, more accurately, exercisable—by everyone. Thus it is a right to life, an affirmation of living.

This radical inclusivity of right can easily be castigated as a determinism that removes the individual's freedom.[41] But this completely ignores the context of Spinoza's argument. Spinoza opposes here the tradition of political thought that determines sovereignty through exclusions—the thanatopolitics that determines sovereignty with recourse to the written law and the right of life and death to which Hobbes and Rousseau belong. There is, in fact, no rejection of freedom in Chapter 16 of the *Tractatus*: "It is from the necessity of this order alone [i.e., natural law] that all individual things are determined to exist and to act in a definite way" (528).[42] Not only is freedom not rejected in this statement that summarizes Spinoza's description of right; on the contrary, the danger is that Spinoza's radical inclusivity—the insistent affirmation of living—may be interpreted as allowing for too much freedom. It could be seen as superseding any notion of written law, thereby leading to unrestricted freedom—to a pervasive anarchy. Not only does this image of anarchy reintroduce the fear of democracy as it was described in the Platonic metaphor of the ship with the drunker sailors, but, more importantly, the privileging of the law of nature over the written law can posit freedom again as an ideal.[43] To dispel this misunderstanding Spinoza needs to address the relation between written law and natural law. Spinoza immediately turns to this relation: "However, there cannot be any doubt as to how much more it is to men's advantage to live in accordance with the laws and sure dictates of our reason, which, as we have said, aim only at the true good of men" (528). Even though one's power is the means to achieving what one desires, still the laws of nature and the rights of the individual are not disconnected from written laws. On the contrary, Spinoza insists on the expediency of a conformity of rights with the written laws. Spinoza continues: "Furthermore, there is nobody who does not desire to live in safety free from fear, as far as is possible" (528). The individual has a rightful desire for order, peace, and stability. But it is precisely the correlation between natural and state law that prevents that desire from becoming an end in itself: "But this cannot come about as long as every individual is permitted to do just as he pleases, and reason can claim no more right than hatred and anger. For there is no one whose life is free from anxiety in the midst of feuds, hatred, anger and deceit, and who will not therefore try to avoid these as far as in him lies" (528). It is the individual's right to be subject to passions—that is, to express its natural right—but this expression itself is not sufficient for freedom. Freedom requires an elimination of the illusion that there is pure desire "free from anxiety." Or, differently put, freedom requires an elimination of the illusion that the distinction between natural and written laws entails that one law is more significant than the other. Rather, the alleviation of anxiety, according to Spinoza, requires reason and obedience to assist in the regulation of free desire. And this consists in eliminating the possibility that desire can be an end in itself. Written law prevents natural law from positing itself as an end.

There is neither an end to the power indicated by the laws of nature nor an end in privileging the laws of nature over written law. The absence of an end means that the radical inclusivity of written law—the fact that everyone is capable of obedience—is correlated with the radical inclusivity of natural law—the fact that everyone has a determinate power. The former inclusivity points to community, or the love of one's neighbor, that, according to Spinoza, entails the emptiness of the law. The latter inclusivity points to the power of the individual. As soon as Spinoza argues that the inclusivity of state law eliminates the end from natural law, he proposes a sense of community that is more nuanced than that described two chapters earlier: "And if we also reflect that the life of men without mutual assistance must necessarily be most wretched and must lack the cultivation of reason . . . it will become quite clear to us that in order to achieve a secure and good life, men had necessarily to unite in one body" (528). What Spinoza calls here the unity of the people "in one body" corresponds to the assertion in the *Tractatus Politicus* that the multitude is united in "one mind" (3.2).[44] Even though Spinoza develops his account of the multitude in detail only in his second political *Tractatus*, one point is made clearly in the earlier *Tractatus Theologico-Politicus*—namely, the delimiting of natural law through written law: "They therefore arranged that the unrestricted right naturally possessed by each individual should be put into common ownership, and that this right should no longer be determined by the strength and appetite of the individual, but by the power and will of all together" (528). Natural right is not simply "unrestricted," but rather delimited through the presence of the other. It is the other, then, that points to the radical inclusivity of both laws in Spinoza and in such a way as to eliminate the end in both of them. The other is the condition of the possibility of the modalities, not only of necessity and contingency—as we saw in the previous section—but also of possibility. And the inclusivity that points to the other marks in Spinoza the erasure of an end.

The "common ownership" of right that allows for the radical inclusivity without end is also responsible for a nonidealized conception of freedom that ultimately leads to Spinoza's conception of democracy. According to the famous Proposition 67 of Part IV of the *Ethics*, "A free man thinks of death least of all things, and his wisdom is a meditation of life, not of death" (355). A lot can be gleaned from this complex statement.[45] In the context of Spinoza's conception of the political and of sovereignty, this proposition on freedom needs to be juxtaposed to the following statement from the *Tractatus Theologico-Politicus*: "the less freedom of judgment is conceded to men, the further their distance from the most natural state, and consequently the more oppressive the regime" (571). Freedom is related to judgment, and in such a way as to determine the quality of the regime. Freedom of judgment is related to democracy. But the question, then, arises about the connection between the fear of death and its obverse, the ability to judge. This is taken up by Spinoza immediately after the quoted passage above, where he discusses the "common ownership" of right. He introduces judgment as an issue that is crucial "so as to ensure its [the covenant's] stability and validity" (528). Spinoza draws attention to the point that he is about to make: "Now it is a universal law of human nature that nobody rejects what he judges to be good except through hope of a greater good or fear of greater loss, and that no one endures any evil except to avoid a greater evil or to gain a greater good" (528–29). Freedom consists in being in a position to judge on the economy of gain and loss. If we consider this statement in relation to the proposition from the *Ethics* that a free individual "thinks of death least of all things," then the freedom of judgment consists in a state wherein the individual need not worry about its self-preservation. Or, to put the same point in positive terms, freedom consists in a state where the individual is given the opportunity to judge how to realize its possibilities—how to exercise its power so as to affirm life. This state is called "democracy" by Spinoza. To recall the definition from the beginning of the present section, democracy is the regime that strives for the maximum operative presence of natural law—without, however, striving for the overcoming of written law.

Spinoza raises exactly the same point about freedom, judgment, and the allowing of the modality of possibility in describing what he calls "the purpose of the state."

> It follows clearly from my earlier explanation of the basis of the state that its ultimate purpose is not to exercise dominion or to restrain men

by fear and deprive them of independence, but on the contrary to free every man from fear so that he may live in security as far as is possible, that is, so that he may best preserve his own natural right to exist and to act, without harm to himself and to others. It is not, I repeat, the purpose of the state to transform men from rational beings into beasts or puppets, but rather to enable them to develop their mental and physical faculties in safety, to use their reason without restraint and to refrain from the strife and the vicious mutual abuse that are prompted by hatred, anger, or deceit. Thus the purpose of the state is, in reality, freedom. (567)

The purpose of the state is to allow the individual as much as possible to exercise one's power, and that is only possible if one can exercise the judgment about the economy of gain and loss. Democracy is a politics of living. Again here, in Chapter 20, the concluding chapter of the *Tractatus*, Spinoza insists that freedom is ultimately the purpose of the state. This is not a freedom to justify power. Rather, it is a freedom to exercise judgment in order to enjoy one's natural right or power. The justification of power turns humans into puppets, whereas the exercise of judgment makes them free. Democracy is the political regime that provides the institutional and legal matrix that allows for judgment. Or, differently put, democracy is the regime that recognizes that written laws are delimited by natural law, and hence they are inherently open to change. Or, in yet another formulation, democracy is the regime that welcomes the revolutionary.

It is at this point, after we have established that the elimination of the end in Spinoza entails the creation of the multitude or the "common ownership" of right, the inscription of freedom within the domain of natural right, and the identification of freedom as the "purpose" of a democratic state, that the question of the comparison to Rousseau becomes pressing. Is Spinoza's freedom an ideal? Does the fact that it is referred to as a "purpose" reinscribe an end to freedom and hence allow for a return of the vicious circle that characterizes the logic of sovereignty?

The most revealing way to answer these questions and to illuminate the comparison with Rousseau is to rephrase these questions in terms of justification. Does Spinoza's freedom justify violence the way that Rousseau's idealized freedom justified violence against the "wrongdoer"? Spinoza, unlike Rousseau, is careful to confine freedom within natural law—that is, within the realm of the possible. This is not to say that state laws are unrelated to the way that freedom is realized, but rather that ontologically the right to freedom is coextensive with the possibility of its articulation in life. Spinoza argues this point in terms of what he calls "the natural right to act deceitfully" (529). This right is described with recourse to an example of breaking one's promise. Imagine, says Spinoza, that you are assaulted by a robber. Because "right is determined by power alone" (529), Spinoza argues that one has the right to use any means at one's disposal to free oneself from the robber, including promising something to the robber without any intention of keeping the promise. From the perspective of natural law, says Spinoza, "I have the sovereign right to break faith and go back on my pledged word" (529).[46] Spinoza's freedom affirms the economy of living power—an economy that makes judgment possible without adherence to an ideal. Kant avers in the *Groundwork on the Metaphysics of Morals* that the keeping of the promise is compulsory because one should always act in such a way as to adhere to the ideal, universal moral law.[47] The Kantian categorical imperative functions in a way analogous to Rousseau's liberty: they are both ideals that must be followed. Conversely, Spinoza insists on the utility of following one's promise: "the validity of an agreement rests on its utility, without which the agreement automatically becomes null and void" (529). Spinoza is not pointing here to an ideal that justifies action. Instead of adhering to an ideal end, Spinoza's notion of the promise operates in the realm of means.[48] The criterion is whether the promise keeps open the possibility of judgment: "It is therefore folly to demand from another that he should keep his word for ever, if at the same time one does not try to ensure that, if he breaks his word, he will meet with more harm than good" (529). Judging on the economy of loss and gain is not the same as justification, because judgment requires a consideration of the singular moment, whereas justification requires a universal end. On this basis Spinoza can infer that the right to act deceitfully "is particularly relevant in considering the constitution of the state" (528). Deceit is permissible so long as it supports the state. And this means that the right to be deceitful is permissible so long as one exercises the power at one's disposal. The freedom that is derived from natural law is connected with the contingency that characterizes the necessary rebel: they both privilege the moment of the now—the participating in the circumstances that enhance the "common ownership" of the polity's rights. The right to be deceitful is the right to live in singularity.

This "right to act deceitfully" should also not be confused with Machiavelli's argument in the *Prince* that we encountered in the previous chapter. Machiavelli argues that the sovereign has no obligation to keep his promises, because his subjects are inherently deceitful, and hence, in order to perpetuate his power, the sovereign is justified to use whatever means at this disposal. Machiavelli's argument does appear similar to Spinoza in the sense that they both emphasize that keeping one's promise is related to power. The difference is, however, that the breaking of the promise for Machiavelli is justified in order to support the sovereign's effort to maintain himself in his position—and this includes the sovereign's right of life and death. Conversely, the breaking of the promise for Spinoza points to the exercise of power as a pure means. This power is not determined by state law, as is Machiavelli's sovereign, who stands above the law. Instead, power in Spinoza is determined by natural law. As intimated at the beginning of the present section, it is a category mistake to confuse power and state law while at the same time, as also argued earlier, it is important to relate the two in such a way that neither law is more primary. By establishing this distinction without separation of state and natural law, Spinoza can show that power creates the space of judgment, the space of the expression of freedom—a space that does not rely on justification.[49] In constitutional terms the regime that makes this space possible is democracy. Democracy is the regime of broken promises. It creates the space for the expression of power, but that power has no aim other than living. Whatever it promises to deliver never comes. It always falls short of the plenitude of the universal. It never realizes the promise of order, peace, and stability because it stubbornly responds to the singular moment. The broken promise is democracy's power.

Spinoza then succeeds in avoiding justification and the circular logic that absolutizes sovereignty by eliminating the end of the political. The written law is given through its being opposed by the necessary rebel who taps the singular moment. And the natural law shows that power, freedom, and judgment can flourish within that singular moment of living. Thus Spinoza emerges as the first philosopher we have encountered thus far who defends a democratic conception of the political. He is the first philosopher who provides an account of how to conceive the participation in the conflict, the *stasis*, that Solon defines as the democratic exigency. This *stasis* is the agonistic relation to written law that is conducted by the necessary rebel, leading to an account of the community through Spinoza's theory of natural law.

One question, however, arises at the point when the space of sovereignty has been distinguished from the space of democracy—a question that pertains to the core of the idea of agonism and the revolutionary in Spinoza. What is the relation between sovereignty and democracy? Or, in the terms employed here, what is the relation between the juridical conception of power and the determination of power as freedom? Or, more specifically, what is the relation between the logic of justification and the possibility of judgment? The difficulty in determining the relation between justification and judgment consists in that one of the main characteristics of justification—the right of life and death—is the operation of exclusion. Augustine excluded the pagans, Hobbes excluded the madman, Rousseau excluded the wrongdoer. All of them justified violence against those excluded by identifying them as the internal enemy. But then is it possible to say that a genuine democracy is possible if it excludes sovereignty? Would not then sovereignty function as the internal enemy of democracy? Derrida recognizes the gravity of this question when he points out in *Rogues* that when it concerns the other, "a certain unconditional renunciation of sovereignty is required a priori."[50] From which, however, it follows that "The great question . . . of all democracy . . . is that the *alternative* to democracy can always be *represented* as a democratic *alteration*."[51] Heinrich von Kleist's unrepeatable rebel, Michael Kohlhaas, can be shown to tackle this "great question" within the purview of Spinoza's conception of the democratic.

THE PAROXYSM OF THE ALEATORY: KLEIST'S *MICHAEL KOHLHAAS*

The relation between sovereignty and its other can be approached by asking the question: Is Michael Kohlhaas a justified rebel? In the first paragraph of his novella, Heinrich von Kleist answers this question in the negative. This is not, however, a simple castigation of Kohlhaas, but rather indicates that Kohlhaas is not containable within sovereignty's logic of justification. Kleist writes that the horse dealer who "lived beside the banks of the River Havel . . . was one of the most honourable as well as one of the most terrible men [*einer der rechtschaffensten zugleich und entsetzlichsten Menschen*] of his age" (114/2).[52] Up to the age of thirty Kohlhaas conducted his life in such as way as to be admired and respected by everyone. Being virtuous, says Kleist, "the world would have had cause to revere his memory, had he not pursued one of his virtues to excess. But his sense of justice made him a robber and a murderer" (114). Kohlhaas suffered an injustice that led him to become a rebel. Kleist suggests that this rebellion was not justified. His pursuit of justice was excessive, so much so that he was in fact "a robber and a murder." However, Kleist's verdict is not unambiguous. Even though the last sentence of the first paragraph rejects the claim that Kohlhaas was a justified rebel, it is complicated by the preceding sentence, which claims that if he had led his life in peace and quiet, "the world" would have celebrated his memory. This is a paradoxical claim, since if Kohlhaas had not led a rebellion, it is inconceivable that anyone would have remembered him in the first place.[53] If he had not asserted his claim to justice, he would have been merely a horse dealer during the Reformation. A memory of Kohlhaas is justified only because Kohlhaas himself lacks justification. In other words, justification requires the unjustified. There is no justification without exclusion. There is no justification without thanatopolitics.

We have encountered this circularity of justification numerous times already. It was described in Chapter 1 as the circle of the logic of sovereignty that absolutizes it. In Chapter 2 we saw how Augustine's justified war of the pilgrims could only be conducted because of the existence of the pagans. The absolute sovereignty propagated by Hobbes rehearsed this circularity, since it is impossible to determine whether its principle "might is right" means that might justifies justice, or whether it is the control of the discourse on the order, peace, and stability of the state that determines who is the most mighty. Finally, Rousseau's perpetual revolution sought to justify the ideal of freedom, yet that freedom was articulated by the exercise of violence against the wrongdoer. Kohlhaas's two attributes emphasized by Kleist at the very beginning—honorable and terrible—indicate this circularity between means and ends, law and justice, the violence in particularity being justified by, as well as justifying, a transcendent value. Kohlhaas is honorable because he adheres to certain transcendent values of justice as an end, and yet he is terrible because he uses the means of violence to pursue his claim to justice. Thus the question—is Kohlhaas a justified rebel?—cannot be answered by a simple "yes" or "no." The question is not so much whether he is a justified rebel, but rather the manner in which justification operates in his case. For instance, is he justified because the means justify the end—as is the case with modern sovereignty—or rather, in the manner of ancient sovereignty, whereby the end justifies the means? In other words, how does Kohlhaas articulate the circularity of justification? Only after the nature of justification is considered will we be in a position to consider whether a space is posited that is different from justification. Might Kohlhaas be not a justified, but rather a *necessary* rebel, in Spinoza's terms?

The plot of the novella is relatively straightforward. As Michael Kohlhaas, a horse dealer, crosses the border to Saxony, two of his horses are confiscated because he does not have a passport. After he determines that he did not need a passport, he requests the return of his horses. When his request is not satisfied, he pursues various legal avenues, all of them fruitless. His wife, Lisbeth, volunteers to assist him by petitioning the elector of Brandenburg, but she is accidentally killed by one of the elector's guards. At this point Kohlhaas leads a rebellion that seeks retribution for the injustices committed against him. After much bloodshed as well as the arson of Wittenberg, Kohlhaas starts to be viewed favorably by the population. Due to the intervention of Martin Luther, Kohlhaas is granted amnesty to pursue his claim to the Saxon courts, but eventually this fails, and he is sentenced to the death penalty. The Brandenburg elector claims Kohlhaas as his subject, demanding to have him tried again in Berlin. At that point the elector of Saxony realizes that Kohlhaas holds a secret upon which his own life as well as the continuation of his dynasty depends. He offers to help Kohlhaas escape from prison, but Kohlhaas is bent on retribution—he has, as Kleist suggests, an excessive sense of justice, and is there justice without retribution?—so Kohlhaas rejects the offer and destroys the information sought by the elector of Saxony just before he is executed. Upon witnessing the destruction of the evidence, the elector of Saxony collapses—retribution has, indeed been achieved, but at the cost of Kohlhaas's own life.

This relatively linear plot is complicated by the various positions in relation to the law that Kohlhaas occupies. These positions vis-a-vis the law and justice raise the question whether Kohlhaas is a justified rebel. In his *Theory of the Partisan*, Carl Schmitt unambiguously rejects the claim that Kohlhaas is a justified rebel: "Michael Kohlhaas, whom the feeling of justice made a robber and murderer, was no partisan because he was not political and fought exclusively for his own, private justice, rather than against a foreign conqueror or for a revolutionary cause. In such cases, irregularity is unpolitical and becomes purely criminal because it loses the positive interconnectedness with a somewhere available regularity. This is how the partisan is distinguished from a—noble or ignoble—robberchief."[54] The key distinction that Schmitt relies on is that a justified rebel, or a partisan, in his terminology, is one who defends or aspires to sovereignty. Thus Schmitt argues that Kleist's "*Die Hermannsschlacht* is the greatest partisan work of all time," since it offers an anti-Napoleonic narrative that defends the principles of Germanic sovereignty.[55] This is not the case with *Michael Kohlhaas*. The horse dealer does not aspire, according to Schmitt, to any political motivation. In Schmitt's terms from *The Concept of the Political*, Kohlhaas has no enemies, he only has foes.[56] To be political the exercise of power must be related to sovereignty, and sovereignty in turn is justified in relation to its standing above the law.[57] Thus, within the legalistic tradition, the justification of rebellion can only entail the justification of the means of violence. Schmitt essentially avers that Kohlhaas, to the extent that he is "noble," acts by privileging a sense of justice over the means and laws of exercising justice. In other words, Kohlhaas's end seeks to justify his means. He acts according to the precepts of ancient sovereignty. Schmitt's interpretation agrees with Luther's. After Kohlhaas had burned parts of Wittenberg as part of his rebellion, Martin Luther issued a statement in which he sought to dispel the idea that Kohlhaas was justified to conduct a just war. The proclamation, addressing Kohlhaas, stated: "Know that the sword which you bear is the sword of robbery and murder; you are a rebel and no warrior of the just God" (150). The greatest spiritual authority of the age intervenes to lay to rest any idea that the injustices committed against Kohlhaas can justify his actions within the logic of ancient sovereignty. Kohlhaas has no authority to claim that he is acting out of an end that justifies his means—in the manner that the pilgrims justify their violence against the pagans, according to Augustine. Kohlhaas does not represent a divine sense of justice that justifies his violence. Therefore, if he does not aspire to sovereignty, in Schmitt's terms, and is not justified out of a sense of divine justice, in Luther's terms, then Kohlhaas has no justification to take the law in own hands. There is no justification for him to stand above the law and wage a war in a pseudo-sovereign manner.[58]

Upon reading the proclamation, Kohlhaas decides to visit Luther. In the middle of the night the horse-dealer sneaks into the spiritual figurehead's study. In the exchange that ensues, Kohlhaas denies that he has conducted a just war. He refuses to position himself within the logic of ancient sovereignty. Instead, he insists that he has been excluded from the law. "'The war I am waging against human society becomes a crime if . . . society had not cast me out!'" (152), Kohlhaas tells Luther. He defines himself in a position of exclusion analogous to that of the madman in Hobbes or the wrongdoer in Rousseau, thereby insisting that he is conducting himself in accordance with the principles of modern sovereignty. Luther does not seem to grasp this positioning: "'Cast you out!' cried Luther, staring at him. 'What mad idea has taken possession of you? Who do you say has cast you out from the community of the state in which you have lived? Has there ever, so long as states have existed, been a case of anyone, no matter who, becoming an outcast from society?'" (152). Luther maybe misunderstands Kohlhaas because he is still thinking in terms of the logic of ancient sovereignty that leads to justified war.[59] "'I call that man an outcast,' answered Kohlhaas, clenching his fist, 'who is denied the protection of the law! For I need that protection if my peaceful trade is to prosper; indeed it is for the sake of that protection that I take refuge, with all the goods I have acquired, in that community. Whoever withholds it from me drives me out into the wilderness among savages'" (152). Whoever excludes Kohlhaas from the law, and thereby denies him the means of achieving a peaceful and prosperous life, effectively throws Kohlhaas back into the state of nature—"into the wilderness among savages." Kohlhaas insists that his rebellion is justified because the "outcast" or the oppressed has a right to rebel against the oppressors. The excluded has the right to rise up against the sovereign. This rising up can be pictured as the image of the sovereign standing above the law and the outcast being positioned below the law. Kohlhaas proclaims that all those excluded from the law have a right to challenge the sovereign who excludes them—a sentiment that would have been shared by the revolutionaries in France a couple of decades before Kleist wrote his novella, as well as most revolutionaries since then.

Kohlhaas's rebellion against his being placed outside the law shows that he wants to be treated according the logic of modern sovereignty. His desire appears straightforward—namely, to be placed within the law from which he has been excluded.[60] We can divide the novella into four parts: The first includes his horses being confiscated and his attempts to regain them legally (114–37). The second part describes his rebellion and ends with the dialogue with Luther (137–56). The third opens with Luther's letter to the elector of Saxony asking him to grant amnesty to Kohlhaas, thereby permitting him to reopen his legal case, and ends with his death sentence (156–85). In his letter to the elector of Saxony, Luther argues that "the situation would best be remedied if Kohlhaas were treated not so much as a rebel in revolt against the crown but rather as a foreign invading power" (156).[61] Luther's suggestion that Kohlhaas is treated "as a foreign invading power" means that he is no longer positioned as an outcast, as the one excluded from the law, but rather as another sovereign who legitimately stands above the law. In the first three sections, then, Kohlhaas insists on being placed within the law, and he repeats this request in each section by saying that he wants punishment of the Junker who confiscated his horses illegally, restoration of his horses to their original condition, and compensation for damages suffered (127, 153, and 163). This persistent demand, articulated every time in almost identical words, indicates that Kohlhaas led a rebellion as a means of regaining the means afforded to citizens to live their lives in peace. He wants to be a subject. His desire to enter the law and to be judged according to the logic of modern sovereignty is so strong that when, in the fourth section of the novella Kohlhaas is given the opportunity by the elector of Saxony to help him escape his conviction in Berlin, he declines and prefers to be decapitated instead—and, as it will be shown at the end of the present section, this decision that prefers death over life rehearses the relation between justification and judgment.

But the fourth section, which includes Kohlhaas's extradition to Brandenburg and his execution (185–213), paradoxically seems to lend credence to Schmitt's and Luther's conviction that Kohlhaas is conducting a just war that is amenable to the logic of ancient sovereignty, according to which the end justifies the means. On the scaffold, the elector of Brandenburg tells him: "'Well, Kohlhaas, the day has come on which justice will be done to you! Look: I here deliver to you everything [you requested] . . . Are you satisfied with me?' Kohlhaas took the court's verdict which was passed to him . . . when he also found a clause condemning Junker Wenzel to two years' imprisonment . . . he joyfully assured the High Chancellor that his dearest wish on earth had been fulfilled" (212–13). Kohlhaas has achieved punishment of the Junker, restitution of his horses, and compensation. But in addition, he has managed to exact retribution from the elector of Saxony by depriving him of the prophecy of "the name of the last ruler of your

[Saxon] dynasty, the year in which he will lose his throne, and the name of the man who will seize it by force of arms" (201). This retribution, however, is not derived by legal means, and hence it is not amenable to the logic of modern sovereignty. Instead, it is precipitated by the intervention of a mystical figure, the old woman. Now, there are clear indications that there are links between this fortuneteller and Kohlhaas's own departed wife. Not only is the old woman called Elizabeth, while his wife's name was Lisbeth, and not only does the old woman appear only days after his wife died, as if she were her ghost, moreover, they resemble each other: "The horse-dealer noticed a strange resemblance between her and his deceased wife Lisbeth, so much so that he almost asked her if she was her grandmother; for not only did her features and her hands, which though bony were still finely shaped, and especially the way she gestured with them as she spoke, remind him most vividly of his wife, but he also saw on her neck a mole like one that Lisbeth had had on hers" (206). Thus Kohlhaas's desire to be a subject is coupled by his participation in a process that starts by positing an end—the just retribution of the enemy—the attainment of which is accomplished through the intervention of powers beyond this earth—that is, powers that pertain to a transcendent justice.

Is Kohlhaas a justified rebel? This question, as already intimated, necessitates to distinguish the sovereign logic according to which Kohlhaas seeks justification. Is Kohlhaas's position outside the law because he is excluded from the law and thereby denied the means to lead his life? Or is he outside the law because he acts by privileging the end or justice? In other words, is his rebellion justified according to the logic of modern or of ancient sovereignty? Kohlhaas's legal demand on punishment, restitution, and compensation points to the modern justification of sovereignty, but the desire for retribution points to the ancient justification. These two justifications move in opposite directions—from the means to the end and vice versa. And yet they cannot be taken simply as contradictory, because they describe the circularity of the logic of sovereignty. The separation of law and justice is only possible because of their reunification through the coincidence of power and a transcendent sense of peace. Thus the two justifications are contradictory to the extent that they dejustify the logic of justification that legitimizes sovereignty. Or, to put it another way, the "resurrection" of Kohlhaas's wife in the figure of the old mystical woman, Elizabeth, indicates the resurgence of ancient sovereignty in the most trenchant, the most stubborn proponent of modern sovereignty, Michael Kohl-haas. (We will see in the following chapter that Foucault recognizes the circularity of sovereignty as such as resurrection.) As a figure Kohlhaas shows that the sovereign decision can be taken only because it pivots between two senses of justification *and* because it fails to recognize that. In fact the decision consists not so much in the justification of power, either according to the modern or the ancient logic of sovereignty, but rather as the repression mobilized to obfuscate the circularity and complementarity between ancient and modern sovereignty. Recognizing these contradictory justifications as well as their repression consists in a radical dejustification of sovereignty. From this perspective Henry Sussman is perfectly correct to compare *Michael Kohlhaas* to *Hamlet*, since the dejustification of sovereignty produces a fragmentation of subjectivity that is paramount in both works.[62]

Alongside the narrative that indicates this dejustification, however, Kleist constructs a different space that is not amenable to the logic of sovereignty—and it is because of this parallel narrative that Kleist's novella goes beyond *Hamlet*.[63] This narrative overlays sovereignty with the power of the aleatory.[64] Every important event happens by accident. The whole story is propelled by a pervasive and all-encompassing contingency. Let us list some indicative accidents in the four parts of the novella. In the first part the confiscation of the horses by the warden and the steward of the Troka castle required the support of the Junker himself, which is described in the following manner: "But at that very moment a gust of wind drove a great sheet of rain and hail through the gateway, and to put an end to the matter the Junker shouted: 'If he refuses to leave the horses, throw him back over the toll-gate,' and went in" (118). The one endowed with sovereign powers is impelled by contingent circumstances—rain and hail—to put an end to the dispute wishing to protect himself from the winter weather. Also in the first part, Kohlhaas's claim was rejected by the Saxon court because of a coincidence, namely, that the cupbearer and the chamberlain to the Saxon elector were related to the Junken von Tronka (128). The death of Kohlhaas's wife that leads to the second part of the novella is also an accident, since "through no fault of his [*ohne Verschulden desselben*], a rough and over-zealous member of his [the elector of Brandenburg] bodyguard had struck her a blow on the chest with the shaft of his lance" (136/16). It was not an intentional act that led to her death, but an accident. In the third part of the novella, Kohlhaas ends up being convicted because he desires to leave Saxony and his enemies manage to present this desire as a plan to resume his revolution, even though he was granted amnesty. But the actual reason remains unclear. Kleist says that Kohlhaas wanted to return to his home in Brandenburg "and motives of another kind may also have been at work, which we may leave for all who know their own hearts to surmise" (177). In the fourth part the extradition to Brandenburg is achieved only by a political accident—namely, that von Gessau, the chancellor of Brandenburg, exploited the animosity between Saxony and Poland (186). These are only some indicative accidents. Every turn of the plot is in fact based on contingent circumstances.

Now, recall that contingency is that force that opposes the necessity of the law in Spinoza. In our reading of the *Tractatus Theologico-Politicus*, the necessary rebel is the one who can intervene in the emptiness of the law by asserting the importance of responding to the contingent circumstances. Necessary rebellion entails that the figure that defends the law by standing above the law is also subject to the contingent. The coupling of contingency with sovereignty is registered in the novella as the involuntary reaction to the aleatory of those who stand above the law. Again, indicatively, we can support this claim with the following examples. When confronted by Kohlhaas complaining about the mistreatment of his horses, the "Junker dismounted, blanching for an instant [*indem ihm eine flüchtige Blässe ins Gesicht trat*], and said: 'If the damned fool won't take his horses back, let him leave them here'" (121). Going pale because of the horse dealer's embarrassing accusation in front of his friends, the Junker just avoids making a decision. In the second part, already acting as an "invading foreign power" or as a sovereign, Kohlhaas catches sight of Luther's proclamation calling him a robber, and his "face flushed deep crimson" (151), an involuntary reaction that prompted him to seek the audience with Luther. In the third part, the amnesty is granted to Kohlhaas after Luther's intervention, but this is agreed upon by the elector of Saxony only because Prince Christiern of Meissen argued in the council that if they were going to punish Kohlhaas, the Saxon state should also punish the chamberlain who had dismissed his case originally: "At these words the Junker [i.e. the Chamberlain] looked in dismay at the Elector, who turned away, blushing deeply [*indem er über das ganze Gesicht rot ward*], and moved over to the window" (158–59). This blushing at the reminder of the misjudgment of his friend and confidant led the elector to grant amnesty to Kohlhaas. All decisions of any weight taken by those who stand above the law—the sovereign in the modern sense—are caused by an abrupt eruption to the aleatory. The decision requires intentionality. The sovereign can decide on the exception because his standing above the law is meant to provide him with the prerogative to intentionally intervene when the circumstances are not codified in statute or when they are not even codifiable. Here, however, Kleist presents every significant decision as being caused by a collision of the contingent and sovereign power. The effects of this collision are involuntary physical reactions such as paling and blushing. The term used for these effects in the first chapter was the "sovereign discomfort." George W. Bush looking stunned while Andrew Card whispered in his ear during the visit at Booker Elementary is like a Kleistian sovereign whose power is assaulted by the aleatory and who reacts in an involuntary way that discloses the fact that his law is dependent upon its being challenged by contingency. This does not mean, of course, that the challenge is justified. Rather, the challenge is the force of dejustification, thereby indicating a space distinct from the logic of sovereignty. The sovereign discomfort shows that necessary rebellion, in Spinoza's sense, is not amenable to a legalistic definition of sovereignty that posits it as standing above the law. As we saw in Spinoza, it is only because of this challenge that the law of the state can achieve any content—which means that all the positions defined in relation to the law, such as when the sovereign is conceived above the law, are caused by that challenge.

This collision between contingency and sovereignty or, rather, the intrusion of contingency in sovereign power, achieves a paroxysm in the fourth part of the novella through the figure of the old woman. The accidents proliferate to an uncontrollable degree through the intervention of the mystical. Indicatively, again, the encounter between the elector of Saxony and the old woman is riddled with coincidences. The elector happens to find himself in Jüterbock, he happens to encounter the fortuneteller, the proof of her prophetic powers is the coincidental theft by a dog of a roebuck's head from the butcher, and Kohlhaas happens to be present on his way to attack the Tronka castle, only to be handed over the prophecy by the old woman (199–202). Also, it is by an elaborate series of coincidences that the elector of Saxony discovers that Kohlhaas was the man who was handed over the prophecy—the carriage deporting Kohlhaas to Brandenburg was delayed because one of his children fell ill, at the border "it happened" (188) to encounter a hunting party with the Saxon elector, and "it happened" (189) that the elector was goaded by his old love to spy on Kohlhaas, and again by chance during that spying he discovered that Kohlhaas had "happened" (191) to be holding the secret. This proliferation of coincidences culminates when the chamberlain is dispatched by the elector of Saxony to Berlin in order to steal Kohlhaas's secret and he recruits an old woman to assist him, but she happens to be the same old woman, Elizabeth, who had given the secret to Kohlhaas. Kleist introduces this coincidence thus: "indeed (for probability and reality do not always coincide) it chanced that something had happened here which we must report, though anyone who so pleases is at liberty to doubt it" (205–6). Doubting this further coincidence is not, as one would expect, because chance and reality hardly coincide, but rather the opposite—namely, that "probability and reality do not always coincide." By this stage in the novella coincidence has become the norm. This paroxysm of the aleatory can be interpreted in two ways. It may be taken as a divine intervention that rectifies the injustices committed against Kohlhaas. In this sense the contingent is the mark of transcendence. However, if we follow Spinoza in interpreting religious laws on an equal footing as state laws, then another interpretation becomes possible. Then contingency is the mark of the necessary rebel. It marks the giving truth content to the law by being the counterpart of necessity as the affirmation of singularity that, as argued earlier, is devoid of an end.

In fact, the two interpretations about the relation of the aleatory and the divine point to the relation between sovereignty and its other. By taking coincidence to be the mark of the divine, transcendence is retained. This sustains the logic of sovereignty that requires an end that either justifies or is justified by the means—the circular relation between the universal and law. Conversely, by taking coincidence to be the mark of the necessary rebel, no end is affirmed other than the exercise of the agonistic relation between necessity and contingency in the now. We can recognize the former interpretation in Kohlhaas's desire for retribution against the elector of Saxony, which is extracted only by Kohlhaas accepting the death penalty. In the Spinozan interpretation of contingency we recognize instead an affirmation of possibility—the individual whose power is coextensive with its right. In other words, we recognize an affirmation of life. When Elizabeth, the old woman, gave Kohlhaas the secret, she admonished him to keep it safe, because "'one day it will save your life!'" (192). While visiting Kohlhaas in the Berlin prison, Elizabeth suggested that it "would be wise" to put the secret into use by accepting the Saxon elector's offer to be handed the prophecy "in exchange for life and freedom" (207). This suggestion is the same as the advice of his dying wife, Lisbeth, to "forgive your enemies" (137) only to the extent that they both affirm the exercise of power by including the other. Life is the living with, the love of one's neighbor in Spinoza's sense. There is no end to it. It consists in the exercise of one's power, in the pursuit of the realization of one's possibilities. Kohlhaas is called upon to judge according to the economy of loss and gain—and the ultimate gain is living.

Kohlhaas does not heed the old woman's advice. He pursues his desire to retribution against his "enemy" (207), the elector of Saxony. This may appear as divine retribution, as an assertion of the logic of ancient sovereignty. But it is only possible because of Kohlhaas's other stubborn desire—namely, to be placed within the law, to be a subject—and that means subjected to the power of the law, which is articulated as the right of life and death. The moment of his execution represents both the retribution against the Saxon elector and the enactment of the death penalty. Therefore, the execution—the exercise of the sovereign right of life and death—combines the logics of ancient and modern sovereignty. Kohlhaas keeps his promise to rectify the injustice and to renounce his right of life in order to remain within the social contract. It is not the figure of Kohlhaas who presents that circularity on the scaffold, but rather the *death* of Kohlhaas. It is only with his submission to the logic of sovereignty and its thanatopolitics that he can remain within the law—state and religious.[65] His dying is the keeping of his promise. His death enshrines his rebellion as justified—that is, as operating within the logic of sovereignty. Conversely, Elizabeth's suggestion to accept the offer of escape "in exchange for life and freedom" would have consisted in the breaking of Kohlhaas's promise. But this broken promise would have been the judgment to live. It would have been the affirmation of *life*.

Elizabeth's prompting of Kohlhaas to break his promise functions as the caesura of the novella. It shows that the figure of Kohlhaas could be a necessary rebel. This requires him to judge for life over death—to judge in favor of judgment instead of justification. Thus the appeal to break his promise indicates the rupture between the two different realms—sovereignty and its other. The aleatory makes it possible to judge in favor of life—it makes it possible for one to assume one's singular responsibility and to act in the moment, in the now. The judgment is between death and life, between sovereignty and democracy, between the exclusion of and exercise of violence against the enemy and the living with the other. The judgment is between the possibility of evading judgment through justification and sustaining it through an indefinite deferral of an end—through a rejection of a final judgment. Thus the structure of judgment cannot come into effect without the threat of death—the threat of the end. It is only in an agonistic relation to the logic of sovereignty that its other can appear. Democracy exists through the enactment of that agonism. Elizabeth's appeal to a judgment that would have consisted in Kohlhaas breaking his promise in favor of life and freedom is only possible because it can be rejected if Kohlhaas keeps his promise to retribution and to the adherence of his being a subject to the law. The caesura indicated here is not an exclusion. Instead, it is the recognition that one's singular responsibility can only ever be dispensed with by resisting the justification that rejects judgment. Thus the agonism between judgment and justification is the incessant rebellion against thanatopolitics—a battle of life and death that, however, contains dying as an inherent possibility. If the other of sovereignty is democracy, still that otherness cannot exist without sovereignty. But this is not to say that the choice between the two—the judgment that has to choose between justification and the structure of judgment—is eternally undecidable. To the extent that the aleatory was shown to be the condition of the possibility of justification and to the extent that the aleatory is part of the structure of judgment, then judgment is more primary than justification. This means that judgment is enacted through its contestation with justification, but it does not mean that it can never be decided. Kohlhaas had his chance, but he did not take it. Judgment does not mean that one should break their promises all the time. Rather, it means that one must break the promises when that sustains living—when that breaks with thanatopolitics.

5

DEMOCRACY AND ITS OTHER
Biopolitical Sovereignty

NORMALIZING THE EXCEPTION

The transition to biopolitics is characterized by the starting point of justification shifting to the side of the exception. Sovereignty, as described
thus far, exhibits a consistent logic that justifies violence and that relies
on the relation between means and ends. At the same time, distinctions
between different forms of sovereignty are drawn, depending on whether
justification privileges an end or the means—justice or the law. According
to ancient sovereignty, the end justifies the means. This is articulated, as we
saw, as the just war of the pilgrims against the pagans that Augustine describes in the *City of God*. The formulation in Chapter 2 that encapsulated
this description was that there must be pagans for Augustinianism to exist.
There must be those who can be subjected to violence for the end of a perpetual peace in the city of God to be able to justify violence against all
those who are perceived not to advance toward that transcendent peace.
According to modern sovereignty the relation is reversed, so that now the
means justify the end. Violence is justified against anyone who is excluded
from the social contract because he threatens the perpetuation of sovereign power that is assumed as the defender of order, peace, and stability.
Thus we saw that, according to Hobbes, "there must be madmen" who are
excluded from the social contract so that absolute sovereignty can exist. As
I will be showing in the present chapter, a biopolitical justification privileges neither the means nor the end, but rather relies on a justification of

means by further means. It is this biopolitical justification that is signified by the normalization of the exception.

"The tradition of the oppressed," writes Walter Benjamin in Thesis VIII of his "On the Concept of History," "teaches us that the 'state of emergency' in which we live is not the exception but the rule."[1] Benjamin is implicitly addressing Carl Schmitt, who had defined the sovereign as he who decides on the exception.[2] Benjamin, however, reverses Schmitt's point.[3] Schmitt's definition suggests that there are threats to the existence of the state that cannot be codified in law and to which it is the role of the sovereign to respond. These circumstances are uncodifiable precisely because they are not normal. Schmitt avers that the sovereign can use any means at his disposal in order to attain the end of the perpetuation of the state—so that Schmitt clearly assumes the modern modality of sovereignty. Claiming that the exception is the rule turns Schmitt's point upside-down. It is not an unpredictable threat, but rather the normal that is uncodifiable. This means that the unpredictability of life—the contingent, the accidental, the aleatory—is now linked to the exception. Benjamin's point can easily be misunderstood. He is not suggesting that the exception is the same as the aleatory, thereby ascribing sovereign power to that which is contingent. That would have simply consisted in an apotheosis of the accidental that would have endowed it with divine justice—to recall Kleist's *Michael Kohlhaas*, it would have consisted in collapsing the distinction between justice and contingency. Benjamin, however, states that it is the "tradition of the oppressed" that indicates the ontological coincidence between the exception and normalcy. In other words, *pace* Schmitt, the exception is not a response to an unpredictable threat to the state, but rather the means used by a sovereign power to repress any resistance, to quench any revolutionary drive, and thus to perpetuate itself in power. When the exception is the rule, in Benjamin's sense, then the exception becomes the means that justifies legality as the means of power. This perpetual justification of means by means distinguishes biopolitics from ancient and modern sovereignty.

The normalization of the exception is distinctive of the biopolitical modality of justification. Instead of the means justifying an end, or vice versa, now the means justify the means. The exception is all-pervasive and functions as the means that justify the exercise of power. In a "post-" world—postmodern, posthuman, postindustrial, and so on—where metaphysics is said no longer to be possible, or at least credible—there is a desire to show that we have liberated ourselves from transcendent ends. Thus the creation of public narrative is now put in the service of power for the maintenance and perpetuation of power. But narrative can become a means that sustains power only if that narrative justifies power's perpetuation through the use of law and its institutions—such as the police, the education system, and the medical system. And it is narratives of the exception that can attain this justification of means by means. The exception is normalized because it refers—or, rather, represents itself as referring—to the immanent situation, not to a transcendent end. The privileging of the exception over law or justice demarcates the distinctive feature of biopolitical justification.

This biopolitical desire to overcome an end to the political can lead, however, to contrasting outcomes. Recall that in Chapter 4 we encountered Spinoza's resistance to transcendence and to imposing an end to the political. It was shown there that thereby Spinoza managed to create a space of judgment that is distinguishable from the sovereign space of justifications. Thus the "postmodern" desire to eliminate transcendent ends can be viewed as affiliated to the democratic impulse in Spinoza. Significantly, however, the normalization of the exception does not necessarily resist transcendence and the end of the political. Rather, it merely *represents* a desire to resist transcendence. As we will see in the following section of the present chapter, the exception becomes the norm by creating fabulatory ends— ends that are so imbued with the workings of power that there is no longer any point in presenting them as transcendent. The fabulatory ends, created through the exceptional narrative, justify the means of power. Thus the agonism against transcendence can be viewed from two opposing perspectives. First, it can be seen as an approximation to Spinoza's extrapolation of necessary rebellion. The necessary rebel in the *Tractatus Theologico-Politicus* showed that the law was empty, a pure necessity, thereby allowing for its being challenged by the individual who recognized the importance of judging according to the singular moment—the necessary rebel who is responsive to the contingent circumstances of each historical moment. Second, biopolitics can be seen as an attempt to control this Spinozan necessary rebel. If transcendence is no longer believable, then biopolitics decides to disguise transcendence into immanence. Transcendence is now dressed up to perform its part in the representations of exceptionality— to play its role in a historical "farce," as Marx calls it in the *Eighteenth*

Brumaire. In other words, biopolitics can be seen as the most sophisticated attempt to contain the democratic possibility that was inherent in the Spinozist theory of judgment. Thus the biopolitical desire to overcome transcendence, on the one hand, posits the possibility of democracy, but also retains, on the other hand, the threat that the other of democracy—sovereignty—will prevail.

Since the normalization of the exception can be appropriated both by democracy and sovereignty, it can function as the hinge that will allow an understanding of biopolitics in terms of the relation between democracy and its other. But biopolitics places this relation on a different basis. In biopolitics the initial impulse to bypass any politics that relies on an end betrays a direction toward democracy. The reason is that, as we saw in the previous chapter, the elimination of an end in Spinoza and its corollary, the insistence on the aleatory in Kleist, can make a thinking of the democratic possible. The question, then, about the relation between democracy and sovereignty returns in biopolitics, but it is posed from a basis that presupposes the democratic. Because the democratic presents itself as a visible possibility, the sovereign impulse to oppress it becomes stronger.

The most glaring symptom of the biopolitical desire to repress the democratic consists in the biopolitical drive to control life—to control the sphere of the aleatory that determines the relations of the living.[4] As Foucault has argued in the first volume of his *History of Sexuality*, the old sovereign right of life and death is now transformed in a right to make life and let die—into the sovereign right to control life.[5] In other words, the control of life is associated with the transformation of the traditional sovereign right of life and death. The right of life and death has been already identified as a decisive feature of sovereignty's logic of justification. For instance, we saw in *Michael Kohlhaas* how the horse dealer remained within the logic of justification by submitting himself to the death penalty. Ancient and modern sovereignty can be described as the justification of the sovereign's control of death. In this thanatopolitics, as it was called earlier, the control of the means of power or the control of the law is represented as the retention of the right of life and death. Now, as the emphasis shifts in biopolitics and the means justify the means, the privileging of the side of the exception entails that it is no longer possible to identify the means of power simply as the standing above the law. Controlling the exception signifies the control of the political narrative that provides the means of the exercise of power. And this signals that sovereign power now aims at controlling life—it aims at domesticating the modality of contingency that had pointed to the possibility of singularity and the necessary rebel in Spinoza. Or, to put it in a different formulation, the normalization of the exception aims at controlling the way the living incorporate the representations of the political—as I will show through a reading of Marx's *Eighteenth Brumaire*.

Biopower's aim at controlling life is not to say that the right of life and death disappears; rather, it changes tenor. As Roberto Esposito describes this change in thanatopolitics, "in the biopolitical regime, sovereign law isn't so much the capacity to put to death as it is to nullify life in advance."[6] We saw earlier how the sovereign right of life and death led to a conception of power in Spinoza that was premised on the emptiness of the law that required, as a consequence, its other, the necessary rebel, in order to achieve any content. Necessary rebellion was understood as the modality of contingency. We also saw the role of contingency in *Michael Kohlhaas*, where the sovereign powers continuously found themselves in a position of discomfort due to accidental occurrences. As argued, the aleatory dejustified sovereign power, both in its ancient and in its modern manifestation. Thus the challenge that biopolitical power seeks to rise to by normalizing the exception is the challenge of the aleatory. Biopower seeks to evade the dejustifications enacted by the aleatory. The aleatory, however, is constitutive of life—the unpredictable possibilities that are singular to the circumstances and to the individuals immersed in the now. Thus control of life is in fact control of the aleatory—or an attempt to mold life to accord with the representation of power, a nullification of life "in advance," as Esposito puts it.

It is not surprising that biopolitics participates in the same thanatopolitics that characterized ancient and modern sovereignty. As already argued, alongside the distinguishable modalities of justification of violence that the different forms of sovereignty denote, there is a consistent structure in the logic of sovereignty. This is a constant circularity in the logic of justification that, as already intimated, absolutizes sovereignty. As argued in Chapter 1 and as shown subsequently, justification operates by separating the law as the means of power from justice as the end of power, only in order to provide an account of violence that immediately reunites them. This separation and reunification of means and ends leads to a pervasive circularity. For instance, to recall one example from Chapter 4, Rousseau criticizes the vicious circle of the principle "might is right" that characterizes Hobbes's sovereignty because it bases "the right of life and death on the right to enslave, and the right to enslave on the right of life and death." In other words, the sovereign's standing above the law and thus having control of the means of power—or being able to decide on the exception, in Schmitt's sense—including the right to kill those who oppose his sovereignty, is premised on the subjects already having renounced their rights and hence having submitted themselves to the power of the sovereign. But, objects Rousseau, it is unclear what comes first, the sovereign's right of life and death as the symbol of the absolute control of the means of power or the enslavement of the subject that transfers all right to the sovereign. Rousseau endeavors to eschew this vicious circle, as we saw in Chapter 4, by arguing that the individuals transfer their association to the general will in order to strive for civil freedom, thereby allowing the citizen to retain their right and to avoid enslavement. However, Rousseau retains the sovereign right of life and death. The death penalty is now justified against anyone who opposes the general will by asserting his individual desires. Thus Rousseau recreated the circularity of sovereign power whereby the exercise of power is the means that is justified, as well as justifies, the end of order, peace, and stability. The circularity that absolutizes sovereignty has been a constant feature of the logic of justification.

Three inferences can be drawn at this point. The first indicates what was called in the Preamble the cosupponibility of the three modalities of justification. The reason that ancient, modern, and biopolitical sovereignty can revert to each other is that they all rely on a logic that has the same objective—namely, the justification of violence—and that it is circular. For instance, the normalization of the exception, which is taken here as a defining feature of biopolitics, can be understood as a perpetual civil war.[7] Demea indicates that such a "perpetual war is kindled amongst all living creatures."[8] The interlocutor in Hume's *Dialogues on Religion* who most approximates a Christian position presents humanity after the Fall as being in such a state of perpetual war. This is not surprising if we recall that Augustine had also described the present in terms of a perpetual and incessant conflict between the passions and spirituality, between the pagan and the pilgrim. And it is the same figure of civil war as the state of nature in Hobbes that premised his account of state formation. To the extent that biopolitics, like modern sovereignty, signifies a justification of violence,

Agamben is correct to point out that the "state of nature and the state of exception are nothing but two sides of the same topological process."[9] In all these different cases the justification may be carried out in different ways, but what remains constant is, first, a justification of sovereign violence as a response to the civil war/the exception, and second, a circularity between the state described as war/the exception and the violence that is justified. Because of this circularity the distinct modalities of justification can actually support each other.

Second, the biopolitical control of life can be seen as the culmination of the justificatory logic of sovereignty. Biopolitical violence is not necessarily physical violence. The regulation of life entails controlling the narrative of justification—as we will see with reference to Marx—or through forms of policing—as we will see with reference to Foucault. For instance, the control of life through campaigns such as the "war on drugs" does not put violence on the stage the way that Foucault describes the violence of the sovereign in Chapter 1 of *Discipline and Punish*—the violence that is expressed in torture and the death penalty.[10] The violence exercised by biopolitics is not on display in the same way as the ancient and the modern sovereign justifications of violence. Instead of exercising itself directly on the body, biopolitical violence seeks to control the representations of good life and to normalize behavior. At the same time, given the cosupponibility of the different justifications, biopolitics is not inherently against the use of blood violence. In fact, we will see later that Foucault insists that, even though biopolitics appears to have rejected the sovereign right of life and death, in fact it retains it through what he calls "racism."

Third, interpreting the normalization of the exception in terms of the circularity of the logic of justification retains a legalistic determination of sovereignty. The political implication of the legalistic determination of biopolitics is the seeming inescapability of the machine of biopower. When the exception functions as a means that justifies the law as the means of the exercise of power—that is, when the construction of representations generates sovereign power—then it is difficult to envisage an escape from the circularity of sovereignty. Differently put, when the end of sovereignty—the universal of order, peace, and stability—is perceived as a dispensation of the contingencies of life, hence there is nothing inherently just in it, then it is hard to interrupt the way that the means (the exception) justifies further means (the legal order). If the exception is approached from the legalistic perspective, it is impossible to envisage anything other than a pernicious normalization process pervading every aspect life.[11] The circle of justification remains closed; biopolitical sovereignty is absolutized—even when an attempt is made to break that circle. For instance, Giorgio Agamben works on a definition of the exception that relies on a topology of inside and outside the law.[12] This topology is premised on an absolute separation between bare life and political life—that is, between a pure physical body outside the law and a political body subject to the law. As he puts it in *Remnants of Auschwitz*, "Biopower's supreme ambition is to produce, in a human body, the absolute separation of the living being and the speaking being, *zoe* and *bios*."[13] Sovereignty reunifies that separation that was precipitated by the normalization of the exception in law. At this point Agamben encounters the problem of how to escape this biopolitical logic, which consists in a coincidence between the circularity of sovereignty and the exception that has become the norm. He responds by seeking to recuperate a sense of eschatology, which ultimately means that he seeks to reinstitute an end. This gives rise to an almost apocalyptic tone, an incantation of moments that demonstrate the "decisive event of modernity," as Derrida observes, and that ultimately rehearse the rhetorical tenor of the exception from which Agamben wants to escape.[14] Therefore, so long as the biopolitical characteristic of justification and the circularity of justification are interpreted from the legalistic perspective, then the constant feature—absolutization— of sovereignty persists.

We can glean an alternative interpretation of the link between the normalization of the exception and the circularity of sovereignty by taking seriously Walter Benjamin's suggestion from Thesis VIII: "it is our task to bring about a real state of emergency."[15] Such a real state of emergency becomes a political task in conjunction with historiography. Benjamin admonishes the understanding of history as a linear series of events that are represented by the historian in his account. This process of representation is complicit in the legalistic determination of the normalization of the exception, since the exception functions as a means only when it controls the narrative of the political. From this perspective Benjamin's advice consists in a reversal of the exception. The real state of emergency would consist in the derailment of the structures of representation that normalize the exception. Then a task such as the one advocated by Benjamin in his theses on history would be nothing other than what we have been calling "dejustification." Dejustification consists in an antirepresentational narrative in the sense of a narrative that is not co-opted in the control of life or in the control of the aleatory. I will argue later that this is only possible if power is examined from the perspective of whom it effects—the "oppressed," in Benjamin's terminology. Through such a historical account the space of judgment can be opened up, leading to the possibility of democracy.

The "Theses on History" are Benjamin's notes for a theory of historiography for his aborted research on Paris during the Second Empire. This incomplete research has been published as *The Arcades Projects*.[16] One of Benjamin's major concerns in this work is how space is constructed in such a way as to represent power, or, more specifically, how the Haussmannization of Paris was a representation of the rule of Louis Bonaparte no less than the rise of the bourgeoisie.[17] What underlies this discussion of architecture and representation is a political commitment to a "real state of emergency," to a rupture of representation. Benjamin could have appropriated this idea from Karl Marx's *The Eighteenth Brumaire of Louis Bonaparte*, where Marx describes Bonaparte's rise to power as a manipulation of the exception. We need to turn, then, to Marx's text in order to determine with greater precision the task that Benjamin designates as the creation of the real state of emergency.

THE UNSAVABLES: MARX'S WAGER

Carl Schmitt identified the most intriguing difficulty in the relationship between democracy and biopolitical sovereignty when he observed that, in the aftermath of the 1848 revolution in Paris, "in opposition to parliamentary constitutionalism, *not to democracy*, the idea of a dictatorship that would sweep parliamentarism regained its topicality."[18] In *The Eighteenth Brumaire of Louis Bonaparte*, Marx concurs with Schmitt's diagnosis of the dangerous proximity between dictatorship and representative democracy.[19] Marx describes how the "centralization of governmental power" ultimately led to the concentration of power in the hands of one man, a dictator, so much so that "under Louis Bonaparte does the state seem to have made itself completely independent" (186). However, Marx also observes that Bonaparte's rise to dictatorship was in fact supported by the people: "revolutions perfected this machine instead of breaking it" (186).[20] Both thinkers point out the way that the majority of the French population lent their support to Louis Bonaparte to assume dictatorial powers and eventually to establish the Second French Empire. Both thinkers recognize the proximity between representative democracy and dictatorship. Nevertheless, there is an important difference: Marx does not condone dictatorship. Instead, Marx utilizes this paradox in order to offer a critique of how representation can lead, through the normalization of the exception, to the creation of such an "appalling parasitic body" of governmental power that coordinates the executive, governmental bureaucracy and the military (185). Through this critique an alternative notion of the democratic emerges—a notion that is not amenable to representation and hence to dictatorship, a notion that points to the "real state of emergency" in Benjamin's sense.

Marx proffers a critique of representation that is at the same time a critique of political representation—that is, in Karatani's terms, Marx points to the nexus between narrative representation (*Darstellung*) and representation in the legislative body (*Vertretung*).[21] "In the story of Bonaparte's victory [i.e., his becoming emperor], one sees precisely the first instance of the crisis of representation and the imaginary sublation of the contradictions therein."[22] Marx presents this doubling of representation in the famous opening to the *Eighteenth Brumaire*: "Hegel remarks somewhere that all facts and personages of great importance in world history occur, as it were, twice. He forgot to add: the first time as tragedy, the second as farce. Caussidière for Danton, Louis Blanc for Robespierre, the Montagne of 1848 to 1851 for the Montagne of 1793 to 1795, the Nephew for the Uncle" (103). The events starting with the revolution of February 1848 and concluding with the "Nephew," Louis Bonaparte, becoming a dictator in December 1851, are likened to a theatre and are analyzed as a representation. But this representation is double because it mirrors the events of the original French Revolution in 1789 and the ascension to power of the "Uncle," Napoleon Bonaparte. This suggests that a representation is never a representation of something, but also a representation of something already represented. Representation is always double—a representation always has a representative. History is always historiography, politics is already a dispensation of rhetorical strategies, power is always already imbued in exceptional narratives. Marx's *Eighteenth Brumaire* tackles the relation between democracy and sovereignty by extrapolating this problematic contained in the doubling of representation.

Karatani points out that Marx uses the figure of the double representation in order to show how the politicians at the time did not function as the representatives of the class that elected them to power. In Karatani's words, "the relation between representative and represented is radically severed, and becomes arbitrary."[23] For instance, as we will see later, Louis Bonaparte was supported by the peasants, even though he was not representing their interests. Thus Karatani identifies the nebulous relation among dictatorship, democracy, and the doubling up of representation. His analysis stops short, however, from explicitly addressing how the exception can be manipulated and ultimately normalized, not simply because of deficiencies in the process of representation, but rather because representation is always double. It is not only the bureaucracy and the executive and their policing and military apparatuses that Marx refers to as an "appalling parasitic body." Marx also refers to the way that the doubling of representation makes it possible for exception to denote not simply a state of emergency for the state (as Schmitt defines it in *Political Theology*), but rather a phantasmagoria of a state of emergency that is used to co-opt, and ultimately usurp, power. It is not the doubling of representation that constitutes the farce of the events following the revolution of 1848. Rather, it is the explicit generation and manipulation of this doubling that was farcical. Marx summarizes this critique in the assertion that "Society is saved just as often as the circle of its rulers contracts, as a more exclusive interest is maintained against a wider one" (111–12).[24] Saving society—that is, determining what order, peace, and stability consist in—is not a real outcome; it is not a real end. Rather, it signifies the perpetuation of power. This means that the end is imaginary, a theatrical farce. And the more society is saved or the more the exceptional narrative is normalized, then the less numerous are the saviors, resulting ultimately in a single individual—a dictator—usurping power. The greatest farce unfolds when the dictator dupes a majority to represent them. This justifies dictatorial powers through a process that appears democratic. Farce, then, signifies the perilous entanglement of dictatorship and democracy that is made possible through representation. The question then arises whether anyone remains who is not savable and hence does not contribute to the farce that leads to the contraction of the circle of power. Maybe it is through such an unsavable that democracy has a chance to disentangle itself from dictatorship. Marx's democratic wager consists in describing such a figure of the unsavable in the *Eighteenth Brumaire*.

A quick summary of the historical events surrounding the 1848 revolution is necessary because the journalistic tenor of the *Eighteenth Brumaire* assumes a significant contextual and historical knowledge on the part of the reader. Only then will it be possible to explore the implications of Marx's assertion about the normalization of the exception and the founding of dictatorship through popular support. After the election of Louis Philippe as monarch in 1830, there were high hopes for the implementation of democratic measures, such as universal suffrage, election of parliamentary representatives, and freedom of the press. These hopes were quickly doused. Louis Philippe privileged only the elite. For instance, only landowners were given voting rights, curtailing the political aspirations of the ambitious bourgeoisie. At the same time economic and employment policy was increasing the hardship of the lower classes. Due to bad crops, poverty in the land forced labor into the cities, thereby increasing unemployment. Simultaneously, in other countries such as England, workers were gaining significant rights. Resentment led to unrest in February 1848. During a demonstration the National Guard opened fire, leaving scores of dead and wounded protesters. In response the streets of Paris were barricaded. Soon after, on February 26, the king was forced to abdicate and a provisional government comprising all the different liberal parties was formed. Marx describes this first phase of the revolution as wholly "provisional" (108). Nobody would make any real decisions. The only significant development was that the proletariat—who in economic terms Marx defines here narrowly as the workers in the cities—was still entertaining hopes of change while "the old forces of society had grouped themselves, rallied, reflected and found unexpected support in the mass of the nation, the peasants and petty bourgeoisie, who all at once stormed on to the political stage" (109). Thus the "first act" of the revolution is characterized by the haphazard introduction of numerous political actors who, however, initially struggle to define their roles as well as their allies. The roles of the protagonists become clearer with the formation of the National Assembly on May 4, but only to the extent that it was "a living protest against the aspirations of the February days and was to reduce the results of the revolution to the bourgeois scale" (109). Barely two months after the February uprising the revolution has been hijacked by the bourgeoisie, who use the newly formed parliament to assert their interests.

The proletariat disenchantment with the National Assembly leads to the "second act" of the political play, which is the June insurrection. Marx calls this uprising "the most colossal event in the history of European civil wars" (110). This statement may initially appear incomprehensible, since the uprising was an utter failure. As Marx himself admits, "The bourgeois republic triumphed" (110). Marx places such great importance on the June insurrection because it discloses the manipulation of the exception through representation: "On its [i.e., the bourgeois republic's] side stood the finance aristocracy, the industrial bourgeoisie, the middle class, the petty bourgeois, the army, the lumpenproletariat organized as the Mobile Guard, the intellectuals, the clergy and the rural population. On the side of the Paris proletariat stood none but itself" (110). There are two aspects of representation highlighted here. First, the bourgeoisie succeeded in becoming the representative of all the other classes, even though they did not represent their interests. We will see shortly how they managed to do that by offering themselves as the saviors of society. Second, the proletariat was not represented by anyone. In other words, everyone except the proletariat was duped by a narrative—a representation—that did not accord with—that did not represent—their interests. Everyone except the proletariat was participating in a normalization of the exception. The proletariat's incapacity to be represented will turn out to be the reason they are the unsavables, which will explain the unique importance that Marx accords to the failed insurrection of June 1848.

The normalization of the exception is signified as the saving of society, which leads to a contraction of the circle of power. The first occurrence of this move takes place during the June uprising: "During the June days, all classes and parties had united in the *Party of Order* against the proletarian class as the *Party of Anarchy*, of socialism, of communism. They had 'saved' society from 'the enemies of society'" (111). So the precondition of the construction of a narrative of the exception is the determination of order, peace, and stability. This is made possible by identifying a threat from which the state must be defended—declaring that a class is "enemies of society." The universal of order, peace, and stability aspires solely to the maintenance and perpetuation of power. There is no "real" universality here—the universal becomes represented and utilized by a single group, the "Party of Order." The figure of order, peace, and stability becomes a trope in the rhetorical strategy that precipitates the normalization of the exception. "Order" is no longer an end, but rather a part of the means that justify the means of power—that is, the violence unleashed against those participating in the June uprising. Louis Bonaparte followed the example of the bourgeoisie in claiming to be the savior of society. After the June insurrection, Bonaparte gradually represented himself as the symbol of order, peace, and stability, even though his actions were intended to produce instability. For instance, he continuously destabilized the Legislative Assembly that was formed in May 1849. As Marx puts it, Bonaparte "produces actual anarchy in the name of order" (197). Ultimately the bourgeoisie were undone by their own tactics: "The bourgeoisie kept France in breathless fear of the future terrors of red anarchy [during the June Uprising]; Bonaparte discounted this future for it when, on December 4 [1851], he had the eminent bourgeois . . . shot down at their windows by the liquor-inspired army of order. The bourgeoisie apotheosised the sword; the sword rules it. . . . It imposed a state of siege; a state of siege is imposed upon it. . . . It transported people without trial; it is being transported without trial" (182). The result of this creation of a fabulatory order, peace, and stability directed by Louis Bonaparte was the coup of December 1851, followed by the granting of universal suffrage and a referendum in which Bonaparte was triumphantly elected emperor. The representations of order, peace, and stability discover their representative in the protagonist and director of the play about the saving of France that started in early 1848 and was concluded in late 1852. Plato's metaphor of the ship in the *Republic* described democracy as anarchy. Marx here reverses Plato's point. He shows that anarchy lies with the person who controls the narrative and hence represents himself as the savior of the people. Only the representative encapsulates the double meaning of the word *anarchia*—namely, being above the law and instituting a state in which the law is transgressed.

The normalization of the exception through the transformation of transcendence into a means of power facilitates the control of life. Life is controlled through different tactics, one of which is fashion. Marx articulates this point in relation to the June uprising more explicitly in *The Class Struggles in France 1848 to 1850*. There he discusses how the lumpenproletariat—the young unemployed and mostly homeless men roaming Paris—who should have been the natural allies of the proletariat that rose up in June, in fact fought against the uprising and were instrumental in the bloodbath of the insurgents. This is explained by the way in which the lumpenproletariat was guided into the theatre of representation. After the February events the National Guard was forced to withdraw from Paris. In order to protect itself, the provisional government sought "to play off one part of the proletariat against the other."[25] Thus it formed a new force, the Mobile Guards, by conscripting the lumpenproletariat. The government paid them a daily wage, thereby buying their loyalty. But, even more significantly, the government "gave them their own uniform, that is, it made them outwardly distinct from the blouse-wearing workers."[26] The proletariat regarded the lumpenproletariat as their own guard "in contradistinction to the bourgeois National Guard" because they shared common social objectives— "Its error was pardonable."[27] However, the uniform—the costume—that the Mobile Guard was dressed in functioned as a means of controlling their alliances. Their dress functioned as a marker of their chosen representative. Marx extends this critique of fashion to the subsequent use of the same tactic by Louis Bonaparte in order to enlist the peasantry's support: "the uniform was their [the peasant's] own state dress" (192). In addition, at the third paragraph of the *Eighteenth Brumaire*, Marx embarks on a critique of fashion in the French Revolution: "the heroes as well as the parties and the masses of the old French Revolution, performed the task of their time in Roman costume and with Roman phrases" (104). This fashion is determinative of the historical actors' decisions.[28] This "resurrected Romanity" might have aspired to republicanism, but only led to "Caesar himself" (104)—that is, the usurpation of power by Napoleon Bonaparte on the 18th Brumaire (or November 9) of 1799, leading to the establishment of the First Empire in 1804. Thus from the perspective of the control of life, there is not much difference between the 1789 and 1848 revolutions: "the resurrection of the dead in those revolutions served the purpose of glorifying the new struggles" (105). Note that Marx is referring here to ghosts, to specters from the past, that cannot possibly aspire to an eschatological future or to a transcendent end.[29] And it is in turn the aspiration toward such an end regardless that induces the "phantasmagoria before the one man" (108) who becomes a dictator by controlling the exceptional narrative and the "hallucinations" (193) of the peasants, whose "idées napoléoniennes" (189–93) helped anoint Louis Bonaparte as their savior. Fashion, then, constitutes a means of controlling the aleatory and of managing populations and classes, thereby supporting the exceptional narrative that transformed the transcendent goals of order, peace, and stability into the immanent means for the contraction of the circle of power around the "saviors" of society. Fashion is one of the means used for the normalization of the exception.

The two aspects of the normalization of the exception that Marx identifies—transcendence as a fabulation and the control of the aleatory—both rely on representation. But representation itself relies on a representative, as already intimated. Representation is double—a narrative and its political manifestation. Marx describes in detail how Louis Bonaparte manipulated representation in its double sense to gradually usurp power, even to the point of being triumphantly elected emperor in a referendum. Thus Marx conducts a radical polemic against representative democracy. But this polemic is not directed against democracy understood as agonism, but rather only against representative democracy. After analyzing the machinations that led to the coup of December 1851, Marx observes that "the overthrow of the parliamentary republic contains within itself the germ of the triumph of the proletarian revolution" (184). This will consist, as we will see later, in the vision of the possibility of agonistic democracy. But for this to be possible, Marx first pursues a critique of representation whose "immediate and palpable result was the victory of Bonaparte over parliament, of the executive power over the legislative power, of force without words over the force of words" (184–85). Bonaparte became a dictator showing the triumph of "force without words." Marx suggests that Bonaparte's rule was premised on the principle that "might is right." Yet, unlike the Hobbesian use of this principle, here there are no rational agents transferring their right to the sovereign. Instead, the executive usurps the other branches of government through election, through the support of a majority that acts irrationally against their own interests. Marx continues: "In parliament the nation made its general will the law, that is, it made the law of the ruling class its general will" (185). The general will, according to Rousseau, is always right, meaning that the general will has the right to control change. However, when the general will is represented in parliament, then this right to change is transferred to the representatives. Ultimately one individual can wrest control, thereby narrowing the circle of power even further. That is what happened when Louis Bonaparte took control of the parliament: "Before the executive power it renounces all will of its own and submits to the superior command of an alien will, to authority" (185). The representative is further deflected, the circle of saviors further contracts, so that now a single savior no longer represents a "general will," but rather an "alien will" that derives its authority solely through this system of representations. This will is alien because the "executive power, in contrast to the legislative power, expresses the heteronomy of a nation, in contrast to its autonomy" (185). The alien will is heteronomous because it consists in the "despotism of an individual" (185) that does not really represent anyone except himself—or, rather, he does not represent anyone except representation itself. "Bonaparte would like to appear as the patriarchal benefactor of all classes" (195), because that consists in a thorough control of the representation by a sole representative. The exception is here—at the point when the dictator and the people coincide, when the alien will fully incorporates the general will—thoroughly normalized.

With the coincidence of the general will and the alien will—or the collapse of representative democracy into dictatorship—the state apparatus becomes an "appalling parasitic body" that "chokes" French society (185), to the extent that the "state seems to have made itself completely independent" (186). It is here, in the midst of the profoundest failure of political processes, that Marx insists on a redemptive possibility—a possibility that arises through the definition of class: "And yet, the state power is not suspended in mid air. Bonaparte represents a class, and the most numerous class of French society at that, the small-holding peasantry" (186–87). Even though Marx calls the peasants a "class," he immediately retracts or at least refines that determination: "Insofar as there is merely a local interconnection among those small-holding peasants, and the identity of their interests begets . . . no political organization among them, *they do not form a class*. They are consequently incapable of enforcing their class interests in their own name. . . . *They cannot represent themselves*, they must be represented" (187, emphasis added). So long as a group is subject to representation in the double sense—that is, representation as narrative formation and as electing a representative for that narrative—then a group does not form a class, writes Marx. The peasants "do not form a class" because they are represented. And representation means that their political organization enforces a normalization of the exception. At the same time, their representative is their savior: "Their representative must at the same time appear as their master, as an authority over them, as an unlimited governmental power that protects them against the other classes and sends them rain and sunshine from above" (187–88). When a single man, almost like a deity, like a savior, saves a majority, then not only do democracy and dictatorship coincide, but also those who belong to the majority that elects their savior can no longer form a class.

But as soon as Marx argues that a group does not form a class when it is subject to representation and the exception, he immediately provides a definition of class as a group of people who are unrepresentable: "Insofar as millions of families live under economic conditions of existence that separate their mode of life, their interests and their culture from those of the other classes, and them in hostile opposition to the latter, they form a class" (187). The definition of class here is akin to Spinoza's definition of the necessary rebel.[30] A class is defined in terms of its contingent circumstances. It is the recognition of one's "mode of life" that refers to the singularity of one's existence that forms the basis of the definition of a class. But this definition does not, and cannot, ascribe a specific content to class, since class is determined through the "economic conditions of existence"—that is, through the laws of capital that are empty—a circulation of use value, exchange value, and surplus.[31] The opposition between the laws of capital and the mode of one's life creates a sense of participation in the community. When this participation is "in hostile opposition" to groups of formed interests, then there is the formation of a class. This agonistic element is crucial. Class is possible, insists Marx, only if there is opposition to other classes—not as an opposition to groups of people as such, but rather as opposition to the laws of capital. This opposition resists representation in the sense that representation and the normalization of the exception that it ultimately leads to require control of life and of the aleatory. Conversely, class hostility is precisely the assertion of life and the aleatory as ineliminable elements in the way that people relate to each other and form communities. Further, this agonism, this "hostile opposition," asserts dynamic relations between the elements of the society. No one can then rise up to become the representative of this agon, because no one offers himself to be saved. Elements of society are unsavables in the sense that they are incompatible with the category of salvation. Instead of salvation, the category that pertains to them is agon, "hostile opposition."

It is instructive to compare at this point Marx's famous letter to Joseph Weydemeyer, who was the editor of the periodical *Die Revolution*, for which Marx wrote the *Eighteenth Brumaire*. In the letter dated March 5, 1852, Marx informs his editor that he has just completed the final part of the *Eighteenth Brumaire*—the part where the above discussion of class can be found—and makes some insightful observations about his work centered around "the dictatorship of the proletariat."[32] This expression, which is actually not common in Marx's writings, has caused heated debates that we cannot review here.[33] However, the source of the debates was already identified by Kautsky, who indicated the paradoxical nature of the expression. According to Kautsky, dictatorship "signifies the suspension of democracy" and yet, at the same time, Kautsky wants to argue that the dictatorship of the proletariat is a transitional phase toward the classless society that "is certainly not possible without Democracy."[34] In other words, this paradoxical expression raises precisely the problem of the proximity between dictatorship and democracy that the normalization of the exception and the events following the revolution of 1848 dramatize. A careful reading, however, of Marx's wording on the dictatorship of the proletariat shows that Marx is thinking of class in the agonistic terms described above. Marx starts his observation by stating that "No credit is due to me for discovering the existence of classes in modern society or the struggle between them. Long before me bourgeois historians had described the historical development of this class struggle and bourgeois economists the economic anatomy of the classes." There is nothing new in identifying different groups that have competing interests, observes Marx. He continues: "My own contribution was 1. To show that the *existence of classes* is merely bound up with *certain historical phases in the development of production*."[35] The first novelty in his thought that Marx identifies pertains to the importance of living in the determination of class. Just as he argued in the *Eighteenth Brumaire* in the passage quoted above and that could have been in his mind as he was writing to Weydemeyer, class articulates itself in hostility or in a struggle against other classes. But this is only possible when the laws of production are recognized as not having an inherent telos, opening them up to challenge by the living conditions in which people find themselves. The second point consists in the creation of the dictatorship of the proletariat through this class struggle: "2. That the class struggle necessarily leads to the *dictatorship of the proletariat*."[36] According to the *Eighteenth Brumaire* again, every time society is saved, the circle of power contracts, resulting ultimately in a single person becoming the dictator by feigning to represent the whole of society. The expression the "dictatorship of the proletariat" signifies the opposite movement: there is an expansion of the circle of power and a contraction of the circle of representation. Representation must contract because, as we saw above, class struggle is only possible for those who cannot be represented. Instead of the tyrannical rule of one sovereign, we now have the dictatorship of a class. The expression "dictatorship of the proletariat" is obscure because of the way that Marx uses both terms. We have already seen that class in the *Eighteenth Brumaire* signifies the agonistic participation in common affairs by a group of people. Dictatorship does not refer to a tyrannical regime, but rather to the Roman sense of an institution of power that becomes responsible for the state during a time of emergency.[37] In other words, the term "dictatorship" denotes here precisely the normalization of the exception. Thus the dictatorship of the proletariat is the intensification of the agonistic opposition *against* representation and a representative *during* the time that an end of action and governance is lacking. Differently put, the dictatorship of the proletariat signifies the unsavables who cannot be represented.

Recall here Solon's notion of participation, which was identified in Chapter 1 and discussed throughout. According to Solon, participation in a conflict within society is the defining feature of democracy. From this perspective Marx's "dictatorship of the proletariat" describes precisely the conflict—the stasis—between different groups and the struggle that ensues between them as a form of political praxis that welcomes opposition—that welcomes the other. Further, this participation is only possible when there is an assertion of singularity—an assertion of life that escapes measure and control. But this process will always be incomplete without the curtailing of the biopolitical form of justification—namely, the normalization of the exception. Benjamin had suggested that the political task was the constitution of a real state of emergency. This perpetual conflict, which persists through the dictatorship of the proletariat, is that different state of emergency that Benjamin had envisaged. Here, within contingency, within life and singularity, the agon is ineliminable and indefinite. Democracy is the name that this agon can receive. But in this real state of emergency democracy is practiced by those who do not need a savior, who resist and fight the assimilation of democracy to dictatorship.

A final question arises at this point: How can a transition be enacted from the normalization of the state of emergency to the real state of emergency—from representation to agonism? It is at this point that the June uprising is crucial in Marx's plot. Recall that Marx called the June uprising the most significant moment in the history of European civil wars and that the rise of Louis Bonaparte to dictatorship was a phase toward the revolution. Marx introduces a passage that makes explicit reference to *Hamlet* with the following remark: "But the revolution is thorough. It is still journeying through the purgatory" (185). The revolution is here placed in the purgatory—a low position, below the surface of the earth. This signifies the oppressed, but also all those who are excluded from power. "It does its work methodically. By December 2, 1851, it has competed only one half of its preparatory work; it is now completing the other half. First it perfected the parliamentary power in order to be able to overthrow it. Now that it has attained this, it perfects the executive power, reduces it to its purest expression, isolates it, sets it up against itself as the sole target, in order to concentrate all its forces of destruction against it" (185). What is required is a process that allows for the recognition of—or the awakening to—the structures of representation that permit the perfection of the executive power in the guise of a dictatorship such as the one established with Louis Bonaparte's coup.[38] From this perspective the failure of the June uprising was illustrative of the tactics of representation—for instance, the dressing up of the lumpenproletariat in the uniform of the Mobile Guard only in order to control them. The whole process from February 1848 to December 1851 was illustrative of how the circle of power contracts every time there is a savior of society, every time the exception is normalized. Marx continues: "And when it has done this second half of its preliminary work, Europe will leap from its seat and exultantly exclaim: Well burrowed, old mole" (185). The final sentence is a citation from *Hamlet*, Act 1, Scene 5, line 162.[39] It is spoken by Hamlet, who is addressing the Ghost, who had just asked Hamlet's friends to swear that they will not reveal the encounter at the fortifications of Elsinore that night when the old king's murder was communicated to the living. The Ghost is likened to a mole because he is not on the stage, but rather standing beneath the stage, from where he has just spoken. The murdered in *Hamlet* has an equivalent position to the proletariat in the *Eighteenth Brumaire*—the proletariat was also murdered in the June insurrection, and it is in the "purgatory," or below the earth.

But here there is a crucial difference from *Hamlet*. Shakespeare's play, as shown in Chapter 3, enacted through the figure of melancholia a destabilization of the hierarchies that support absolute sovereignty. Hamlet, as the melancholic prince, occupied simultaneously all three positions of the hierarchy of power: the most high—the heir to the throne, the potential sovereign—the middle position of the subject that suffers passions, and the lowest position of the madman who is excluded from the social contract. Thus *Hamlet* enacted a dejustification of the logic of justification that supported absolute sovereignty. Here, however, Marx does not describe such a melancholic destabilization of hierarchies. Instead, he avers that "Europe will *leap* from its seat and *exultantly* exclaim: Well burrowed, old mole." First, the leap of Europe is like a startled awakening. Europe will come to recognize the structure of representation that underlined dictatorship. It will be jolted into action by the oppressed, the unseen and unrepresentable ones, the unsavables—the murdered actors of history that persist beneath the stage of the politics of a normalized exception. At the same time, this is an "exultant" awakening—a joyous moment instead of a melancholic disposition. The reason for this joy is the possibility of sustaining the agonistic struggle that distinguishes the real, democratic state of emergency from the normalization of the exception. Unlike the melancholic up-and-down movement along the scales of hierarchical power, Marx posits a joyous ontology of struggle. There is also a third novelty about his conception of the class struggle that Marx indicates in his letter to Weydeyer: "3. That this dictatorship itself constitutes no more than a transition to the *abolition of all classes* and to a *classless society.*"[40] Maybe the "abolition of all classes" is the figure of Europe leaping up joyously when it wakes up from its slumber induced by representation. Maybe there is indeed joy in that moment when the farce of the normalization of the exception is recognized. But this joy is only possible because the political is no longer trapped in a hierarchical structure whose only avenue for a change of power consists merely in the substitution for one sovereign by another. It is no longer the vertical movement along the hierarchical axis that characterizes absolute sovereignty. Rather, it is the invitation to everyone to rise to the stage of the political, to leap up from the low position of oppression, and to assert their right to struggle. Everyone is allowed on the stage, so long as that stage is one where there is joy and possibility of attaining one's singularity.[41] A joyous singularity that can only be sustained by those who do not expect salvation and hence rejoice in their "hostile oppositions," their agonistic participations. Such a joyous participation to the happenings on the stage is a far cry from the farce of representation that Marx describes in the *Eighteenth Brumaire*.

Marx's wager consists in identifying the figure of the unsavable—that is, the unrepresentable—as the only chance of democracy. If the unsavable is, however, only ever possible through the perpetuation of agonism, then Marx's wager can never be cashed in. Democracy can never be fully realized. This leads to two inferences. First, it sharpens the distinction between the sovereign logic of justification and a democratic insistence on agonistic participation. Whereas justification consists in the circularity between the separation and reunification of means and ends, of law and justice, the agonism of the democratic consists in the disjunction between the two, in the resistance to any conciliation. The circularity of democracy consists instead in the way that the means of power are related to the aleatory and hence the unrepresentable unfolding of living. Second, whereas the sovereign logic ultimately always retains an end—no matter how phantasmagorical—that justifies violence, the fact that Marx's wager can never be "won" entails the absence of an end. This inexhaustibility of the wager means that the democratic is that which is presupposed by the unfolding of the political. Every thought and every action participates in the conflict instituted by the wager. In the vocabulary used by Marx above, class conflict is paramount. In this sense sovereignty is a product of the struggle between means and end, between law and justice. Sovereignty is a derivative of democracy. The other of democracy is, indeed, democratizeable. Democracy is more primary than sovereignty.

ACTS OF DEMOCRACY: THE PRIMACY OF THE EFFECT IN FOUCAULT'S THEORY OF POWER

In the famous debate with Noam Chomsky on Dutch television in 1971, Michael Foucault summarized his conception of resistance to power in the following manner: "the real political task . . . is to criticise the workings of institutions, which appear to be both neutral and independent; to criticise and attack them in such a manner that the political violence which has always exercised itself obscurely through them will be unmasked, so that one can fight against them."[42] The institutions of power appear "neutral and independent" when they are assumed to defend society. Power acts in such a way as to defend society from threats—an aim commensurate with the maintenance and perpetuation of its power. From this perspective the sovereign right of life and death is neither good nor bad. It is rather, as Foucault puts it in *The Will to Knowledge*, a "right of rejoinder"—that is, a right to respond to a threat, a right of self-defense.[43] This right to protect the state in fact justifies its acts of violence by protecting them from critique, since they are presented as "neutral and independent." Foucault suggests that an attempt to resist power by engaging with its institutions of power will sooner or later encounter the limit of the justification of one's self-preservation.[44] This is part of the mechanism of the logic of sovereignty, and it cannot be resisted. Foucault indicates an alternative way of "fighting" power. The "political task," he says, is to "criticise the workings of institutions." Only then will it be possible to identify the "political violence" that is exercised "obscurely" through them. A critique of power should not start with the cause—the holder of power who justifies violence through neutrality. Rather, a critique should start with the effect—namely, with the violence exercised on bodies. A critique of power without presupposing power's neutrality is possible only when the effect is recognized as more primary than the cause—that is, only through a genealogy that repudiates any origin to power, recording instead "the singularity of the events."[45] Only such an agonistic stance will achieve what Foucault calls elsewhere a "critical ontology of ourselves" that can offer a positive conception of the political.[46]

The primacy of the effect, however, can lead to two divergent outcomes. First, the normalization of the exception indicates precisely such a primacy of the effect over the cause. The reason is that the justificatory logic that privileges the exception no longer has—or pretends to have—recourse to an end. The upshot is that there is no ultimate aim in the exercise of power other than the allowing of power to operate. In Spinoza's terms, the sole purpose of the law is obedience. Or, in terms of justification, when the means justify the means, there is nothing outside the sequence of effects. In biopolitics the exception is no longer a response to a threat against the state, as Carl Schmitt had conceived it. Rather, in biopolitics the exception is, as we saw in the analysis of the *Eighteenth Brumaire*, the construction of a phantasmagorical representation whose aim is to justify the violence of the representative—the sovereign—of the people. Such a phantasmagoria requires neither a sufficient nor a final cause. It only requires the link between representation (narrative) and the representative (sovereignty). Second, the primacy of the effect also points to the possibility of asserting one's singularity. In the absence of predetermined or determinable causes, when power is divested of an end, the subject is given a chance to shake off the shackles of transcendental illusion—and the greatest such illusion in politics is the neutrality of sovereignty that exercises itself through the right of life and death for the defense of the order, peace, and stability of the state. The affirmation of singularity affords the possibility of the critique of power that seeks to control life by propagating the pure necessity and obedience at the heart of the law. A critique of biopolitics needs to show how biopower turns this emptiness of legality—the void of the political—into a phantasmagoria. Besides critique, however, there is an additional possibility inherent when the effect is recognized as more primary than the cause—one that Spinoza recognized, but that Foucault refrained from acknowledging.[47] This consists in the potential to form judgments about the effects of power. This possibility of singular judgments resonated in Chapter 1 with Solon's description of agonistic democracy. In Spinoza's terms, it is the possibility of the necessary rebel.

Thus the primacy of the effect gives rise to two contradictory spheres. First, there is the sphere of justification. Here the primacy of the effect indicates the shift from the sovereign right of life and death that characterizes the neutrality of sovereignty to the justification of sovereignty's control of life. The political game consists in making populations obedient. Second, there is the sphere of judgment. This does not only allow the critique of the nonneutrality of power; in addition, it points to a space distinct from sovereignty—the space of democracy. Judgment consists in the affirmation of sites of resistance of, or rebellion against, justification. The political task, then, is to describe the conditions under which it is possible to disentangle these two ways in which the primacy of the effect operates. Such a political task requires the recognition that biopolitics is not merely a new form of power—if that were the case, then biopolitics would have been recognized only in its first aspect indicated above, that is, as a form of justification. Instead, biopolitics in Foucault is a method of analysis and critique of power that proceeds from the primacy of the effect over the cause of power. Examining how the historical is articulated in terms of a critical methodology in Foucault will lead ultimately to the dejustification of power. But for this to be possible, Foucault's historical distinctions need to be recognized as part of his critical methodology—not merely as a description of ruptures in forms of power.

Even though Foucault's genealogies of power appear to indicate different technologies of power, still he is also careful to always qualify the ruptures by pointing to continuities in the way that power is exercised—that is, continuities in the way that the power's effects are registered. For instance, Foucault writes: "Whereas the end of sovereignty is internal to itself and possesses its own intrinsic instruments in the shape of its laws, the finality of government resides in the things it manages and in the pursuit of the perfection and intensification of the processes which it directs; and the instruments of government, instead of being laws, now come to be a range of multiform tactics."[48] The tactics used by governmentality point to the justification of means by further means. The reason is that, unlike strategies, tactics have no end beyond the effect that they produce. They are expedient operations concerned with the effects of power. Such statements may give the impression that Foucault adumbrates a clear rupture between modern sovereignty and biopolitics, since the tactical element is not predominant in earlier forms of sovereignty. However, such statements should be read in conjunction with statements like the following one: "We need to see things not in terms of the replacement of a society of sovereignty by a disciplinary society and the subsequent replacement of disciplinary society by a society of government; in reality one has a triangle, sovereignty—discipline—government, which has as its primary target the population."[49] The historical or genealogical differentiations between different forms of power do not simply posit ruptures between different regimes of power. Such ruptures would have presupposed a method that interrogates power from the perspective of its cause. Instead, Foucault is concerned to interrogate the ways in which the effects of power are registered. Power has no primary aim. Instead, there is a "primary target," the population. Or, differently put, there is a common logic of power that can take different modalities. Distinguishing these different modalities is the condition of the possibility of their dejustification.

The dejustification that has been suggested in this book as a possible marker of resistance to sovereignty is commensurate with Foucault because he also distinguishes, but does not separate, the different technologies of power. Instead, Foucault insists on several places that older and newer forms of sovereignty do not exclude each other. In the *Will to Knowledge* Foucault says explicitly: "It is not a question of claiming that this [i.e., biopolitics] was the moment when the first contact between life and history was brought about."[50] This claim is incompatible with a strictly historical perspective that seeks to differentiate sharply between different historical forms of sovereignty. Instead, if biopolitics is characterized by the operation of the law "as a norm," then that operation is intensified at a certain historical moment and through the development of certain technological apparatuses used by power. However, this normalizing function can also be detected in earlier forms of sovereignty. For instance, as explained in Chapter 2, the distinctive feature of ancient sovereignty is the privileging of end or justice over the means of power and the laws. With Paul's injunction to "love thy neighbor," justice subsumed the law. According to the Augustinian model, it was one's fellow pilgrim that could be one's neighbor, whereas the pagans should be persecuted. Crucially, the same injunction of neighborly love can be reformulated to conform to either modern or biopolitical sovereignty. Thus one's fellow countryman, a citizen who exists within the same social contract, would be one's neighbor. And the injunction itself, through its moralistic implications, produces normalizing effects—neighborly love might be possible only under certain proscriptions in certain communities, and in general only when the conduct of living adheres to certain values or "moral laws." The normalization of the exception has been a perennial feature of power. All this shows that biopolitics is not simply a new phase of sovereign power that is separated from previous ones. Rather, biopolitics is the intensification of the control of life and of normalization.[51] Significantly, this control of life can only be recognized when power is divested of its transcendent ends and it is interrogated instead by focusing on its effects.

The corollary to treating biopolitics as a methodology of interrogating the effects of power that shows the inseparability of the three forms of sovereignty is that biopolitics extends power to a wide, dispersed field that seeks to cover everything. The effects of power seek to be applied to everyone. The last lecture of Foucault's *Society Must Be Defended*, where Foucault uses the term "biopolitics" (243) for the first time, is also perhaps the most clear expression of his position that the resurgence of previous forms of sovereignty in biopolitics is linked to a radical inclusivity of power.[52] After a detailed discussion of different ways in modern times that power has used the apparatuses of security to justify sovereignty, this final lecture adopts a more speculative tone that is premised on the following observation: "the basic phenomenon of the nineteenth century was what might be called power's hold over life" (229). In the course of this lecture, Foucault contrasts the biopolitical control over life with the right of life and death that characterized earlier forms of sovereignty. The sovereign right of life and death, which "is actually the right to kill," means that "life and death . . . fall outside the field of power. . . . [I]n terms of his relation with the sovereign . . . the subject is neutral" (240–41). The neutrality of the subject mirrors the neutrality of the sovereign right of life and death as a response to a threat against the state. The subject is simply subjected to psychology and the state—to the laws of nature and human laws. The sovereign stands above the law in order to defend the law. Thus in relation to the subject, sovereign power is neither good nor bad. The *law of the state subjects the subject* as a means of protecting the state. And if the subjection fails, the sovereign has the right to kill the subject in order to protect the state. This means that the life of the subject, so long as it does not threaten the state, is not a concern of the sovereign. Foucault expresses this old sovereign right also as the "right to take life and to let live" (241), in the sense that the subject either does not conform to the law, in which case the sovereign can take its life, or it does conform to the law, in which case the sovereign lets the subject live. Foucault introduces the perspective that counters the neutrality of sovereignty thus: "one of the greatest transformations political right underwent in the nineteenth century was precisely that, I wouldn't say exactly that sovereignty's old right—to take life or let live—was replaced, but it came to be *complemented* by a new right which does not erase the old right but which does *penetrate* it, *permeate* it. This is the right, or rather precisely the opposite right. It is the power to 'make' life and 'let' die" (241, emphasis added). The old right is not simply transformed into a new right. The transition to the right to "make life and let die" signifies the control of life. Sovereignty no longer polices the subject's adherence to the law. Rather, sovereignty now polices how the subject lives its life—sovereignty concentrates on the effects of power. It is no longer a question of the law subjecting the subject; it is rather about the subject *subjecting itself* to the sovereign's normalizing processes. But Foucault emphasizes that the right of life and death is not superseded—in fact, as we will see in the following section, Foucault argues that the control of life and the right to kill coincide in racism. Here he insists that biopolitical control of life complements, penetrates, and permeates the older right to exercise violence against the excluded. Whoever does not conform to the norm is not necessarily excluded—his life is not under threat. Instead, the biopolitical control of life means that everyone is *potentially* included; everyone is *potentially* normalized. Hamlet's melancholia dejustified absolute sovereignty because it could not fit within the hierarchy of power instituted by the law. But this is no longer a problem for biopolitics. Melancholia has now turned to depression—it is pathologized, and as such is treated by social services and by medication.[53] Prozac is the response to "To be or not to be." Thus the resurgence of all three forms of sovereignty in biopolitics means that everybody is determined through the effects of power, hence everybody is potentially included.

This potential inclusion of everybody in biopolitics is the principle that Foucault can use to delineate the main characteristics of biopower. The individual subject is no longer the focus of power. Power shifts its attention to the population as a whole. "Biopolitics deals with the . . . population . . . as a problem that is at once scientific and political, as a biological problem and as power's problem" (245). The subject does not subject itself to a law, but rather to norms derived by the scientific knowledge of the entire population. When "power ignores death" (248), then the emphasis shifts from the individual to groups of people, from the subject to the population, from capital punishment to the "mortality rate" (245). The potential to include or to normalize everyone by making all part of a population or a statistic operates by targeting the contingent, the accidental, or the aleatory. "The phenomena addressed by biopolitics are, essentially, aleatory events that occur within a population that exists over a period of time" (246). Or, as Ian Hacking puts it, probability tamed chance in the nineteenth century.[54] For instance, an individual death may be unpredictable, but not so the mortality rate. Thus the phenomena controlled by biopolitics "are aleatory and unpredictable when taken in themselves or individually, but which, at the collective level, display constants that are easy, or at least possible, to establish" (245). Even though it is not possible to determine when an individual will die, still it is possible to determine with certain statistical accuracy the survival probability for a particular kind of cancer.[55] This control of the aleatory is formalized through regulation: "regulatory mechanisms must be established to establish an equilibrium, maintain an average, establish a sort of homeostasis, and compensate for variations within this general population and its aleatory field" (246). Regulation becomes the substitution for a transcendent end. Instead of a universal order, peace, and stability, the aim now is a "homeostasis" of the political field. The regulatory tactics justify the exercise of the means of power. The biopolitical attempt to repress contingency and singularity is a response to the destabilizing and dejustifying power of the aleatory. For instance, in *Michael Kohlhaas*, the distinct forms of sovereignty all sought to justify their violence in response to unpredictable, contingent events. In fact, it was the intensification or paroxysm of the aleatory in Kleist's novella that showed the limits of sovereignty. Thus the biopolitical is sovereignty's response to the threat posed by the aleatory to its justification of violence.

The control of the aleatory indicates that the cosupponibility of the different modalities of justification is the other side of the radical inclusivity that characterizes biopolitics—the fact that potentially everyone can be included. Foucault himself uses an example to illustrate how the control of the aleatory is connected to the copresence of different forms of sovereignty. He prefaces his comments by observing that different mechanisms of power—in this instance the older disciplinary power and the newer regulatory power—"are not mutually exclusive and can be articulated with each other" (250). Then he says that he will take the example of the rationally ordered town that was actually constructed in the nineteenth century—and even though he does not mention Paris, it is as if he looks out of the window of the Collège de France to discuss the transformation of the city after the usurpation of power by Louis Bonaparte and the establishment of the Second Empire. Foucault concentrates on the effects of city planning on the population that was forced to move from the medieval center of Paris to the housing estates in the periphery of the city. The examination of power starts from the effects of power. Foucault describes these effects as twofold. Initially they are shown to be disciplinary: "One can easily see how the very grid pattern . . . of the estate articulated . . . the disciplinary mechanisms that controlled the body . . . by localising families (one to a house) and individuals (one to a room). . . . It is easy to identify a whole series of disciplinary mechanisms in the working-class estate" (251). The estates that were constructed in the outskirts of Paris, away from the palace, conformed to patterns that allowed for the disciplining of the individual. For instance, not only were the lower classes relocated away from the palace; in addition, if the inhabitants of the estates entertained thoughts of erecting barricades in the manner of 1789 or 1848, then they would no longer have the advantage of the narrow, winding streets of medieval Paris, and they will be no match for the regular army in the long, straight streets of the estates.[56] But alongside discipline, Foucault also recognizes biopolitics: "And then you have a whole series of mechanisms which are . . . regulatory . . . which apply to the population as such. . . . Health-insurance systems, old-age pensions; rules on hygiene that guarantee the optimal longevity of the population" (251). Foucault recognizes the improved living conditions of the poor population. For instance, whereas the medieval streets of Paris were filthy, without sewage or running water, the estates regulated "rules on hygiene." At the same time, such regulations also are mechanisms of control of the aleatory—they are normalizing the population. Thus we see in this example how the copresence of different forms of sovereign power is intimately tied with a critique of power that starts from its effects and that analyzes the policing function of power. The biopolitical control of the aleatory is a description of power that presupposes that power can be criticized through its effects.

The possibility to critique power's hold over life and the aleatory, however, does not indicate only that dejustification accompanies power. We have also encountered the aleatory in relation to the rise of democracy. According to Solon, as we saw in Chapter 1, democracy is characterized by the exigency of participation, which means that every citizen must take sides when there is a political dispute in the now, in the contingent circumstance that they find themselves in. Agonism is part of the unpredictable, aleatory aspect of life. Agonism requires the primacy of effect, because agonism is incompatible with neutrality—as Solon says, one participates by taking sides, and those who remain neural are expelled from the polis. Further, Spinoza insists that the necessity of the law is only possible because of the resistances offered by the necessary rebel who bases his judgments on the now, on the contingency of the situation. The emergence of the judgment in Spinoza, and hence the possibility of democracy, is predicated on the political import of singularity or the fact that life resists its submission to a transcendent end. Thus the biopolitical desire to control the aleatory is also a desire to control democracy. The question then arises: What is the relation between democracy and the regulation of the aleatory, whose symptom is the resurgence of different forms of sovereign power? How can judgment arise in contrast to the interknitting of different modalities of justification? Foucault, as already intimated, refrains from raising these questions.[57] However, it is possible to explore them through expanding his method, and in particular by drawing out the implications of the nexus between the primacy of the effect and the dejustification enabled by the resurgence of the different forms of sovereignty.

To show the relation among the three modalities of justification, their dejustification, and the possibility of the democratic judgment, I will use here as an example an abortion case in Cairns, a town in the north of the state of Queensland in Australia. I am choosing an abortion case because, according to Foucault, "sexuality exists at the point where body and population meet" (251–52). In other words, the different justificatory modalities of sovereignty overlap in sexuality. I will start by providing the factual as well as legal background to the case. A young couple, Tegan Leach and Sergie Brennan, decided to terminate an unplanned pregnancy. Brennan's sister obtained for them the termination drug RU486 from Ukraine. When the police stumbled upon the pharmaceutical evidence, they questioned the couple. According to the interview transcript, Leach stated: "I heard from other people how they do it here. They scrape it out, suck it out." Leach did not want to go through a termination procedure in a hospital because of an abject abhorrence of the procedure. "It wasn't really that much of a big deal. . . . Just decided that I wasn't ready for a child."[58] Instead of going to the hospital, Leach decided to use RU486 because it was not "much of a big deal." However, terminating a pregnancy in Queensland is still a criminal offense. Leach was charged under section 225 of the 1899 Queensland Code, which states, "Any woman who, with intent to procure her own miscarriage . . . unlawfully administers to herself any poison or other noxious thing . . . is guilty of a crime."[59] George Williams indicates that the laws under which Leach and Brenan were charged are "based on superseded acts of the British Parliament" dating back to an 1803 "English statute that imposed the death penalty for undertaking the procedure." Since then, the law has changed in Britain as well as Australia, with the exception of the states of Queensland and New South Wales. In those states "women are only able to seek an abortion because, when prosecutions have been brought, courts have given the law a liberal interpretation." According to Williams, the turning case was when "Judge Levine held in 1971 that an abortion is not unlawful if the doctor 'had an honest belief on reasonable grounds that what they did was necessary to preserve the women involved from serious danger to their life, or physical or mental health.'"[60] Leach was essentially brought to trial in October 2010 because there was no certification by a doctor of such a "serious danger" to herself.

This case shows the cosupponibility of the three modalities of justification. First, modern sovereignty is operative in the way that the subject is positioned outside the law. There is a law from 1899 prohibiting self-procured abortion. However, there are court judgments that qualify abortion on the grounds of the health of the mother. Thus it did not matter that RU486 was actually legalized in Australia in early 2006.[61] All that mattered from the perspective of modern sovereignty was that the subject had not acted within the purview of the qualification of the law, since Leach had admitted during the police interview that "it wasn't a big deal." This statement contradicts the qualification of "serious danger," thereby placing the subject outside the law. At the same time, ancient sovereignty is also operative. Pro-life groups participated in the public engagements regarding the case, for instance, by making statements on the media and by being present in court. What motivated them was a just end, the sanctity of life of the unborn fetus.[62] In response to the not-guilty verdict returned by a jury on October 14, 2010, Teresa Martin from "Cherish Life Queensland" called for more counseling of women who consider abortion in order "to be shown firstly what is being aborted."[63] As Foucault observes in the Will to Knowledge, the church retains its power in modernity through the compulsion to confess. As he puts it, "Western man has become a confessing animal."[64] The confessee is subjected to an authority based on transcendent values. This is exactly the situation that the compulsion to counseling as advocated by Martin sought to reproduce. Finally, the biopolitical element in this case is also operative. Leach and Brennan were essentially tried because they did not follow regulations. The procedure that would have normalized their behavior would have consisted in Leach visiting a doctor, who would have referred her to a specialist in order to certify that Leach's mental health was in peril, thereby justifying the abortion. This threat to Leach need not have been true. Rather, the exceptional narrative operates through phantasmagorias, and from this point of view it would have been perfectly acceptable if Leach had lied about her mental condition. Only the normalization of the exception matters—the construction of a narrative that would have normalized Leach's behavior, thereby controlling her life. These three aspects of power—modern, ancient, and biopolitical—can be distinguished by recognizing the primacy of the effect and its link to the resurgence of the three different justificatory modalities of sovereignty. In this particular case, all three justifications would have been satisfied if Leach had physically taken herself to a doctor, thereby following a normalizing procedure. The pregnancy would have been terminated, but Leach would have acted as a lawful subject who adheres to the counseling process showing respect for the sanctity of life, and thereby her behavior would have been regulated.

Far from indicating three separate forms of sovereignty, the three distinct justifications intermingle the various modalities of justification of violence. And yet, by recognizing the methodological import of biopolitics, whereby the effects of power are more primary than the causes, the three modalities of justified power can be made distinct so as to criticize them individually. This is the moment of dejustification. But alongside dejustification, there is also democratic judgment. Ultimately the judgment consists in responding appropriately to the resurgence and interknitting of different forms of justification. This response requires the recognition of the three different modalities of justification leading to dejustification, but it is not the same. With judgment, the interknitting of justifications itself is taken as the justification of practices that legitimate power. It is not each justification on its own, but rather the circularity of the three modalities of justification that calls for judgment. This necessitates an alternative imperative to action—an ethics of response that is not reliant on a logic of justification. The difficulty always is that that response can only be unique—it is always a response to contingent circumstances. This is not to say that we are bereft of any categories to make judgments. In Spinoza's terms, contingency is never separated from the law. There is always a legal context. However, the logic of justification requires the universalizing purpose of the law—a law such as "you shall not kill" contains a proscription that applies to everyone and in every situation. Judgment is made possible by first recognizing the emptiness of the law—meaning that that law is just necessary or that, so long as there is more than one person, there is a series of proscriptions that operates. But that recognition entails that there must be something more primary than the law and the cycles of justification. There must be an ontologico-ethical imperative that is presupposed by justification—and in fact, justification consists in the oppression of that imperative. And here the only criterion at this ontologico-ethical level that becomes available is—as we have already seen in the discussion of Spinoza—

the preservation of life.[65] Justification is the giving of reasons for exercising violence, whereas judgment is both the response to this giving of reasons as well as—and here is where democratic judgment is indispensable—the recognition that the justification of violence is always directed against that which resists the universalizing impulse of sovereignty—namely, life, contingency, singularity. To put this the other way around, judgment is the decision to side with an ontology that privileges life over death.

As the response to justification, judgment is the affirmation of agonism. Agonism relies on nonneutral participation and the possibility to question any rule or law. At the same time, such an agonism is only possible in contradistinction to the control of the aleatory that biopolitical sovereignty strives for. Therefore, judgment is the recognition—every time singular—that the primacy of the effect of power entails the ineliminability of contingency. Or, differently put, judgment is the assumption of one's responsibility to respond to the emptiness of the law—to the void at the heart of sovereignty. Thus a judgment is an affirmation of singularity. It is this singularity that sovereignty cannot tolerate and hence seeks to control. Conversely, judgment distinguishes a space distinct from the space of justification and presupposed by sovereignty. This space of judgment and singularity can be called democracy.

The decision of the jury in the Leach abortion case can be taken as a judgment that affirms singularity. Despite the nineteenth-century law that prohibited abortion, contrary to the regulatory judgment from 1971 that justified abortion only when there was a "serious danger" to the pregnant woman, and regardless of the call to counseling as a means of effecting the way that a young woman should behave, the jury delivered a not-guilty verdict. The fact that the decision was achieved within the legal system and as such within a branch of sovereignty does not contradict the inference that the singularity of judgment creates a sphere that is distinct from that of sovereignty. Sovereignty and democracy cannot be wrenched apart. There is no suggestion here that democracy requires a banishment of sovereignty. For instance, as Spinoza said, the presence of laws is an expedient for the organization of a community—legality provides the means for achieving objectives. The point is rather that, because legality is artificial, because sovereignty is not "natural," it needs to identify something more primary that allows for its construction. That is the sphere of agonism, judgment, singularity, and democracy. From this position democracy asserts that critique is preserved and presupposed by power *because* justification is opposed to critique, judgment, and singularity. Democracy, then, is not simply a regime in politics—a constitutional arrangement of the state. Rather, it is the political regime that indicates the ethical mode of being that affirms agonism. Democracy is a different understanding of existence—or a different ontology, as I will argue in the Epilogue.

Agonistic democracy is not simply a defense of resistance—even though rebellion is necessary, to recall Spinoza once again. Nor, to repeat, does it entail the overcoming of sovereignty, as if it were possible to create a utopian—and ultimately religious—space that is outside the law. Rather, democracy is the exigency to act, the imperative to take sides in the instances of disagreement that unfold in a community. There is no democracy as such separate from the enactment of agonism. There is no democracy without acts of democracy. Such acts can take place within the institutions of the state—for instance, the verdict in the Leach case judged against the control of life, judged in favor of living. Or, they can be acts that oppose institutions calling for their transformation. But, to return to the initial point in the debate between Foucault and Chomsky, such acts cannot be contained within the workings of the institutions. The reason is that assuming the neutrality of the institutions is always a justification for the control of life that seeks to elide the act of judgment. What exceeds the operation of control, however, are the effects of power as the basis of acts of judgment that are both resistances to sovereignty and affirmation of the democratic.

THE UNEXCEPTIONAL: COETZEE'S MICHAEL K. AND RESISTANCE

We saw in the previous section that democracy appears as acts that are agonistic against the logic of justification within a framework that does not simply reject or expunge sovereignty. At this point the figure of resistance returns by considering the question of the relation between this agonism and the operation of exclusion and inclusion that is generated by justification. If biopower, as the culmination of the logic of sovereignty, potentially includes everyone, then how can one resist power without excluding oneself from power, thereby playing into the hands of exclusion and inclusion and hence reaffirming the logic of sovereignty? An outright rejection of sovereignty ends up presupposing and reproducing its logic of justification of violence. As Foucault puts it, "To imagine another system is to extend our participation in the present system."[66] I call this the problem of counter-resistance.[67]

We saw this counter-resistance earlier when Michael Kohlhaas sacrificed himself in order to extract retribution. Even though he inflicted damage on his enemy, the elector of Saxony, still Kohlhaas positioned himself within the same logic of justification by failing to preserve his life and submitting himself to the death penalty. J. M. Coetzee's *Life and Times of Michael K.* is not simply a retelling of the story of Michael Kohlhaas in a state where emergency has become the norm.[68] Moreover, it is an attempt to negotiate the problem of counter-resistance within the purview of biopolitics. To address the issue of resistance in biopolitics it is important not to conflate the resistances offered by Michael Kohlhaas and by Michael K. For this we can compare the way that the border—and hence exclusion and inclusion—operate in the two novellas. Like *Michael Kohlhaas*, so also Coetzee's novella is about borders. Kohlhaas's story starts as an attempt to cross the border of Saxony. Michael K.'s story starts when he wants to escape from Cape Town to the country. Michael K. is a simple man working in the public gardens. When the civil war is becoming unbearable, he decides to escape to the countryside with his ailing mother. The mother soon perishes, but Michael K. continues with his trip in the countryside, constantly evading the civil war. In *Michael Kohlhaas*, the border signifies the transition between two states, Brandenburg and Saxony. Further, the border is crossed in a time of peace—indeed, in a time of relative prosperity, as the horse dealer's flourishing trade suggests. Conversely, in *Life and Times of Michael K.*, there is only one sovereign state. Michael K. does not want to cross a border, but rather several checkpoints that are set up to contain the population within the Cape Town area. (We will see shortly that there is another sense of the border, associated with the mouth, that determines whether the individual is conceived of as a subject or as a member of a population.) The reason that the population needs to be controlled is that there is a civil war raging. There is, in other words, a generalized exception. Within the single state of Coetzee's *Life and Times of Michael K.*, everyone is included in that civil war. In this radical inclusivity of the state where the entire novella unfolds, Michael K. resists the logic of the generalized civil war. There are, however, two ways of approaching his resistance.

First, resistance can be understood as a refusal to be included in the generalized civil war—in the normalized exception. The possibility of a successful resistance is at the heart of Michael Hardt and Antonio Negri's turn to *Life and Times of Michael K.* at a crucial juncture of *Empire*. Hardt and Negri define Michael K. as "a figure of absolute refusal." This refusal has the character of movement: "he is continually stopped by the cages, barriers, and checkpoints erected by authority, but he manages quietly to refuse them, to keep moving."[69] Hardt and Negri identify in Michael K.'s "perpetual motion" a political project, since it "cannot but appeal to our hatred of authority"—or, more emphatically, "the refusal of voluntary servitude, is the beginning of liberatory politics."[70] The refusal of borders is both a "hatred" of sovereignty and a love for freedom. But refusal is not enough for Hardt and Negri: "This refusal certainly is the beginning of a liberatory politics, but it is only a beginning. The refusal in itself is empty." The reason for this emptiness is that Michael K.'s refusal is "completely solitary." They continue: "What we need is to create a new social body, which is a project that goes well beyond refusal. Our lines of flight, our exodus must be constituent and create a real alternative. Beyond the simple refusal, or as part of that refusal, we need also to construct a new mode of life and above all a new community."[71] Hardt and Negri envisage a being that is not pure refusal, but rather a constituent community. As the rest of *Empire* makes clear, such a constituent community is separate from constituted power. In other words, liberation hinges on being able to overcome sovereignty. Such a constituent power does not simply endeavor to refuse the borders that demarcate constituted power. Moreover, a constituent community eradicates borders; it dismantles constituted power. The problem with this position that radically separates constituent power from sovereignty is twofold. First, it reerects a border between constituent power and constituted power, or—in Hardt and Negri's terms—between democracy and sovereignty.[72] Hardt and Negri, like Michael Kohlhaas, declare their hatred for sovereign power, but this hatred itself is articulated within a logic that reintroduces the exclusions that they wish to preclude. Second, this vision of a free society without borders is perilously close to the kind of theology that substantiates ancient sovereignty. For instance, the chapter that immediately follows the section entitled "Refusal" starts with an epigraph by Augustine about the Heavenly City on earth, and Augustine returns in the final chapter of the book, "The Multitude Against Empire," when Hardt and Negri compare the universalism of the City of God precisely to the constituent community's overcoming of sovereignty.[73] Such a community reintroduces the universalism of ancient sovereignty. There is, on the one hand, the complete exclusion of sovereignty, and on the other, the absolute inclusion of everyone in the new constituent community—thereby reanimating the dialectic of exclusion and inclusion.[74] Therefore, the account of a constituent society that overcomes sovereignty ultimately suffers from precisely the accusation that Hardt and Negri level against Michael K.—namely, it fails to resist sovereignty in such a way as to avoid being co-opted by its logic. Yet, for all that, Michael K. then emerges as a figure that addresses precisely the problem of how to negotiate the border, or, differently put, how to articulate resistance without presupposing and preserving that which is resisted. Michael K. becomes a figure that allows for an investigation of counter-resistance.

The second way of understanding Michael K.'s resistance departs from the radical inclusivity that characterizes biopolitics, according to Foucault, linking it to the generalized state of exception—the civil war in the novella.[75] Foucault describes this radical inclusion in a state of civil war as racism.[76] It is necessary to turn to that description of racism in order to delineate how the potential inclusion of everyone that characterizes biopolitics in fact leads to the reanimation of exclusion and hence to the right of life and death. By delineating the way that the potential for everyone's inclusion becomes the principle for exclusion, it will become possible to differentiate between counter-resistance and resistance.

In the final lecture of *Society Must be Defended*, Foucault accords a special importance to the Nazi state. The reason is that it denotes the intensification of the control of life, and hence of biopolitics. In Nazi Germany there is an omnipotent control of life "if only because of the practice of informing" (259). Everyone could inform on one's neighbors if they did not conform to the norm, such as the racial types guaranteeing the "purification" of the German *Volk*. This unlimited expansion of the power to control life can be described as a generalized civil war to the extent that everyone is subjectable to it—which is to say, everyone is potentially included by biopower. Paradoxically, this culmination of biopower coincides with the reintroduction of the right to kill—the old sovereign right of life and death. When control is generalized, "murderous power and sovereign power are unleashed through the entire social body" (259). Killing is unleashed through life—hence the figure of civil war. Or, as Foucault puts it more succinctly, the generalized civil war signifies "a society which has generalized biopower in an absolute sense, but which has also generalized the sovereign right to kill. *The two mechanisms . . . coincide exactly*" (260, emphasis added). In other words, the absolutization of the control of life coincides with the resurgence or resurrection of the older forms of sovereign power. This resurgence is constitutive of biopower's control of life, as we saw in the previous section. A generalized civil war indicates the biopolitical modality of justification, where the different forms of sovereignty can support each other in normalizing the exception.

This generalized civil war is different from state war or war between sovereigns. As already intimated, in *Life and Times of Michael K.* there are no borders to defend. Instead, there are thresholds of the control of life. Foucault indicates the difference of biopolitical violence by pointing out that the killing effected by biopower does not necessitate the spilling of blood. "When I say 'killing,' I obviously do not mean simply murder as such, but also every form of indirect murder . . . political death, expulsion, rejection, and so on" (256). The culmination of the control of life would be most successful when it precisely obfuscated the fact that it was such a culmination—that is, when it masked its killing. In other words, the generalized civil war is a manifestation of the phantasmagoria that characterizes the normalized state of emergency. Foucault designates as racism the way that power effects bodies in such a state. "[W]hat gives it [i.e., racism] its specificity . . . is bound up with the technique of power. . . . We are dealing with a mechanism that allows biopower to work" (258). As such a technique of power, which starts from the effect on the body that is to be included in the exercise of control, racism need not rely on visible signifiers such as biological or dermatological differentiations. Rather, just as any normalization of the exception, it relies, in Marx's terms, on a "farce," that is, on the creation of fabulations that justify the violence of its power. Foucault describes this fabulation as a narrative of purification: "The fact that the other dies does not mean simply that I live in the sense that his death guarantees my safety: the death of the other, the death of the bad race, of the inferior race (or the degenerate, of the abnormal) is something that will make life in general healthier . . . and purer" (255). The abnormal is anything that is not normalized—and this means anyone who fails to be included. The common—and unbearably otiose—complaint about the state of culture, society, and politics we often hear by our contemporary "intelligentsia" is a symptom of their own self-determination as "abnormal" within a normalizing society. This observation returns us directly to Hardt and Negri's point about refusal. A simple refusal of normalization entails the positioning of the one effected by power as the one excluded. As such, refusal plays into the hand of the normalization of the exception because it positions the refusing individual within the "unhealthy" population and thereby animates the mechanism of racism. Refusal is not resistance, but counter-resistance. By analogy to the principle that "there must be pagans for Augustinianism to exist" and the Hobbesian "there must be madmen for modern sovereignty to exist," we can say here that "there must be refusalists for biopolitics to exist." The possibility of realizing Walter Benjamin's real state of emergency is stalled by such a counter-resistance. The political task consists instead in how to evade the mechanism that perpetuates the normalization of the exception. Marx's unsavables must also be described as unexceptional. In the sense of indicating a space in excess of the exception, Michael K. is a figure of this unexceptionality that does *not* refuse, but rather *enacts* evasions of the justificatory logic of sovereignty.

The difference between refusal and acts of evasion can be described in spatial terms. Refusal is the delusion that a position *outside* sovereign power can be discovered. Conversely, acts of evasion, just as the democratic acts described in the previous section, hold that there is no outside the law—there are only moments that affirm singularity and thereby puncture the universalizing and absolutizing logic of justification. Further, such an unexceptional enactment requires an engagement with and resistance to, not only each modality of justification, but to justification as such—that is, to all forms of sovereign power. In the generalized civil war that includes everyone in Coetzee's novella, Michael K. presents both the refusal that only leads to counter-resistance and evasion as the possibility of an unexceptional resistance.

Life and Times of Michael K. was published in 1983, at the height of the resistance to apartheid.[77] As a prominent intellectual in South Africa, Coetzee was expected to continue being a vocal opponent of the racist regime. The novella, however, made him a target of criticism for not representing clearly enough the interests of the struggle.[78] The reason was that *Life and Times of Michael K.* is located in an unspecified time, and the generalized civil war that it describes did not exactly fit the "real" situation in South

Africa. For instance, the color of Michael K.'s skin is never explicitly mentioned.[79] Thus it was deemed that Coetzee's refusal of apartheid was not articulated clearly enough. The novella will be misunderstood if it is taken as a commentary just on apartheid. Rather, its target is the logic of sovereignty and in particular the thanatopolitics that arises out of the different modalities of justification. The title provides a crucial clue—the missing definite article. Coetzee says, "'The Life' implies that the life is over, whereas 'Life' does not commit itself."[80] Michael K. is a figure of life. He is oppressed by the logic of sovereignty, and he exhibits all three different forms of sovereignty. But ultimately Michael K. remains a figure that affirms life—and it is in this affirmation that he does not lapse into the counter-resistance that characterized Michael Kohlhaas's self-sacrifice.

Before showing the way that this affirmation of life operates in *Life and Times of Michael K.*, it is necessary to show how the effects of the three modalities of justification are registered on Michael K. This will indicate how a simple refusal of them all is nothing but a counter-resistance.

The modern sovereignty's exclusion of those who cannot fit is introduced to Michael K. by Robert, who is a fellow inmate in Jakkalsdrif camp. Robert takes it upon himself to educate Michael K. He aims to teach him precisely the mechanism of exclusion. Michael K. heeds the message: "Standing against the wire looking out over the veld, K. brooded on Robert's words. He no longer found it so strange to think of the camp as a place where people were deposited to be forgotten" (94). Michael K. has been taught that exclusion does not simply mean that the excluded do not have access to power. Moreover, there is no power without such an exclusion. At the same time, however, Michael K. cannot fully incorporate the lesson on the exclusion and power: "It seemed more like Robert than like him, as he knew himself, to think like that" (95). Thus Robert appears as a figure that wants to educate Michael K. of his position of exclusion below the law in order to provide him with the means to resist, but at the same time Robert, by that very educating, is located in a position of authority above or power over Michael K.

Ancient sovereignty is introduced through the way that the medical officer glorifies Michael K. at the medical camp where he is interned: "only you, following your *idiot light* . . . have managed to live the old way, drifting through time . . . no more trying to change the course of history than a grain of sand does" (151–52). The discourse of the "idiot light" refers to the figure of the holy fool. According to Paul, "If any man among you seemeth to be wise in this world, let him become a fool, that he may be wise. For the wisdom of this world is foolishness with God."[81] The tradition of the holy fool introduces in a different way the distinction that we saw in Augustine between the earthly city of God that can never be completely pacified and the heavenly city, where there is perpetual peace. Since it is impossible to incarnate the heavenly city on earth, the earthly city of God is always deficient—and so is its wisdom that is "foolishness to God." Those who are "fools" recognize this perpetual deficiency and thereby refuse all wisdom as well as earthly goods—what Nietzsche refers to as the ascetic ideal. But again, as in the construal of modern sovereignty, Michael K. here too encounters the imposition of power. "I am the only one who can save you" (151) says the medical officer. He proposes to save him by writing his story: "the truth is that you are going to perish in obscurity . . . unless you yield and at last open your mouth. I appeal to you, Michaels: *yield!*" (152). The medical officer wants to write an hagiography of the holy fool, but that would only make him the savior—the author who occupies the position of authority, the *authoritas* or sovereign of the discourse.[82]

The figure of the mouth is prevalent throughout the novel. It does not open for the "holy fool" who does not want to speak, and it has a different construal for biopolitics. Here the non-opening mouth is a symptom of illness—the marker of a person who belongs to a population that needs to be excluded for society to be purified. Michael K. hardly ever has the urge to speak (see 47–48, 96, 131), mostly remaining silent. Contrast here Michael Kohlhaas, who is never diffident, proclaiming his revolutionary demands and asserting his opinions strongly, even to Luther, the highest spiritual authority of his time. Michael K.'s inability to speak points to the fact that, unlike Michael Kohlhaas, he does not hold any strong opinions, and others perceive him as simple, even as an idiot. In addition, the mouth points to physical lack of health. As the first sentence of the novella declares, he was born with a hare lip. Moreover, when he opens his mouth, most of the time it is in order to retch (see 54, 70, 121, 123, 130, 173). Another aspect of the physical illness denoted by the mouth is the refusal of nutrition. Thus, in all these cases, the mouth functions as a boundary or a border that separates Michael K. from the mentally and physically healthy—or, in Foucault's terms, the mouth is the sign that makes Michael K. subject to racism.

Michael K. harbors the illusion that he can escape all these different ways that power effects him by moving away from its reach. His escapes to the mountains or his hiding in the cottage are supported by the idea of "living here for ever" (46, 99), isolated from the rest of humanity. In isolation he is described as "living beyond the reach of calendar and clock in a blessedly neglected corner" (116). This ideal is expressed in the following way: "A man must live so that he leaves no trace of his living" (99). This ideal is an illusion, of course, and it shutters every time with Michael K.'s repeated arrests. This is not surprising—it is this ideal that Hardt and Negri describe as refusal. This is a thorough refusal of sovereign power in whatever way it is expressed. But by its being so thorough, it reproduces the exclusion that it wants to eliminate. In this refusal, all three forms of sovereignty are reinscribed: modern sovereignty as the evasion of the law, ancient sovereignty as the escape of the holy man to the desert, and biopolitics as the refusal of potential inclusion that is the precondition of racism. Thus refusal becomes a counter-resistance that supports the justification of sovereignty, not in any one of its forms, but in its totality. Counter-resistance performs the circularity of the three modalities of justifications, showing that the different forms of sovereignty work in tandem to co-opt any desire to position oneself outside power.

At the end of the novella, however, Michael K. indicates a different form of resistance—one that does not desire refusal. Michael K. recalls how he tried to escape power by achieving self-sufficiency in the country through planting fruit, such as pumpkins, for sustenance.

> my mistake was to plant all my seeds together in one patch. I should have planted them one at a time spread out over miles of veld in patches of soil no larger than my hand and drawn a map and kept it with me at all times so that every night I could make a tour of the sites to water them. Because if there was one thing I discovered out in the country, it was that there is time enough for everything. (183)

This is a complex passage. It points to a conception of both spatiality and temporality. In terms of space, Michael K.'s realization can be articulated through a distinction between cultivation and gardening. He recognizes that his mistake was to seek self-sufficiency through planting his "seeds together in one patch." In other words, he sought to cultivate the land. Cultivation has political implications. According to the *Genesis*, God granted the humans dominion over cultivated lands. "God said unto them . . . replenish the earth, and subdue it: and have dominion over . . . every living thing that moveth upon the earth."[83] Cultivation asserts a transcendent authority.[84] Also, a cultivated land denotes a locale with borders. Rousseau writes: "The true founder of civil society was the first man who, having enclosed a piece of land, thought of saying, 'This is mine,' and came across people simple enough to believe him."[85] This act of establishing borders around a land in order to cultivate leads to modern sovereignty's determination through the territory it controls. Finally, the cultivation of the land becomes subject to regulation, something measurable and hence controllable, thereby animating biopolitics. Thus all forms of sovereignty surge in a land that is cultivated. Instead of this cultivation, Michael K. recognizes that he should have deterritorialized his planting.[86] He should have planted his seeds "one at a time spread out over miles of veld." This figure of unorganized cultivation—what can be called gardening—undoes the mechanism of control and thereby derails the resurgence of the different forms of sovereignty. Gardening, then, functions as a kind of dejustification—it recognizes and deconstructs the different ways that land is used for the justification of power. Gardening introduces a figure of being that is singular. Each plant grows in its own unique patch. Thus it evades the control that always seeks to universalize through transcendence, borders, and normalization. But it does so without refusing power, thereby lapsing into counter-resistance. Instead, this singular gardening practice recognizes the primacy of the effect. One is always within power, one is always effected by power, but this power requires as its precondition a singularity that it seeks to tame through control. In accepting the primacy of the effect of power, gardening dispels the illusion that one can step outside the law, and at the same time points to a spacing—a relational space or a "map," as Michael K. calls it— that affirms the modality of contingency. Or, more precisely, he conceives of a way that the aleatory can evade the control of the law—without entertaining the illusion of an escape from the law.

In terms of temporality, Michael K. recounts his discovery that "out in the country . . . there is time enough for everything." This is not simply a plenitude of time, but rather the countering of emergency time. The normalization of the exception requires the emergency. A threat—be it the "pagan," the "madman," or the "refusalist"—is always imminent. Or, differently put, the threat to sovereignty is always the now, the affirmation of singularity. This temporality of the present is an affirmation of the unexceptional. It is a judgment in the Spinozan sense—namely, as the decision to act in such a way that privileges life over the thanatopolitics of sovereignty. Further, this is a judgment in the sense that it is an awakening to the phantasmagorias that construct an exceptional narrative that fabricates emergency in order to support saviors that thereby assert their power. Or, differently put, the judgment that there is plenty of time points to the potential inherent in the seeds of gardening. Potential can grow, or one can grasp its constituent power, not by stepping outside sovereignty, but rather by making judgments that sustain that growing of power. This judgment in favor of singularity can be articulated in many different contexts and in an unpredictable variety of ways—the seeds *can* grow differently depending on contingent factors such as the soil and the weather. But gardening *can* happen only by embracing that contingency—that is, only by resisting either a complete submission to justification or, what is really the obverse side of the same coin, the complete refusal of power. The temporality of the now is unexceptional because it affirms potentiality by renouncing control through the recognition of the importance of contingency.[87]

The coimplication of judgment and resistance points to one further observation. The primacy of the effect and the affirmation of singularity that accompanies it indicate the primacy of judgment over justification. Cultivation was a mistake, as Michael K. recognizes, because it aimed at self-sufficiency. We encountered that self-sufficiency in Pericles's "Funeral Oration." Self-sufficiency was the principle that allowed Pericles to describe the greatness of Athens and its citizens within an exceptional narrative. The totalizing power of biopolitics that aims to include everyone relies, as already argued, on such exceptional narratives. The narratives that normalize the exception prescribe ends that are supposed to be self-sufficient, complete, universal. But these universals are nothing but phantasmagorias that justify the exercise of violence. The sovereign logic is one of thanatopolitics.

Conversely, a narrative can be understood as unexceptional precisely as the affirmation of life. This is a narrative that insists that "there is time enough for everything." This is a temporality of the now that affirms life.[88] Michael K. ultimately wants to live. His political import is not as a literary figure that refuses apartheid, but rather as showing a way of living that is not commensurate with thanatopolitics. He does so by recognizing his repeated mistake of trying to refuse power as such and thereby lapsing into counter-resistance. When at the end of the novella Michael K. returns to Cape Town, this return is a fight for his life, a fight to live away from the various camps where he had been interned. But it is also a fight to regain a sense of living that is not a simple flight in the desert, where he had hoped to persist in perfect isolation. He does not lapse into counter-resistance any longer, because he recognizes that there is no outside to the law. The law as empty, as pure necessity, is a condition of the living, as Spinoza recognizes. In addition, Michael K.'s affirmation of life is also an affirmation of a space that exceeds the thanatopolitics of sovereignty. This is a space of the now, a space of the "there is time enough for everything." Living in the now, one becomes unexceptional. One's life is no longer determined through ideals—one's story is not, as the doctor was hoping for Michael K., a hagiography. But this unexceptionality opens up the possibility of a living with others. The affirmation of such a politics of life is Michael K.'s contribution to the series of literary figures who resist.

EPILOGUE

A Relational Ontology of the Political

A man walks across this empty space whilst someone else is watching
him, and this is all that is needed for an act of theatre to be engaged.
—Peter Brook, *The Empty Space*

Peter Brook's assertion that theatre takes place when at least two people
encounter one another in an empty space does not describe what is or
must be present for theatre to exist. The filling of the empty with two bodies does not function as a predicate. Rather, Brook delineates a complex
set of relations. Theatre happens when relations unfold between at least
two people. What matters is not the mere presence, but rather the operative
presence of two people in the empty space. What matters is how the two
people relate—how one waits in the empty space, watching the other
appearing. Brook delineates a relation that carries an ontological weight.
Something does exist because of the relation. But the ontology remains
open because the relations are not predetermined—they are different every
time that the empty space is occupied. In other words, the relations are
singular. I call this ontology of unfolding singular relations a "relational
ontology."

This book has constructed a relational ontology of the political that
starts from the same principle as Brook's delineation—namely, the unfolding of singular relations. The question has always been about how to conceive of the encounter between people. The question has not been about
being; rather, it has been about being-with. What kind of power relations

unfold when people are with each other? I have distinguished two forms of relation: relations that affirm either sovereign power or democracy.

I have called justification the relations that characterize sovereign power. A man or group of men assert their power against—they subject—another man or group of men. As I have argued, justification has three modalities. Ancient sovereignty posits an end that justifies the means of exercising power. Modern sovereignty conceives of the exercise of the means of power as the end of sovereignty—which is another way of saying that sovereignty aims at its self-maintenance. Biopower hides any end by creating fabulatory narratives, thereby appearing as if the means of its power are mere tactical effects. The different modalities of justification have one thing in common: namely, that they justify violence. In other words, justification is a deadly relation. It creates a thanatopolitics, as it was called earlier in the book.

I have called judgment the relations that characterize the democratic. Judgment is agonistic. Its relations express participation and engagement with competing points of view. Judgment has two aspects. First, judgment can manifest itself as resistance to justification—it can be a dejustification. We have seen how every formulation of sovereignty is accompanied by de-justification. There is no justification without dejustification. Second, judgment is an affirmation of life in the sense that the agonistic relations demanded by judgment are of the here and now. The engagement is always a singular response to contingent circumstances. Further, judgment's agonism should not be confused with the violence justified by justification. Whereas justification is a deadly relation, agonism aims at engaging with the other.

From the perspective of a relational ontology of the political, democracy is more primary than sovereignty. Differently put, the relations that characterize sovereignty are derivative. Justification is an effect of judgment. The primacy of judgment follows from the relational ontology's concentration on the unfolding of singular relations. These are relations that affirm the contingency of life. We have seen that justification is an attempt to control the unfolding of singular relations. Ancient sovereignty posits an ideal—such as the city of God—that can never be realized in the now. Modern sovereignty exercises the right of life and death on anyone who does not conform to the imperative of its self-maintenance. And biopolitics is the normalization of the exception as the attempt to control the aleatory.

Thus sovereignty is a reaction to the unfolding of singular relations. Kleist described this reactive relation of sovereignty to life by showing how all important decisions made by the holders of power were accidental—they were always responses to the sovereign discomfort due to an unpredictable event.

Sovereignty is an effect of democracy within the purview of an ontology of power. Such an ontology does not coincide with particular regimes. If democracy is indeed agonistic, if it allows for the expression of singular relations, then it cannot, strictly speaking, ever be fully realized. It is always in a process of transformation—or, in Derrida's formulation, it is always to-come. Further, if sovereignty manifests itself as an effect of democracy, then sovereignty itself can never be complete. Whatever ideal ends, whatever institutions of power, and whatever regulations characterize the sovereign regimes of power, these are only provisional responses to the transformations of justificatory relations. The completeness of sovereignty is an illusion. No regime can ever be perfect; no ideal can ever be fully realized. In *Civilization and its Discontents* Freud examines the Paulian imperative to love your neighbor as yourself. Freud shows that universal love is nothing but a denegation of violence. In other words, the ideal of order, peace, and stability that sovereignty propagates is the repression of the expression of its power through violent means. I am not suggesting that ideals do not have a role to play in politics. Rather, to exercise judgment one has to remain suspicious of ideals that promise completeness, because they have an unappealing underbelly—namely, the justification of violence.

Sovereignty as an effect of democracy shows that the dilemma that has often exercised political theorists—*democracy or sovereignty?*—is in fact a false dilemma. Even if democracy is in a process of transformation, it still materializes in settings that are governed by rules and regulations. We can highlight this by returning to Brook's definition of theatre as the encounter of two people in an empty space. From a political perspective the space is never completely empty. Relations unfold always within certain laws. These laws can be of various kinds—for instance, they can be unwritten laws such as the laws of kinship in *Antigone*, the laws of the state that characterize modern sovereignty, or the rules and regulations of biopower. Regardless of how these laws are conceived, the encounter with the other is never pure. Agonistic relations are always supplemented—and that supplement is sovereignty.

Sovereignty as a supplement of democracy indicates that violence can never be eliminated from the political. The choice is not between democracy and sovereignty, as if the former is nonviolent. This is a false dilemma. Rather, the question of violence is that which shows the necessity for judgment. As it was expressed in the discussion of Spinoza, judgment consists in choosing the relations that allow for the affirmation of singularity—that is, choosing in favor of life over death. But judgment itself is agonistic. It demands engagement with the here and now, which takes the form of an incessant contestation about life. Solon expresses this remarkably in his exigency of participation that we discussed earlier. Whoever does not participate in the various discords of the city is to be disenfranchised, demanded Solon. The corollary to this is that the city does not aim to eliminate discord; rather, without discord there is no polis. Judgments can only be made when there are differing opinions. The political judgment is necessary because the threshold between discord and violence is an unstable one—a threshold that, like democracy and sovereignty themselves, is under transformation.

The precarious relation between discord and violence can be articulated also in a way that recalls Brook's definition of the theater. Two people encounter each other. This encounter has a setting. The space around them is determined by a series of formal or informal assumptions that artificially determine human relations. For instance, one of the people might stake a claim of ownership on the space where the encounter takes place. The supplementary relations such as claims of ownership can provide a justification for violence. For instance, the other person might be construed as a threat. It can also be recognized that prior to the threat, the encounter with the other is an affirmation of a relation. That relation can pose threats. But there is no normative basis that can regulate this relation. The possibility of threat is a necessary condition of the contingencies of life. On the other hand, all of life's potential is also linked to the necessities imposed by human law and their relation to contingency, as Spinoza well recognized. But it is impossible to predict with any certainty whether the other will realize the threat that they pose in such a way as to justify violence or in a way that affirms the inherent unpredictability of contingency.

The contention here is that the only chance for democracy is to embrace the unpredictability of contingency—to embrace life. Only then will it be possible to discern in the relational ontology of the political—in the being-with the other—a site where a variety of concerns intersect and overlaps. These concerns are interpretative, since the encounter with the other calls for a way of understanding the relation to the other in such a way as to evade the justifications of violence that characterizes the logic of sovereignty. The concerns are also ethical—they point to how one ought to conduct oneself in relating with the other. And all these concerns—political, interpretative, and ethical—indicate the labor that one has to undertake in order to maintain the singularity of human relations. The relational ontology of the political does not exist as a mere presence; rather, it is performed through the labor to sustain a relating with the other.

NOTES

PREAMBLE, OR POWER AND ITS RELATIONS

1. The crucial reason of approaching the question of sovereignty through justification and the means-and-ends relation is that it essentially bypasses the presupposition of almost the entirety of the recent literature on sovereignty—namely, that the defining characteristic of sovereignty is exceptionality. This is not to say, of course, that exceptionality is not a characteristic of sovereignty, but rather that exceptionality is a product of the different modalities of justification. Such an approach offers, as I will be showing throughout the book, the chance of a stronger critique of sovereignty than relying on exceptionality.

2. Ultimately this leads to the question of how sovereignty and democracy relate to one another—that is, what is the relation of their relations. This question is present throughout the study. It comes to the foreground in the final chapter. See also the concluding paragraph of this chapter.

3. This is at least a common view expressed in the secondary literature. For instance, Andrew McNeal contrasts Agamben's approach to sovereignty with Foucault's on the grounds that the latter offers a "historical critique of sovereignty" in his lecture course *Society Must Be Defended*; Andrew W. McNeal, "Cutting off the King's Head: Foucault's *Society Must Be Defended* and the Problem of Sovereignty," *Alternatives* 29 (2004): 375. I will argue in Chapter 5 that there is a way of reading Foucault that presents his typology of power as being at the same time attuned to the limitations of understanding different forms of power as separated.

4. Even though Foucault continuously reworks the terms of his typology of power, the direction of his thought toward such a typology is already clear in Michel Foucault, *History of Madness*, trans. J. Murphy, ed. Jean Khalfa (London: Routledge, 2006), in which the operative term is that of confinement and hence of the modern power's insistence on territory and the border.

5. The literature here is enormous, so I will only mention some indicative examples. In international relations one of the most interesting books remains Hedley Bull, *The Anarchical Society: A Study of Order in World* Politics, 3rd ed. (New York: Palgrave, 2002), a study on the distinction between internal and external sovereignty; and Stephen D. Krasner's *Sovereignty: Organized Hypocrisy* (Princeton: Princeton University Press, 1999), which is an attempt to show that the development of sovereignty is based on the pragmatic principle that "might is right" instead of any universal principle. Hendrik Spruyt's *The Sovereign State and Its Competitors: An Analysis of Systems Change* (Princeton: Princeton University Press, 1994) seeks to describe the transition from feudalism to modernity through an analysis of sovereignty. And Daniel Philpott's *Revolutions in Sovereignty: How Ideas Shaped Modern International Relations* (Princeton: Princeton University Press, 2001) seeks to account for the transition between different forms of sovereignty according to the development of different conceptions of justice. Works on sovereignty in neighboring disciplines also make a similar set of assumptions. For instance, for a recent book on sovereignty from the perspective of geography, see John Agnew, *Globalization and Sovereignty* (Lanham, Md.: Rowman and Littlefield, 2009).

6. The standard turning point for the separation of internal and external sovereignty according to this approach is the Treaties of Westphalia; see, for instance, Daniel Philpott, "Westphalia, Authority, and International Society," *Political Studies* 48 (1999): 566–89. For a critical, dissenting view about the novelty of Westphalia, see Stéphane Beaulac, *The Power of Language in the Making of International Law: The Word Sovereignty in Bodin and Vattel and the Myth of Westphalia* (Leiden: Martinus Nijhoff, 2004). The distinction between internal and external sovereignty relies on a strong sense of the border that separates states; see Carl Schmitt, *The Nomos of the Earth in the International Law of the Jus Publicum Europaeum*, trans. G. L. Ulmen (New York: Telos Press, 2003). For a critique of the idea of the border that is implicitly a critique of the idea of Westaphalian sovereignty, see two magnificent books: Eyal Weizman, *Hollow Land: Israel's Architecture of Occupation* (London: Verso, 2007); and Wendy Brown, *Walled States, Waning Sovereignty* (New York: Zone Books, 2010). I also argue in Chapter 2 that the distinction between internal and external sovereignty is already implied in the political arrangement of the city states in ancient Greece.

7. For instance, Robert Jackson expresses the historical and substantive characterization of sovereignty according to this approach thus: "Sovereignty is a distinctive configuration of state authority. . . . Sovereignty is a historical innovation of certain European political and religious actors who were seeking to escape from their subjection to the papal and imperial authorities of medieval Europe and to establish their independence. . . . It is a post-medieval and, indeed, anti-medieval arrangement of governing authority"; Jackson, *Sovereignty: Evolution of an Idea* (Cambridge: Polity, 2007), 5–6.

8. Jacques Derrida, *Rogues: Two Essays on Reason*, trans. Pascale-Anne Brault and Michael Nass (Stanford: Stanford University Press, 2005).

9. Derrida, *The Beast and the Sovereign*, vol. 1, trans. Geoffrey Bennington (Chicago: University of Chicago Press, 2009).

10. Giorgio Agamben, *Homo Sacer: Sovereign Power and Bare Life*, trans. Daniel Heller-Roazen (Stanford: Stanford University Press, 1998).

11. As Jens Bartelson avers, "the history of sovereignty ought to be studied not in isolation . . . but in terms of its multiple relations with other concepts within larger discursive wholes, these not necessarily being confined to political ones"; Bartelson, *A Genealogy of Sovereignty* (Cambridge: Cambridge University Press, 1995), 2. One might be tempted to respond to Bartelson by following Carl Schmitt in arguing that the presence of the enemy who posits a threat to the state thereby leading to the "exception"—that is, to the necessity to suspend the law in order to defend the state—puts to rest any notion that sovereignty is not necessarily confined to political authorities; see Carl Schmitt, *The Concept of the Political*, trans. George D. Schwab (Chicago: University of Chicago Press, 1996). However, as Bonnie Honig has shown in her important book *Emergency Politics: Paradox, Law, Democracy* (Princeton: Princeton University Press, 2009), we can retain a notion of emergency without thereby forfeiting the prerogative to suspend the law to a single authority—or, in other words, that the political is dispersed in a much wider spectrum than Schmitt would have accepted. William Rasch also argues that contestability contained in the friend/enemy distinction that defines the political in Schmitt indicates the "primacy of the political" in the sense that "the political can take shape anywhere, not just in the political system of the modern state"; Rasch, *Sovereignty and Its Discontents: On the Primacy of the Conflict and the Structure of the Political* (London: Birkbeck Law Press, 2004), 11.

12. Georges Bataille, *The Accursed Share: An Essay On General Economy*, vols. 1–3, trans. Robert Hurley (New York: Zone Books, 1988–1991). For a recent article on Bataille's conception of sovereignty, see Charles Barbour, "The Sovereign Without Domain: Georges Bataille and the Ethics of Nothing," in *The Politics of Nothing: Sovereignty and Modernity*, ed. Clare Monagle and Dimitris Vardoulakis (London: Routledge, 2013).

13. One such attempt can be found in Bartelson's *A Genealogy of Sovereignty*. Chapter 2 describes the two approaches to sovereignty with recourse to specific disciplines—international relations and structuralist sociology—inferring that they highlight different, but valuable aspects of sovereignty. In the rest of his book, however, Bartelson does not tackle the issue of a rapprochement between them.

14. Michael Hardt and Antonio Negri, *Empire* (Cambridge, Mass.: Harvard University Press, 2000), 37–43.

15. See also Negri's *Insurgencies: Constituent Power and the Modern State*, trans. Maurizia Boscagli (Minneapolis: University of Minnesota Press, 1999).

16. Hardt and Negri, *Multitude: War and Democracy in the Age of Empire* (New York: Penguin, 2004), 340.

17. I take up this issue in greater detail in the chapter on Negri in my forthcoming book on *stasis*, which is the sequel to the present volume. For an outline of the argument about *stasis*, see Vardoulakis, "Stasis: Beyond Political Theology?" *Cultural Critique* 73 (2009): 125–47; and for a short draft of the chapter on Agamben see Vardoulakis, "The Ends of Stasis: Spinoza as a Reader of Agamben," *Culture, Theory and Critique* 51, no. 2 (2010): 145–56.

18. The most important works on Benjamin's influential essay are: Derrida, "Force of Law: The 'Mystical Foundation of Authority,'" trans. Mary Quaintance, *Gardozo Law Review* 11 (1990): 919–1045; Judith Butler, "Critique, Coercion, and Sacred Life in Benjamin's 'Critique of Violence,'" in *Political Theologies: Public Religions in a Post-Secular World*, ed. Hent de Vries and Lawrence E. Sullivan (New York: Fordham University Press, 2006), 201–19; Agamben, *State of Exception*, trans. Kevin Attell (Chicago: University of Chicago Press, 2005); Werner Hamacher, "Afformative Strike: Benjamin's 'Critique of Violence,'" in *Destruction and Experience*, ed. Andrew Benjamin and Peter Osborne (Manchester, UK: Clinamen, 2000), 108–36; Beatrice Hanssen, *Critique of Violence: Between Structuralism and Critical Theory* (London: Routledge, 2000). Peter Fenves's *The Messianic Reduction: Walter Benjamin and the Shape of Time* (Stanford: Stanford University Press, 2011), chap. 7, provides invaluable insights that place Benjamin's essay in a new context.

19. *Gewalt* does not mean only violence, but also constituted power; see Étienne Balibar, "Gewalt," in *Historisch-kritisches Wörterbuch des Marxismus*, ed. W. F. Haug (Berlin: Argument, 2001), 5: 1271.

20. Walter Benjamin, "Critique of Violence," trans. Edmund Jephcott, in *Selected Writings*, ed. Marcus Bullock and Michael W. Jennings (Cambridge, Mass.: Belknap, 2002), 1:237.

21. See, for instance, how Paul Kahn uses the idea of the essential relation between sovereignty and the justification of torture in Kahn, *Sacred Violence: Torture, Terror, and Sovereignty* (Ann Arbor: University of Michigan Press, 2008). For an original account of the link between violence and sovereignty, see Dimitris Papadopoulos and Vassilis Tsianos, "How to Do Sovereignty without People? The Subjectless Condition of Postliberal Power," *boundary 2* 34, no. 1 (2007): 135–72.

22. This conception leads both Benjamin and Spinoza to advocate a politics without ends or, in the language of the "Critique of Violence," a politics of "pure means." I am not taking up this comparison in the present book, but I will do so elsewhere.

23. Walter Benjamin, "Critique of Violence," 1:237.

24. As the brief précis below will indicate, this book does not aim to be an exhaustive account of different theories of sovereignty. Rather, texts have been se-

lected so as to provide a programmatic outline of a theory of sovereignty that takes sovereignty to be, first, the expression of justifications of violence, and, second, an understanding of justification in terms of a means-and-ends relation. Thus the present volume functions as a prolegomena to a new theory of sovereignty. This explains the omission of important philosophical conceptions of power, for instance, by Kant or Hegel—an omission that I intend to address in subsequent publications.

25. Gilles Deleuze and Félix Guattari develop another tripartite typology of power in *Anti-Oedipus*. Their account relies on a Nietzschean account of debt. They argue that there are three systems of debt: the savage, the barbarian, and the capitalist; see Deleuze, and Guattari, *Anti-Oedipus: Capitalism and Schizophrenia*, trans. R. Hurley, et al (London: Athlone Press, 2000). The shift from debt in *Anti-Oedipus* to the justification of violence in the present book has to do with a shifting of the emphasis on sovereignty. Even though such a shift is important, and not withstanding methodological differences, still I regard the project here as compatible with Deleuze and Guattari's account.

26. Sigmund Freud, *Civilization and Its Discontents*, in *The Standard Edition of the Complete Psychological Works*, ed. and trans. James Strachey (London: Hogarth, 1953–74), 21:57–146.

27. Hardt and Negri, *Empire*, 16.

28. Obviously, I am not seeking here to argue either in favor of or against smoking. Rather, I am seeking to describe the way in which power justifies the imposition of normalizing regulatory processes. Further, I do not suggest in any way either that regulation is "bad" as such, or that the absence of regulation is "good." As I will argue in Chapter 5, regulation as such is neither "good" nor "bad." Judgments about regulation can only be drawn based on particular cases. But this does not prevent us from generalizing when we consider the manner in which regulation is justified.

29. For an interesting discussion of identity politics, see Alexander García Düttmann, *At Odds with AIDS: Thinking and Talking About a Virus*, trans. Peter Gilgen and Conrad Scott-Curtis (Stanford: Stanford University Press, 1996).

30. See Étienne Balibar, "Subjection and Subjectivation," in *Supposing the Subject*, ed. Joan Copjec (London: Verso, 1994), 1–15.

31. A full transcript of the speech, as well as an audio copy, can be found at "John Howard's Policy Speech," *AustralianPolitics.com*, http://australianpolitics .com/news/2001/01-10-28.shtml, accessed July 2011.

32. "Convention and Protocol Relating to the Status of Refugees," available at *United Nations High Commission for Refugees*, http://www.unhcr.org/protect/ PROTECTION/3b66c2aa10.pdf, accessed July 2011.

33. For a detailed account of the "children overboard affair," see Andrew Marr and Mirian Wilkinson, *Dark Victory* (Crows Nest, NSW: Allen and Unwin, 2004).

34. The campaign was partly conducted through their website *BoatPeople.org*, at http://www.boat-people.org/, accessed July 2011. The website contains the most important material related to the campaign.

35. I am qualifying this statement because Derrida would tend not to speak of judgment. Is it possible to find a theory of judgment in Derrida's philosophy? This is a question that I cannot take up here, but I hope to return to it on another occasion.

36. Derrida, "Unconditionality of Sovereignty: The University at the Frontiers of Europe," trans. Peggy Kamuf, *Oxford Literary Review* 31, no. 2 (2010): 127.

37. I describe in detail the slippages between the different modalities of justification—what I have been calling here the cosupponibility of ancient, modern, and biopolitical sovereignty—and the absoluteness of sovereignty in Chapter 1.

1. JUDGMENT AND JUSTIFICATION

1. Walter Benjamin, "Critique of Violence," trans. Edmund Jephcott, in *Selected Writings*, ed. Marcus Bullock and Michael W. Jennings (Cambridge, Mass.: Belknap, 2002), 1:236.

2. See Aristotle, *Politics*, trans. H. Rackham (Cambridge, Mass.: Harvard University Press, 1998), book 5.

3. For the theme of fratricide in the Bible, see Pamela Barmash, *Homicide in the Biblical World* (Cambridge: Cambridge University Press, 2005). For the political import of the Cain and Abel story, see George M. Shulman, "The Myth of Cain: Fratricide, City Building and Politics," *Political Theory* 14, no. 2 (1986): 215–38. For the Romulus and Remus story, see Machiavelli's discussion in Niccolò Machiavelli, *Discourses on Livy*, trans. H. Mansfield and N. Tarcov (Chicago: University of Chicago Press, 1996), 116–18.

4. Nikolas Kompridis, *Critique and Disclosure: Critical Theory Between Past and Future* (Cambridge, Mass.: MIT Press, 2006).

5. Michael Hardt and Antonio Negri, *Empire* (Cambridge, Mass.: Harvard University Press, 2000), 40.

6. See, e.g., Carl Schmitt, *Legality and Legitimacy*, trans. Jeffrey Seitzer (Durham: Duke University Press, 2004).

7. Andreas Kalyvas, *Democracy and the Politics of the Extraordinary: Max Weber, Carl Schmitt, and Hannah Arendt* (Cambridge: Cambridge University Press, 2009).

8. Aristotle, *The "Art" of Rhetoric*, trans. J. H. Freese (Cambridge, Mass.: Harvard University Press, 1926), 1354a.

9. I mention here, only indicatively, Michel Foucault's analysis of *Las Meninas* in the opening chapter of Foucault, *The Order of Things: An Archaeology of the Human Sciences* (London: Routledge, 2002).

10. This is related to the idea of a "politics of reading"; see Dimitris Vardoulakis, "Spectres of Duty: The Politics of Silence in Ibsen's *Ghosts*," *Orbis Litterarum* 64, no. 1 (2009): 50–74.

11. For detailed discussions of how a notion of negation can be distinguished from determinate negation and thereby achieve a political significance, see Vardoulakis, *The Doppelgänger: Literature's Philosophy* (New York: Fordham University Press, 2010).

12. Chantal Mouffe, "Deliberative Democracy or Agonistic Pluralism?" *Social Research* 66, no. 3 (1999): 755.

13. Slavoj Žižek is just the latest thinker to argue in Žižek, *Violence* (London: Profile Books, 2009) that symbolic forms of violence can be just as violent as "actual" violence.

14. Carl Schmitt, *Political Theology: Four Chapters on the Concept of Sovereignty*, trans. George D. Schwab (Cambridge, Mass.: MIT Press, 1985), 5.

15. Jacques Lezra offers a remarkable discussion of decisionism in terms of the structure of future contingency in Lezra, *Wild Materialism: The Ethics of Terror and the Modern Republic* (New York: Fordham University Press, 2010), chap. 3. This is, in fact, one of the most potent books on sovereignty, and it would have featured more prominently here if I had read it before the completion of the manuscript.

16. Schmitt, *Political Theology*, 6.

17. Immanuel Kant, "Perpetual Peace," trans. H. B. Nisbet, in *Political Writings*, ed. Hans Reiss (Cambridge: Cambridge University Press, 1991), 93–130.

18. Hannah Arendt, *On Violence* (New York: Harcourt, 1970), 51.

19. Carl Schmitt, *The Concept of the Political*, trans. George D. Schwab (Chicago: University of Chicago Press, 1996), 35; cf. 57.

20. Recognizing this universality of peace, John Milbank correctly associates it with a sense of transcendence and with Christian values. He writes, "from the perspective of Christian virtue, there emerges to view a hidden thread of continuity between antique reason and modern secular reason. This thread of continuity is the theme of 'original violence.' . . . Christianity, however, recognizes no original violence. It construes the infinite . . . as a harmonic peace which is yet beyond the circumscribing power of any totalizing reason. . . . Christianity . . . is the coding of transcendental difference as peace"; Milbank, *Theology and Social Theory: Beyond Secular Reason* (Oxford: Blackwell, 2006), 5–6. As opposed to Milbank's view, it is possible to interpret an "original peace" as a denegation of violence—as Freud contends about Paul's conception of neighborly love—and an "original violence" as a denegation of universal peace and hence as a failed secularism. See, for, instance, the discussion of Hobbes's state of nature in Chapter 3.

21. This holds regardless of whether peace is conceived of as a regulative idea or as an illusion that can never be attained in the political sphere. And this holds

without conceding that such a distinction between peace as a regulative ideal and peace as an illusion can be consistently sustained. In fact the political task of philosophy may be to ask about how to conceive peace independently of a justification of ends. But this also means that peace will no longer function as simply the other side of violence—in such a way that allows for the separation and immediate re-unification of law and justice.

22. Michael Hardt and Antonio Negri, *Empire* (Cambridge, Mass.: Harvard University Press, 2000), xv.

23. Leo Strauss, *Natural Right and History* (Chicago: University of Chicago Press, 1953).

24. Jacques Derrida, *Politics of Friendship*, trans. George Collins (Verso: London, 1997); see also Jürgen Fohrmann, "Enmity and Culture: The Rhetoric of Political Theology and the Exception in Carl Schmitt," trans. Dimitris Vardoulakis, *Culture, Theory and Critique* 51, no. 2 (2010): 129–44.

25. Nick Mansfield, *Theorizing War: From Hobbes to Badiou* (New York: Palgrave, 2008), 165.

26. For an extensive discussion of Mansfield's book, see Vardoulakis, "War and Its Other," *Cultural Studies Review* 16, no. 1 (2010): 267–72.

27. See Derrida, *The Beast and the Sovereign*, trans. Geoffrey Bennington, vol. 1 (Chicago: University of Chicago Press, 2009); and Giorgio Agamben, *Homo Sacer: Sovereign Power and Bare Life*, trans. Daniel Heller-Roazen (Stanford: Stanford University Press, 1998).

28. Ludwig Wittgenstein, *On Certainty*, trans. Denis Paul and G. E. M. Anscombe, ed. G. E. M. Anscombe and G. H. von Wright (Oxford: Blackwell, 1998), §612.

29. Giovanna Borradori, *Philosophy in a Time of Terror: Dialogues with Jürgen Habermas and Jacques Derrida* (Chicago: University of Chicago Press, 2003), 93.

30. Foucault, "Governmentality," in *The Foucault Effect: Studies in Governmentality*, ed. Graham Burchell, Colin Cordon, and Peter Miller (Chicago: University of Chicago Press, 1991), 95.

31. Agamben, *Remnants of Auschwitz: The Witness and the Archive*, trans. Daniel Heller-Roazen (New York: Zone, 2002).

32. Cf. Judith Butler, "Indefinite Detention," in *Precarious Life: The Powers of Mourning and Violence* (London: Verso, 2004), 50–100.

33. From the extensive literature on the Bush doctrine, see Chris J. Dolan, *In War We Trust: The Bush Doctrine and the Pursuit of Just War* (Burlington, Vt.: Ashgate, 2005).

34. See, for instance, Derrida, "Autoimmunity: Real and Symbolic Suicides," in *Philosophy in a Time of Terror: Dialogues with Jürgen Habermas and Jacques Derrida*, by Giovanna Borradori (Chicago: University of Chicago Press, 2003), 96–98.

35. An implication of this possibility of judgment is that the conceptualization of the new is always part of the logic of sovereignty. In other words, the absolutely

new, the totally unprecedented, is incompatible with the possibility of judgment. Even though this point is not expressed precisely in these terms, it is still implied in Andrew Benjamin's *The Plural Event: Descartes, Hegel, Heidegger* (London: Routledge, 1993). For a description of how immediacy is related to this pursuit of novelty, see also Vardoulakis, "A Matter of Immediacy: The Artwork and the Political in Walter Benjamin and Martin Heidegger," in *"Sparks Will Fly": Benjamin and Heidegger*, ed. Andrew Benjamin and Dimitris Vardoulakis (New York: SUNY, forthcoming).

36. Jens Bartelson, *A Genealogy of Sovereignty* (Cambridge: Cambridge University Press, 1995), 2.

37. See Georges Bataille, *The Accursed Share: An Essay On General Economy*, trans. Robert Hurley, vols. 1–3 (New York: Zone Books, 1988–1991).

38. See the Preamble. I will also address this claim further in Chapter 2 while discussing Thucydides conception of the relation between war and the state.

39. I will be analyzing in detail in Chapter 3 the link between sovereignty and the creation of the modern subject.

40. This does not mean, as Hardt and Negri argue, that sovereignty can be overcome. I briefly outlined in the Preamble why I find Hardt and Negri's position problematic. I will return to the distinction between overcoming sovereignty and its rearticulation in the following section of the present chapter.

41. Aristotle, *The Athenian Constitution*, in *The Athenian Constitution; The Eudemian Ethics; On Virtues and Vices*, trans. H. Rackham (Cambridge, Mass.: Harvard University Press, 1935), 8.5 (translation modified).

42. Plutarch is the other ancient, but much later, source of the Solonian law of participation. Plutarch is puzzled by this law, and he seeks to explain it with recourse to a distinction between the private and the public: "Among his [Solon's] other laws there is a very peculiar and surprising one which ordains that he shall be disfranchised who, in time of faction, takes neither side. He wishes, probably, that a man should not be insensible or indifferent to the common weal, arranging his private affairs securely and glorying in the fact that he has no share in the distempers and distresses of his country, but should rather espouse promptly the better and more righteous cause, share its perils and give it his aid, instead of waiting in safety to see which cause prevails"; Plutarch, "Solon," *Lives I*, trans. Bernadotte Perrin (Cambridge, Mass.: Harvard University Press, 1998), 20:1, 457. An argument can be made about the close connection between the exclusion that characterizes sovereignty and the distinction between the private and the public, but I cannot take this up here.

43. See Vardoulakis, "Stasis: Beyond Political Theology?" *Cultural Critique* 73 (2009): 125–47. As I indicated earlier, I am currently developing the concept of stasis further into a monograph that is conceived of as the companion volume to the present study.

44. Jacques Lezra calls this Solonian exigency of participation republicanism rather than democracy. How much depends on such a terminological discrepancy? This is an important question about the relation between a radical democratic and a radical republican conception of agonistic politics. In any case, Lezra's description is close to the idea expressed by Solon: "the role of the radical republic . . . flows precisely from the irreducible capacity that others have, both as political agents and as object in the world, 'to interfere on an arbitrary basis' with every other—that is, to provoke terror in me. To guard and promote in each political subject and in each body of the republic as such, as the defining condition of political subjectivity, the capacity to interfere, the right to arbitrariness . . . is the positive ethico-political norm of the radical republic"; Lezra, *Wild Materialism*, 19.

45. Olivier Roy, *The Failure of Political Islam*, trans. Carol Volk (Cambridge, Mass.: Harvard University Press, 1994); and Roy, *The Politics of Chaos in the Middle East*, trans. Ros Schwartz (London: Hurst, 2007).

46. Carl Schmitt, *The Concept of the Political*, trans. George D. Schwab (Chicago: University of Chicago Press, 1996), 19; see also the collection of papers that I have edited as *Critical Praxis: Or, Is Everything Political?* in *Parallax* 16, no. 4, special issue (2010).

47. For a brilliant discussion of enmity in terms of the relation between Christianity, Islam, and Judaism, see Gil Anidjar, *The Jew, The Arab: A History of the Enemy* (Stanford: Stanford University Press, 2003).

48. Taking the other as a universal does not necessity adopt Levinas's position. Instead, the inquiry here remains vigilant to the possibilities of violence implied in taking the other as universal; see also Derrida, "Violence and Metaphysics: An Essay on the Thought of Emmanuel Levinas," in *Writing and Difference*, trans. Allan Bass (London: Routledge, 2002), 97–192. More than Levinas, I am thinking here of Derrida's "unconditional hospitality" in works such as Derrida, *Of Hospitality: Anne Dufourmantelle Invites Jacques Derrida to Respond*, trans. Rachel Bowldy (Stanford: Stanford University Press, 2000); or of Zygmunt Bauman's concept of the stranger in Bauman, *Modernity and Ambivalence* (Cambridge: Polity, 1991); or of Bonnie Honig's concept of the foreigner in Honig, *Democracy and the Foreigner* (Princeton: Princeton University Press, 2001).

49. Cf. Thomas L. Dumm , "The Problem of 'We': Or, The Persistence of Sovereignty," *boundary 2* 26, no. 3 (1999): 55–61.

50. Foucault, *The Will to Knowledge*, vol. 1 of *The History of Sexuality*, trans. Robert Hurley (London: Penguin, 1990), 88–89 and 90.

51. Derrida, "Unconditionality of Sovereignty: The University at the Frontiers of Europe," trans. Peggy Kamuf, *Oxford Literary Review* 31, no. 2 (2010): 129–30.

52. Nick Mansfield examines in Mansfield, *The God Who Deconstructs Himself: Sovereignty and Subjectivity between Freud, Bataille, and Derrida* (New York:

Fordham University Press, 2010) precisely this relation, arriving at a thesis that resonates with the argument pursued here—namely, that "unconditionality is what makes sovereignty operate, and yet it is the thing in which the challenge to sovereignty is most intensely invested" (*God Who Deconstructs*, 3–4). I refer to this idea as the primacy of democracy over sovereignty, or justification understood as a symptom of judgment.

53. Walter Benjamin, "On the Concept of History," in *Selected Writings*, ed. Michael W. Jennings, et al. (Cambridge, Mass.: Belknap, 2003), 390. This citation is from Thesis II of "On the Concept of History."

2. THE VICISSITUDE OF PARTICIPATION: ON ANCIENT SOVEREIGNTY

1. Leo Strauss, "On Thucydides's War of the Peloponnesians and the Athenians," *The City and Man* (Chicago: University of Chicago Press, 1978), 138–241.

2. All references to Thucydides are to the Loeb edition, *History of the Peloponnesian War*, trans. Charles Foster Smith, vol. 1 (Cambridge, Mass.: Harvard University Press, 1956). All references are given in the text parenthetically. I have on occasion altered the translations.

3. Michel Foucault, *Society Must Be Defended: Lectures at the Collège de France 1975–1976*, trans. David Macey (New York: Picador, 2003), 173.

4. Thomas Hobbes, "Of the Life and History of Thucydides," in *The English Works of Thomas Hobbes of Malmesbury*, ed. William Molesworth (London: John Bohn, 1839), 8: xiii–xxii.

5. Hesiod, *Theogony*, in *Theogony; Works and Days; Testimonia*, trans. and ed. Glenn W. Most (Cambridge, Mass.: Harvard University Press, 2006), 453–91.

6. See, respectively, Marcel Detienne, "The Gods of Politics in Early Greek Cities," in *Political Theologies: Public Religions in a Post-Secular World*, ed. Hent de Vries and Lawrence E. Sullivan (New York: Fordham University Press, 2006), 91–101; and Giulia Sissa and Marcel Detienne, "The Affairs of the Gods and the Affairs of Men," in *The Daily Life of the Greek Gods*, trans. Janet Lloyd (Stanford: Stanford University Press, 2000), 195–207.

7. Nicole Loraux, *The Invention of Athens: The Funeral Oration in the Classical City*, trans. Alan Sheridan (Cambridge, Mass.: Harvard University Press, 1986). Even though I am not concerned here with a reception history of Pericles's funeral oration, I would like to note in passing that it is so important that it has been repeatedly discussed in philosophies of democracy, and its echoes can be heard in Lincoln's Gettysburg Address.

8. The other important tragedy that I cannot discuss here is Aeschylus's *Eumenides*. For a discussion of democracy in both *Eumenides* and *Antigone*, see Jonathan Strauss's book on *Antigone* (New York: Fordham University Press, 2013).

9. Carol Jacobs has convincingly argued that Antigone's sprinkling of dust over her brother's body—the fact that Antigone "neither buries nor fails to bury" her brother's cadaver (901)—disturbs binaries such as state versus kinship laws, universal versus particular, man versus woman, and so on, that have dominated the discussion of the tragedy, especially since Hegel; Jacobs, "Dusting Antigone," *Modern Language Notes* 111 (1996): 889–917.

10. I am using here the Loeb edition, Sophocles, *Antigone*, in *Antigone; Women of Trachis; Philosctetes; Oedipus at Colonus*, trans. Hugh Lloyd-Jones (Cambridge, Mass.: Harvard University Press, 1994). I am quoting parenthetically by line number. I have often modified the translation.

11. The ambiguities and complexities involved in distinguishing between these two senses of participation have determined the discussion of *Antigone* within a political register. Or, to put it the other way round, it is only possible to avoid talking about the political in *Antigone* by avoiding tackling any sense of participation, as the example of Heidegger's discussion of the play, concentrating on the "ode to man," in the *Introduction to Metaphysics* indicates; see Martin Heidegger, *Introduction to Metaphysics*, trans. Gregory Fried and Richard Polt (New Haven: Yale University Press), 156–76. This is not to suggest that Heidegger manages to evade the political, since the very evasion of participation is a political gesture, too, as Creon suggests in the above quotation. Moreover, if the choice is between participation/democracy and decision/sovereignty, then the implication here is that Heidegger sides with the latter—although I cannot take this up in any detail here. For an alternative, excellent reading of the "ode to man" that is attuned to its political import, see Andrew Benjamin's "Placing Speaking: Notes on the First Stasimon of Sophocles' Antigone," *Angelaki* 9, no. 2 (2004): 55–66.

12. Hölderlin's translation of the *Antigone* can be found in the *Sämtliche Werke*, vol. 10, *Briefe und Dokumente*, ed. D. E. Sattler, Bremer Ausgabe (Darmstadt: Wissenschaftliche Buchgesellschaft, 2004), 161–212. His "Aufmerkungen zur Antigonä" can be found in the same volume, immediately after the translation of the play, 212–19; see also Arnaud Villani, "Figures of Duality: Hölderlin and Greek Tragedy," in *The Solid Letter: Readings of Friedrich Hölderlin*, ed. Aris Fioretos (Stanford: Stanford University Press, 1999), 175–99.

13. Walter Benjamin, "The Task of the Translator," in *Selected Writings*, ed. Marcus Bullock and Michael W. Jennings (Cambridge, Mass.: Belknap, 1997), 1:253–63.

14. Friedrich Hölderlin, "Notes on Antigone," in *Essays and Letters*, trans. Jeremy Adler and Charlie Louth (London: Penguin, 2009), 331.

15. Hölderlin, "Notes on Antigone," 331.

16. Hölderlin, "Notes on Antigone," 331.

17. Hölderlin, "Notes on Antigone," 331.

18. There is rarely a recognition of Hölderlin's role in the post–French Revolution reception of *Antigone*. An exception is Georg Steiner's *Antigones* (New Haven: Yale University Press, 1996).

19. For instance, David Gurnham shows that this can lead to a conception of the "complete exteriority of the other" that necessitates that "law and ethics are . . . radically divorced" (334); Gurnham, "'The Otherness of the Dead': The Fates of Antigone, Narcissus, and the Sly Fox, and the Search for Justice," *Law and Literature* 16, no. 3 (2005): 327–51.

20. Indeed, as Carol Jacobs has argued, "*Antigone* . . . perverts . . . any fixed concept of revolution against patriarchy"; Jacobs, "Dusting Antigone," 911.

21. Georg Wilhelm Friedrich Hegel, *Phenomenology of Spirit*, trans. A. V. Miller (Oxford: Oxford University Press, 1977), 280.

22. As Schmitt says, sovereignty "looked at normatively . . . emanates from nothingness"; Carl Schmitt, *Political Theology: Four Chapters on the Concept of Sovereignty*, trans. George D. Schwab (Cambridge, Mass.: MIT Press, 1985), 31–2; see Clare Monagle, "A Sovereign Act of Negation: Schmitt's Political Theology and Its Ideal Medievalism," in *The Politics of Nothing: Sovereignty and Modernity*, ed. Clare Monagle and Dimitris Vardoulakis (London: Routledge, 2012), 7–19.

23. Hegel, *Phenomenology*, 280.

24. Hegel further famously argues in the *Phenomenology of Spirit* that woman is the "everlasting irony of the community" (288), since the public space of reason is constantly opposed to, and hence sublates, the woman. Hegel had Antigone in mind when he expressed his sentiment about "womankind." For a sustained critique of this position of Hegel's, see Luce Irigaray's work on *Antigone*, which spans numerous books—namely, Irigaray, *Speculum of the Other Woman*, trans. Gillian C. Gill (Ithaca: Cornell University Press, 1994); *Sexes and Genealogies*, trans. Gill (New York: Columbia University Press, 1993); *An Ethics of Sexual Difference*, trans. Carolyn Burke and Gill (Ithaca: Cornell University Press, 1993); and *Thinking the Difference: For a Peaceful Revolution*, trans. Karin Montin (London: Routledge, 1994). I cannot deal here with Irigaray's reading of Hegel, but I point the reader to Tina Chanter's masterful engagement with Hegel and Irigaray in Chanter, *Ethics of Eros* (London: Routledge, 1995). Chanter observes that the irony of the position of "womankind," which both defines and yet is excluded from the *polis*, forces Hegel to both define women as beyond being mere "natural beings" and to confine "woman to their naturalness" (88).

25. It should be noted here that Hegel's engagement with *Antigone* is not confined to the *Phenomenology*, but extends to very late works, such as the lectures on religion that were delivered in 1827, twenty years after the publication of the *Phenomenology*; see, e.g., Hegel, *Lectures on the Philosophy of Religion*, trans. R. F. Brown, et al. (Berkeley: University of California Press, 1987), II: 664–66. I cannot deal here with Hegel's compulsion to return to *Antigone*—or, maybe, to Antigone—without a large diversion.

26. Judith Butler, *Antigone's Claim: Kinship Between Life and Death* (New York: Columbia University Press, 2000), 10, emphasis in the original.

27. Bonnie Honig, "Antigone's Laments, Creon's Grief: Mourning, Membership, and the Politics of Exception," *Political Theory* 37, no. 1 (2009): 27; see also Honig, "Antigone's Two Laws: Greek Tragedy and the Politics of Humanism," *New Literary History* 41 (2010): 1–33.

28. Honig, "Antigone's Laments, Creon's Grief," 9.

29. If we take *Moby Dick* to be indeed a political novel—as, for instance, Peter Szendy has argued in *Prophesies of Leviathan*, trans. Gil Anidjar (New York: Fordham University Press, 2010)—then it can be taken as the great novel functioning as a warning against the antidemocratic use of the metaphor of the state as a ship. This is a warning against placing power in the hands of a captain like Ahab, whose obsessions can lead the state to ruin. I intend to develop such a reading of Melville's novel on another occasion.

30. For a similar antidemocratic use of the ship metaphor, see Aegisthus's response to the chorus after the murder of Agamemnon in Aeschylus, *Agamemnon*, in *Agamemnon; Libation-Bearers; Eumenides*, trans. and ed. Alan H. Sommerstein (Cambridge, Mass.: Harvard University Press, 2008), 1649–50. For an argument about the epistemological and political import of the ship metaphor, see Hans Blumenberg, *Shipwreck with Spectator: Paradigm of a Metaphor for Existence*, trans. Steven Rendall (Cambridge, Mass.: MIT Press, 1997).

31. Plato, *Republic*, trans. Paul Shorey (Cambridge, Mass.: Harvard University Press, 2003), 488a–e.

32. Stathis Gourgouris, *Does Literature Think? Literature as Theory for an Antimythical Era* (Stanford: Stanford University Press, 2003), 133.

33. On the permutations of the relation between love and law, see Peter Goodrich, *The Laws of Love: A Brief Historical and Practical Manual* (New York: Palgrave, 2006).

34. Alcaeus, "Fragments," in *Greek Lyric: Sappho and Alcaeus*, trans., ed. D. A. Campbell (Cambridge, Mass.: Harvard University Press, 1982), vol. 1, Fr. 208. Nicole Loraux discusses this fragment in chapter 4 of Loraux, *The Divided City: On Memory and Forgetting in Ancient Athens*, trans. Corinne Pache and Jeff Fort (New York: Zone, 2006).

35. Aristotle, *The Athenian Constitution*, in *The Athenian Constitution; The Eudemian Ethics; On Virtues and Vices*, trans. H. Rackham (Cambridge, Mass.: Harvard University Press, 1935), 8.5 (trans. modified).

36. See Andrew Benjamin's *Place, Commonality and Judgment: Continental Philosophy and the Ancient Greeks* (London: Continuum, 2011).

37. I do not have the space here to go into any detail on the complex history of the concept of neighborly love. I will return to Paul in book my on "stasis," and in the meantime I will mention the following publications: For three recent approaches

to the neighbor that are informed by political theology and psychoanalysis, see Slavoj Žižek, Eric L. Santner, and Kenneth Reinhard, *The Neighbor: Three Inquiries in Political Theology* (Chicago: University of Chicago Press, 2005); for the neighbor in the context of a discussion of enmity, see Gil Anidjar, *The Jew, the Arab: A History of the Enemy* (Stanford: Stanford University Press, 2003). For the way that love continues to play a role in the philosophy of Hegel, see J. M. Bernstein, "Love and Law: Hegel's Critique of Morality," *Social Research*, 70, no. 2 (2003): 393–432.

38. I have used the Greek edition of the New Testament published by the British and Foreign Bible Society (London, 1904).

39. Friedrich Nietzsche, *On the Genealogy of Morality and Other Writings*, trans. Carol Diethe, ed. Keith Ansell-Pearson (Cambridge: Cambridge University Press, 2006), 2: 21.

40. In the extensive and rapidly growing literature on Apostle Paul, I would only like to point to Stathis Gourgouris's "The Present of a Delusion," in *Paul and the Philosophers*, ed. Ward Blanton, Creston Davis, and Hent de Vries (New York: Fordham University Press, 2013), because it traces the non-Greek aspect of Paul's universalism.

41. For the translation of *agape* into *caritas* in Augustine, see Hannah Arendt, *Love and Saint Augustine* (Chicago: University of Chicago Press, 1996).

42. Augustine, *The City of God Against the Pagans*, trans. and ed. R. W. Dyson (New York: Cambridge University Press, 1998). I quote parenthetically by book and chapter numbers.

43. Augustine is the most significant figure in determining the dogmatic account of the Fall; see Kam Shapiro, *Sovereign Nations, Carnal States* (Ithaca: Cornell University Press, 2003), 22–25, for the relation between the Fall and the creation of the concept of the human will.

44. Cf. Todd Breyfolge, "Citizenship and Signs: Rethinking Augustine on the Two Cities," in *A Companion to Greek and Roman Political Thought*, ed. Ryan K. Balot (Oxford: Blackwell, 2009), 501–25; see also Ricardo J. Quinones, *The Changes of Abel: Violence and the Lost Brother in Cain and Abel Literature* (Princeton: Princeton University Press, 1991), 35–40.

45. For a detailed discussion of sexuality in Augustine's work, see Peter Brown, "Augustine: Sexuality and Society," in *The Body and Society: Men, Women and Sexual Renunciation in Early Christianity* (New York: Columbia University Press, 1988), 387–427.

46. Jean-François Lyotard, *The Confession of Augustine*, trans. Richard Beardsworth (Stanford: Stanford University Press, 2000).

47. At this point, in order to support his argument, Augustine quotes Paul: "Even within one man, 'the flesh lusteth against the Spirit and the Spirit against the flesh'" (XV.5). The quotation from *Galatians* is, however, bent to fit Augustine's own argument. In fact the struggle between flesh and Spirit occurs shortly after

the repetition of the law of justice to love one's neighbor, but is mobilized in a very different way by Paul: "For all the law is fulfilled in one word, [even] in this; Thou shalt love thy neighbour as thyself. But if ye bite and devour one another, take heed that ye be not consumed one of another. [This] I say then, Walk in the Spirit, and ye shall not fulfil the lust of the flesh. For the flesh lusteth against the Spirit, and the Spirit against the flesh: and these are contrary the one to the other: so that ye cannot do the things that ye would" (*Galatians*, 5.14–17). Contrary to Augustine's conception, according to which the fallen city of God will never attain to the fullness of the Heavenly City in the sense that it will never be purged of passions, Paul asserts that "Walk in the Spirit, and ye shall not fulfil the lust of the flesh." In Paul's discourse of eternal, universal love, neighborly love does not lead to the distinction between the two cities of God. Conversely, Augustine requires this distinction for his eschatological temporality to be possible.

48. Augustine, *St. Augustine's Confessions*, trans. William Watts (Cambridge, Mass.: Harvard University Press, 1912), VII.19. The last sentence about the necessity of the heretic is a reference to Paul's *First Corinthians* 11:19, and it became a crucial thought in the Middle Ages.

49. William E. Connolly, *The Augustinian Imperative* (Newbury Park, Calif.: Sage, 1993), 78.

50. Connolly, *Augustinian Imperative*, 81.

3. THE PROPINQUITY OF NATURE: ABSOLUTE SOVEREIGNTY

1. Michael Foucault, *Security, Territory, Population: Lectures at the Colle'ge de France, 1977–1978*, trans. Graham Burchell, ed. Michel Senellart (New York: Palgrave Macmillan, 2007), 90. This is the fourth lecture of Foucault's course, and it is better known as the governmentality essay; see Foucault, "Governmentality," in *The Foucault Effect: Studies in Governmentality*, ed. Graham Burchell, Colin Cordon, and Peter Miller (Chicago: University Chicago Press, 1991), 87–104. I prefer to reference the lecture series, since it is a more accurate transcript of Foucault's lecture and lecture notes.

2. Thomas Hobbes, *Leviathan*, ed. Richard Tuck (Cambridge: Cambridge University Press, 1999), 124; all parenthetical references to this edition.

3. Augustine, *The City of God Against the Pagans*, trans. and ed. R.W. Dyson (New York: Cambridge University Press, 1998), Book XV, Chapter 1.

4. "Machiavelli saw the roots of political thought in its anthropological principles. The uniformity of human nature, the power of the animal instinct and the emotions, especially the emotions of love and fear and their limitlessness—these are the insights on which every consistent political thought or action, indeed every science of politics must be based. The positive imagination of the statesman, capable of calculating with facts, has its basis in this knowledge, which teaches us to

understand man as a force of nature and to overcome emotions in such a way that they bring other emotions into play"; from Wilhelm Dilthey's *Weltanschauung und Analyse des Menschen seit Renaissance und Reformation*, quoted in *The Origin of German Tragic Drama*, by Walter Benjamin, trans. John Osborne (London: Verso, 2003), 95–96.

5. Niccolò Machiavelli, *The Prince*, trans. Peter Bondanella (Oxford: Oxford University Press, 2005), parenthetical reference by chapter number.

6. The possible existence of a good person is a significant problem, not only in political philosophy, but also in philosophical anthropology; see, for instance, Hans Blumenberg's concept of the human as *Mängelwesen* in his "An Anthropological Approach to the Contemporary Significance of Rhetoric," trans. Robert M. Wallace, in *After Philosophy: End or Transformation?* ed. Kenneth Baynes, James Bohman, and Thomas A. McCarthy (Cambridge, Mass.: MIT Press, 1987), 429–58.

7. Cf. Marcia L. Colish, "Cicero's *De Officiis* and Machiavelli's *Prince*," *Sixteenth Century Journal* 9, no. 4 (1978): 84–85.

8. See Cicero, *On Duties*, ed. M. T. Griffin and E. M. Atkins (Cambridge: Cambridge University Press, 1991), I.41.

9. Jean Bodin, *On Sovereignty: Four Chapters from the Six Books of the Commonwealth*, trans. and ed. Julian H. Franklin (Cambridge: Cambridge University Press, 1992), 7.

10. E.g., see Quentin Skinner, *The Age of Reformation*, vol. 2 of *The Foundations of Modern Political Thought* (Cambridge: Cambridge University Press, 1978), 285–89.

11. For instance, Mario Turchetti claims that "[w]hen Bodin used the adjective 'absolute' to define a sovereign, he did so as a Romanist, and as an historian of Roman law for whom the word *absolutus* was linked to *legibus solutus*—the prerogative of the one who is sovereign"; Turchetti, "Jean Bodin," entry in the *Stanford Encyclopedia of Philosophy*, revision June 14, 2010, http://plato.stanford.edu/entries/bodin/, accessed August 2011.

12. For a discussion of the Renaissance context within which Bodin developed his theory, see Ann Blair, *The Theater of Nature: Jean Bodin and Renaissance Science* (Princeton: Princeton University Press, 1997).

13. Bodin, *On Sovereignty*, 7–8, emphasis added.

14. See Dieter Wyduckel, *Princeps Legibus Solutus: Eine Untersuchung zur frühmodernen Rechts- und Staatslehre* (Berlin: Duncker und Humblot, 1979).

15. Bodin, *On Sovereignty*, 56.

16. Bodin, *On Sovereignty*, 57–58.

17. Bodin, *On Sovereignty*, 50.

18. Carl Schmitt, *Political Theology: Four Chapters on the Concept of Sovereignty*, trans. George D. Schwab (Cambridge, Mass.: MIT Press, 1985), 36.

19. Plato, *Republic*, trans. Paul Shorey (Cambridge, Mass.: Harvard University Press, 2003), 338c (my translation).

20. Michael Foucault, "Man and His Double," in *The Order of Things: An Archaeology of the Human Sciences* (London: Routledge, 2002), 330–74.

21. Hobbes, *Leviathan*.

22. Carl Schmitt has argued in *The Leviathan in the State Theory of Thomas Hobbes: Meaning and Failure of a Political Symbol*, trans. George Schwab and Erna Hilfstein (1938; Westport, Conn.: Greenwood Press, 1996) for the primacy of law over right in Hobbes, which really means that the commonwealth, which comes after the state of nature, is primary in this imitative paradigm. This leads to an understanding of sovereignty as dictatorship. Conversely, Leo Strauss, in *The Political Philosophy of Hobbes: Its Basis and Its Genesis*, trans. Elsa M. Sinclair (1936; Chicago: University of Chicago Press, 1963), insists that right remains more primary than law, leading to an understanding of Hobbes as a liberal thinker. Miguel Vatter discusses these different interpretations in terms of a confrontation between political theology and liberalism: Vatter, "Strauss and Schmitt as Readers of Hobbes and Spinoza: On the Relation between Political Theology and Liberalism," *New Centennial Review* 4, no. 3 (2004): 161–214; see also C. B. Macpherson, *The Political Theory of Possessive Individualism: Hobbes to Locke* (Oxford: Clarendon Press, 1962). It is also possible to read Hobbes as a republican by denying the primacy of either law or right; see, for instance, Vickie Sullivan, *Machiavelli, Hobbes, and the Formation of Liberal Republicanism in England* (Cambridge: Cambridge University Press, 2004). Samantha Frost has also argued in *Lessons from a Materialist Thinker: Hobbesian Reflections on Ethics and Politics* (Stanford: Stanford University Press, 2008) that Hobbes's radical materialism entails a politics of intersubjectivity, thereby highlighting democratic elements in Hobbes. For another argument about Hobbes as a democratic thinker, see James Martel, *Subverting the Leviathan: Reading Thomas Hobbes as a Radical Democrat* (New York: Columbia University Press, 2007). I intend to take this debate up elsewhere, but I will only indicate here that these different positions hinge on how the transition from law to right can be understood, since Hobbes equivocates on this point.

23. The popularization of the metaphor in the Middle Ages was by John of Salisbury. For a history of ideas, see Cary J. Nederman's *Lineages of European Political Thought: Explorations Along the Medieval/Modern Divide from John of Salisbury to Hegel* (Washington, D.C.: The Catholic University of America Press, 2009).

24. Noberto Bobbio identifies the "transformation of the relation between nature and artifice" as a fundamental difference between ancient and renaissance thought. Specifically for Hobbes, the state is a machine "produced by human beings in order to compensate for the shortcomings of nature, and to replace the deficient products of nature with a product of human ingenuity, that is, an *artificium*"; Bobbio, *Thomas Hobbes and the Natural Law Tradition*, trans. Daniela Gobetti (Chicago: University of Chicago Press, 1993), 36.

25. For the vexed issue of Hobbes's relation to Christianity, see Jeffrey R. Collins, *The Allegiance of Thomas Hobbes* (Oxford: Oxford University Press, 2005). See also the exchange between Collins and Martinich in the *Journal of the History of Ideas*: A. P. Martinich, "Hobbes's Erastianism and Interpretation," *Journal of the History of Ideas* 70, no. 1 (2002): 43–63; and Jeffrey R. Collins, "Interpreting Thomas Hobbes in Competing Contexts," *Journal of the History of Ideas* 70, no. 1 (2002): 165–80.

26. See Schmitt, *The Nomos of the Earth in the International Law of the Jus Publicum Europaeum*, trans. G. L. Ulmen (New York: Telos Press, 2003).

27. Delamare's *Traite de la Police*, the first book on the police, was published in 1705, but began around forty years earlier. For a discussion of the genesis of the police and its function in the maintenance and production of social order, see Mark Neocleous, *The Fabrication of Social Order: A Critical Theory of Police Power* (London: Pluto Press, 2000).

28. As Rancière put it, the police is "first an order of bodies that defines the allocation of ways of doing, ways of being, ways of saying." In other words, the police are the regulator of the realm of means. Rancière continues that he reserves "the term *politics* for an extremely determined activity antagonistic to policing"—an antagonism that pertains to what I have called earlier dejustification; Jacques Rancière, *Disagreement: Politics and Philosophy*, trans. Julie Rose (Minneapolis: University of Minnesota Press, 1999), 29.

29. Cf. Michel Foucault's reading of the Leviathan in lecture 5 of *Society Must Be Defended: Lectures at the Collège de France 1975–1976*, trans. David Macey (New York: Picador, 2003).

30. See Horst Bredekamp, "Thomas Hobbes's Visual Strategies," in *The Cambridge Companion to Hobbes's* Leviathan, ed. Patricia Springborg (Cambridge: Cambridge University Press, 2007), 29–60; cf. also Dario Gamboni, "Composing the Body Politic: Composite Images of Political Representation, 1651–2004," in *Making Things Public: Atmospheres of Democracy*, ed. Bruno Latour and Peter Weibel (Karlsruhe: ZKM; Cambridge, Mass.: MIT Press, 2005), 162–95.

31. Schmitt, *The Leviathan in the State Theory of Thomas Hobbes*, 31.

32. For an opposing view that emphasizes the similarity of the description of civil war in Hobbes and Thucydides, see Gordon Hull, *Hobbes and the Making of Modern Political Thought* (London: Continuum, 2009), 93–98.

33. The fact that democracy is disguised as the state of nature in the *Leviathan* may be explained by the fact that, in Chapter 7 of *De Cive*, Hobbes had argued that the democracy is the first constitutional stage, before the creation of a monarchical sovereignty; Hobbes, *De Cive*, in *the Clarendon Edition of the Philosophical Works of Thomas Hobbes*, vol. 3, ed. Howard Warrender (Oxford: Clarendon, 1983).

34. The causal nature of Hobbes's argument led Leo Straus to compare his political theory to that of a mechanic: "The procedure of political philosophy is,

therefore, much [like] . . . that of the technician, who takes to pieces a machine that has broken down, removes the foreign body which prevents the functioning of the machine, puts the machine together again; and who does all this in order that the machine may function. Thus political philosophy becomes a *technique* for the regulation of the State. Its task is to alter the unstable balance of the existing State to the stable balance of the right State"; Strauss, *The Political Philosophy of Hobbes*, 152. For the antihumanist basis of this scientific impetus in Hobbes, see Quentin Skinner, *Reason and Rhetoric in the Philosophy of Hobbes* (Cambridge: Cambridge University Press, 1996).

35. In his earlier work, *Behemoth*, Hobbes had used the other monster from *Job* to describe the passions that cause civil war. It was these passions that the Leviathan puts under control; see Thomas Hobbes, *Behemoth: The History of the Causes of the Civil Wars of England, and of the Counsels and Artifices By Which They Were Carried On From the Year 1640 to the Year 1660*, in *The English Works of Thomas Hobbes of Malmesbury*, ed. William Molesworth, vol. 6 (London: John Bohn, 1839–45). For Hobbes's use of the mythical monsters, see Johan Tralau, "Leviathan, the Beast of Myth: Ledusa, Dionysos, and the Riddle of Hobbes's Sovereign Monster," in *The Cambridge Companion to Hobbes's* Leviathan, ed. Springborg, 61–81.

36. Stephen L. Collins, *From Divine Cosmos to Sovereign State: An Intellectual History of Consciousness and the Idea of Order in Renaissance England* (New York: Oxford University Press, 1989), 6.

37. Michel Foucault comments on this passage: "The tract of time designates, then, the state and not the battle, and what is at stake is not the forces themselves, but the will, a will that is sufficiently known, or in other words [endowed with] a system of representations and manifestations that is effective within this field of primal diplomacy"; Foucault, *Society Must Be Defended*, 93.

38. Quoted in Ernst Kantorowicz, *The King's Two Bodies: A Study in Mediaeval Political Theology* (Princeton, N.J.: Princeton University Press, 1970), 7.

39. Quoted in Kantorowicz, *The King's Two Bodies*, 9–10.

40. For Kantorowicz's significance in contemporary theories of sovereignty, it is useful to turn to Giorgio Agamben, who has argued in *Homo Sacer: Sovereign Power and Bare Life*, trans. Daniel Heller-Roazen (Stanford: Stanford University Press, 1998), 91 ff., that Kantorowicz's book exemplifies the "paradox of sovereignty"—namely, the "sovereign is, at the same time, outside and inside the juridical order" (15).

41. For a discussion of Kantorowicz's chapter on *Richard II*, see Anselm Haverkamp, "*Richard II*, Bracton, and the End of Political Theology," *Law and Literature* 16, no. 3 (2005): 313–26.

42. For an analysis of the English legal and political context about who can enter a contract, see Skinner, "Hobbes on Persons, Authors and Representatives," in *The Cambridge Companion to Hobbes's* Leviathan, ed. Springborg, 157–80. For an analysis of the philosophical issues of will and individuality, see Justin Clemens,

"Spinoza's Ass," in *Spinoza Now*, ed. Dimitris Vardoulakis (Minneapolis: University of Minnesota Press, 2011), 65–95.

43. Perez Zagorin writes, "Unique to Hobbes as a theorist of sovereignty was also the ingenious argument he developed in the *Leviathan* that since its subjects have authorized the sovereign power to represent and bear their person, its actions are likewise theirs; they therefore contradict themselves should they oppose an action of the sovereign, because its will expresses and contains their will"; Zagorin, *Hobbes and the Law of Nature* (Princeton: Princeton University Press, 2010), 68. This argument has recently been qualified by Suzanne Sreedhar, who argues in *Hobbes on Resistance: Defying the Leviathan* (Cambridge: Cambridge University Press, 2010) that Hobbes retains a "right to resistance" in certain cases of abuse of sovereign power.

44. I am using here the expression "natural men," following Hobbes's terminology. It should be noted, however, that the feminine has consistently been put in that position. Or, following Foucault, we can say that anyone who is designated as "abnormal" would fall into that position of exclusion.

45. William E. Connolly, *The Augustinian Imperative* (Newbury Park, Calif.: Sage, 1993), 81.

46. See, e.g., Agamben, *Remnants of Auschwitz: The Witness and the Archive*, trans. Daniel Heller-Roazen (New York: Zone, 2002); and Eric Santner, *On Creaturely Life: Rilke, Benjamin, Sebald* (Chicago: University of Chicago Press, 2006).

47. Agamben, *Homo Sacer*, 37.

48. See, for instance, Eva Geulen, *Giorgio Agamben zur Einführung* (Hamburg: Junius, 2005), 73–82.

49. See Vardoulakis, "The Ends of Stasis: Spinoza as a Reader of Agamben," *Culture, Theory and Critique* 51, no. 2 (2010): 145–56.

50. Jennifer Rust points out that Agamben has become a significant influence in approaches to highlight Shakespeare's political theology, because "*homo sacer* provides a way to explore the potential link between the most marginalized bodies within a state and the privileged body of the ruler"; Rust, "Political Theology and Shakespearean Studies," *Literature Compass* 6, no. 1 (2009): 177. Although I acknowledge here the importance of looking at these marginalized bodies, it is also important to recognize that for a radical political program the marginalized body cannot be discussed solely from within the framework or logic that marginalizes it. It is that framework itself that needs to be dejustified.

51. William Shakespeare, *Hamlet*, ed. Burton Raffel (New Haven: Yale University Press 2003); all references parenthetically by act, scene, and line number.

52. For an account of the use of the fratricide narrative in philosophical, religious, and literary contexts, see Ricardo J. Quinones, *The Changes of Abel: Violence and the Lost Brother in Cain and Abel Literature* (Princeton: Princeton University Press, 1991).

53. For discussions on the politics of succession in *Hamlet*, see Anthony J. Burton, "An Unrecognized Theme in *Hamlet*: Lost Inheritance and Claudius's Marriage to Gertrude," *The Shakespeare Newsletter* (Fall 2000): 75–78 and 82; and Stuart M. Kurland, "Hamlet and the Scottish Succession?" *Studies in English Literature, 1500–1900* 34, no. 2 (1994): 279–300. The most important of the discussions about Shakespeare making a point about his contemporary politics is Carl Schmitt's *Hamlet or Hecuba: The Intrusion of Time into the Play*, trans. David Pan and Jennifer Rust (New York: Telos, 2009); see also Jürgen Fohrmann's powerful critical reading in "Enmity and Culture: The Rhetoric of Political Theology and the Exception in Carl Schmitt," trans. Dimitris Vardoulakis, *Theory, Culture and Critique* 51, no. 2 (2010): 129–44.

54. Johann Wolfgang von Goethe, *Wilhelm Meister's Apprenticeship*, in *The Collected Works*, trans. and ed. Eric Blackall, in cooperation with Victor Lange (Princeton: Princeton University Press, 1995), 146.

55. Goethe, *Wilhelm Meister's Apprenticeship*, 146.

56. Goethe, *Wilhelm Meister's Apprenticeship*, 146.

57. This interpretation culminates in the other influential interpretation in Germany, August Schlegel's comment that Hamlet represents the self-reflective—and hence, romantic—subject; see Schlegel, *Lectures on Dramatic Art and Literature*, trans. John Black (London: G. Bell and Sons, 1902), 337.

58. Franco Moretti, "The Great Eclipse: Tragic Form as the Deconsecration of Sovereignty," trans. Susan Fischer, in *Signs Taken for Wonders: Essays in the Sociology of Literary Forms* (London: Verso, 1988), 42.

59. Cf. the graveyard scene (5.1), especially when Hamlet contemplates Yorick's skull. Yorick, as a court jester, also operates across the established hierarchies, in particular by being able to challenge and provoke the king without fear of punishment (a discourse that I cannot go into any detail here). Still holding the jester's skull, Hamlet's thought wanders to the death of great sovereigns such as Alexander and Julius Caesar.

60. Jennifer Rust has argued in "Wittenberg and Melancholic Allegory: The Reformation and Its Discontents in *Hamlet*," in *Shakespeare and the Culture of Christianity in Early Modern England*, ed. Dennis Taylor and David N. Beauregard (New York: Fordham University Press, 2003), 260–84, that the worms are also a reference to the Eucharist (261). But we can also recall that it is such an upturning of hierarchies that characterizes the political message of Rabelais, according to Bakhtin; see Mikhail Bakhtin, *Rabelais and His World*, trans. Hélène Iswolky (Bloomington: Indiana University Press, 1984). An interesting aspect of *Hamlet* that cannot be taken up here is to what extent the operative presence this upturning of hierarchies that characterizes comedy can challenge the perception of *Hamlet* as a tragedy—or, rather, that can allow us to discover the strong comic elements in the drama.

61. There are several attempts to explain the presence of this scene within the play. For instance, according to a structural interpretation, the scene is required in order to indicate a passage of time between Hamlet's encounter with the ghost and his perception of being mad in the following scene (Act 2, Scene 2); see, e.g., Eleanor Prosser, *Hamlet and Revenge* (Stanford: Stanford University Press, 1971), 145–47. But this amounts to saying that there is simply a scene whose whole function is to disguise the lack of adequate characterization for Hamlet—that is, the lack of an adequate explanation of why he went mad. In fact, the majority of the interpretations of the scene argue that it functions to delineate either the character of Polonius or that of Laertes; e.g., for the argument for Polonius, see Maurice Charney, *Hamlet's Fictions* (London: Routledge, 1988), 135–36; and James L. Calderwood, *To Be and Not To Be: Negation and Metadrama in Hamlet* (New York: Columbia University Press, 1983), 16. For the argument for Laertes, see Bert O. States, *Hamlet and the Concept of Character* (Baltimore: John Hopkins University Press, 1992), 121–23. But this leads to the further problem of why to devote an entire scene to such secondary characters. Ultimately, all the interpretations of Act 2, Scene 1 that I have been able to consult do not offer a convincing justification for the presence of the scene in the play.

62. I would like to thank Bonnie Honig for pointing out that this sentence can be read as a reference to the ode to man from *Antigone*.

63. For an account of Elizabethan cosmology, see E. M. W. Tillyard, *The Elizabethan World Picture* (Harmondsworth, UK: Penguin, 1982). This cosmology is also reliant on the Christian bifurcation of man's two qualities, his being in the image of God and his being made of clay and becoming dust after death, or what has been referred to as the "homo duplex." For an influential discussion of this duality in the human and its relation to religion, see Emile Durkheim's *The Elementary Forms of Religious Life*, trans. Carol Cosman (Oxford: Oxford University Press, 2001).

64. It is because I want to insist on the impossibility of the two accounts of creaturely life—one asserting sovereignty while the other deconstructing it—that my reading of *Hamlet* differs from Julia Lupton's powerful interpretation, to which I am otherwise deeply indebted, in Lupton, "Hamlet, Prince: Tragedy, Citizenship, Political Theology," in *Alternative Shakespeares*, ed. Diana Henderson (London: Routledge, 2007), 3:181–203. According to Lupton, there are two political axes that define the play's coordinates. The "longitudinal" refers to the high and low movements that I will be describing in detail in a moment and that constitute sovereignty, whereas the "latitudinal" defines relations outside sovereignty, such as friendship, *demos*, and election (187). Lupton argues that *Hamlet*, pace Carl Schmitt's interpretation, conforms more to the latter understanding of the political—that is, the political is understood more in terms of friendship than in terms of sovereignty. But Lupton does not explore the incompatibility between the two. For

instance, Lupton argues that, at the end of the play, Hamlet's "hard-won sovereignty is not based *exclusively* [emphasis added] on kingship and kinship (*pace* Schmitt), but rather on friendship and citizenship in their emancipatory promise" (198). Lupton hesitates making the inference that I want to make here—namely, that what she calls friendship or what I call the creaturely as excess in matter of fact deconstruct sovereignty because they function as its impossible-to-erase and yet infectious supplement. In other words, it is not simply a choice between sovereignty and friendship/creature as excess; rather, sovereignty is, even without knowing it, from the beginning, friendship.

65. See Sigmund Freud, "Mourning and Melancholia," in *Penguin Freud Library* (Harmondsworth. UK: Penguin, 1991), 11:251–68. For the political significance of melancholia, see Rebecca Comay, "The Sickness of Tradition: Between Melancholia and Fetishism," in *Walter Benjamin and History*, ed. Andrew Benjamin (London: Continuum, 2005), 88–101.

66. Walter Benjamin, *The Origin of German Tragic Drama*, 146. For a reading of Benjamin's engagement with Hamlet, see Andrew Curtofello, "'Hamlet Could Never Know the Peace of a "Good Ending"': Benjamin, Derrida and the Melancholy of Critical Theory," in *Nostalgia for a Redeemed Future: Critical Theory*, ed. Stefano Giacchetti Ludoviski (Rome: John Cabot University Press, 2009), 199–216.

67. Benjamin, *Origin of German Tragic Drama*, 142.

68. Benjamin, *Origin of German Tragic Drama*, 71.

4. REVOLUTION AND THE POWER OF LIVING: POPULAR SOVEREIGNTY

1. It was not until the eighteenth century that Montesquieu clearly articulated the distinction of power for the first time in his discussion of the legal system in England in Part 2, Chapter 6 of Montesquieu, *The Spirit of the Laws*, trans. Anne M. Cohler, Basia Carolyn Miller, and Harold Samuel Stone (Cambridge: Cambridge University Press, 1989). The chapter opens with the following statement: "In each state there are three sorts of powers: legislative power, executive power over the things depending on the right of nations, and executive power over the things depending on civil right" (156).

2. Foucault explains the nineteenth-century resurgence of interest in Machiavelli's question of governance in terms of the emergence of the problematic of revolution; Michel Foucault, *Security, Territory, Population: Lectures at the Collège de France, 1977–1978*, trans. Graham Burchell, ed. Michel Senellart (New York: Palgrave Macmillan, 2007), 90.

3. Jean-Jacques Rousseau, *Discourse on Political Economy* and *The Social Contract*, trans. Christopher Betts (Oxford: Oxford University Press, 1994); all references to this edition parenthetically in the text.

4. Bonnie Honig points that in the following sentence Rousseau qualifies this statement by saying this does not entail that what the people want is always right. Honig comments: "Here Rousseau evidences an anxiety that plagues most radical democrats who agitate to give the people power. Popular sovereignty is supposed to *solve* the problems of (il)legitimacy and arbitrariness. But once the people have power, that 'solution' suddenly looks like a problem, for the people, too, can be a source of arbitrariness"; Honig, *Democracy and the Foreigner* (Princeton: Princeton University Press, 2001), 19. We will examine shortly this democratic paradox in Rousseau.

5. This is a conclusion with which Hobbes would have happily agreed: "whosoever has right to the End, has the right to the Means"; Thomas Hobbes, *Leviathan*, ed. Richard Tuck (Cambridge: Cambridge University Press, 1999).

6. Hannah Arendt, *On Revolution* (London: Penguin, 2006), 225.

7. See, on the notion of the refoundation of the revolution, J. M. Bernstein's "Promising and Civil Disobedience: Arendt's Political Modernism," in *Thinking in Dark Times: Hannah Arendt on Ethics and Politics*, ed. Roger Berkowitz, Jeffrey Katz, and Thomas Keenan (New York: Fordham University Press, 2010), 115–27.

8. Arendt, *On Revolution*, 224.

9. Arendt, *On Revolution*, 150.

10. Arendt, *On Revolution*, 116.

11. Arendt, *On Revolution*, 210. For a discussion of the discourse on freedom in *On Revolution*, see Joan B. Landes, "*Novus Ordo Saeclorum*: Gender and Public Space in Arendt's Revolutionary France," in *Feminist Interpretations of Hannah Arendt*, ed. Bonnie Honig (University Park: Pennsylvania State University Press, 1995), 195–219.

12. Jean-Jacques Rousseau, *Discourse on the Origin of Inequality*, trans. Franklin Philip (Oxford: Oxford University Press, 1994), 82.

13. It is of course well-known that, despite his insistence on a modern concept of sovereignty in his political theory, Rousseau's general will is derived from theology; see Patrick Riley, *The General Will before Rousseau: The Transformation of the Divine into the Civic* (Princeton: Princeton University Press, 1986). Jacques Maritain argues in fact that the general will is a perversion of the gospel; Maritain, *Three Reformers: Luther, Descartes, Rousseau* (New York: Thomas Crowell, 1970), 142.

14. Honig, *Emergency Politics: Paradox, Law, Democracy* (Princeton: Princeton University Press, 2009), xvi.

15. Honig, *Emergency Politics*, xvii.

16. Honig, *Emergency Politics*, 15.

17. Honig, *Emergency Politics*, 38–39.

18. I indicated earlier that unlike Hobbes, Rousseau does not rely on a causal chain of emotions that lead from hope to fear. Yet fear remains a dominant emotion in Rousseau. Jacques Derrida cites a passage from the beginning of the *Essay*

on the *Origins of Language* in which Rousseau argues that the savage man's initial reaction in encountering a stranger will have to be fear. Derrida comments: "Does the example of fear come by chance? Does not the metaphoric origin of language lead us necessarily to a situation of threat, distress, and dereliction, to an archaic solitude, to the anguish of dispersion? Absolute fear then would be the first encounter of the other as *other*: as other than I and as other than itself. I can answer the threat of the other as other (than I) only by transforming it into another (than itself), through altering it my fear, in my imagination, or my desire. . . . Fear would thus be the first passion"; Jacques Derrida, *Of Grammatology*, trans. Gayatri Chakravorty Spivak (Baltimore: Johns Hopkins University Press, 1997), 277. I argue here that this archaic, first passion not only does not disappear with the creation of society and the formation of the social contract; rather, the fear is repressed, and therefore all the more intensified. And it is sublimated in the figure of the outlaw.

19. Riley does not indicate in *The General Will before Rousseau* any influence of the juridico-theological metaphor of the king's two bodies on the general will. But the argument here, more generally, is that the king's two bodies are mirrored in the distinction between public and private. Martin Muslow, in "The Libertine's Two Bodies: Moral *Persona* and Free Thought in Early Modern Europe," *Intellectual History Review* 18, no. 3 (2008): 337–47, argues that we can find a "strange parallel (and counter-) history" (346) to the king's two bodies in, among others, Pufendorf's natural law distinction between the private and the public (339–40).

20. In a book that was published after this chapter was written, Eric Santner shows that the tradition of the king's two bodies can be reformulated in the register of popular sovereignty; see Santner, *The Royal Remains: The People's Two Bodies and the Endgames of Sovereignty* (Chicago: University of Chicago Press, 2011). Santner does not discuss Rousseau except to mention in passing that Kenneth Reinhardt suggested in conversation that the general will can be discussed in the purview of the theory he develops in his book (see the note on xxi).

21. Louis Althusser, *Politics and History: Montesquieu, Rousseau, Marx*, trans. Ben Brewster (London: NLB, 1972), 130.

22. Althusser, *Politics and History*, 129.

23. All references to the English translations of Spinoza's works are to Baruch Spinoza, *Complete Works*, trans. Samuel Shirley, ed. Michael L. Morgan (Indianapolis: Hackett, 2002). References will be provided parenthetically in the text. References to the Latin are to the edition of Spinoza's *Opera quae supersunt omnia*, ed. Carolus Hermannus Bruder (Leipzig: Bernhardi Tauchnitz, 1843–1846). When there is a reference to the *Opera*, it will follow the parenthetical reference to the *Complete Works*, separated by a forward slash.

24. See, e.g., Susan James's *Spinoza on Philosophy, Religion, and Politics: The Theologico-Political Treatise* (Oxford: Oxford University Press, 2012), where she

shows the way that Spinoza constructs his argument about the law being human-made.

25. Milad Doueihi describes the difference between the two positions through a juxtaposition of Augustine's theologico-political discourse of grace to a secularized discourse of election developed Spinoza; see Doueihi, *Augustine and Spinoza*, trans. Jane Marie Todd (Cambridge, Mass.: Harvard University Press, 2010).

26. For Spinoza's critique of teleology, see Michael Mack's *Spinoza and the Specters of Modernity: The Hidden Enlightenment of Diversity from Spinoza to Freud* (London: Continuum, 2010); and Mack, "Toward an Inclusive Universalism: Spinoza's Ethics of Sustainability," in *Spinoza Now*, ed. Dimitris Vardoulakis (Minneapolis: University of Minnesota Press, 2011), 99–134.

27. Benoit Frydman, in "Divorcing Power and Reason: Spinoza and the Founding of Modern Law," *Cardozo Law Review*, 25, no. 2 (2003): 607–25, shows how the equivalent of the distinction between state law and the law of natural in jurisprudence—namely, the distinction between positive and natural law—is central in the creation of modern law. He also argues that Spinoza was a central figure in the distinction between positive and natural law: "Spinoza . . . played a major role in the shaping of modern law, which rests upon the *summa divisio* between, on one hand, natural law, embedded in natural reason and discovered *more geometrico*, and, on the other hand, positive law, which expresses the will of the sovereign power" (608).

28. This agonism presupposes that passions are not eliminated from the social contract. This point, which allows for an initial differentiation with Hobbes, has been noted in secondary literature; see, for instance, Aurelia Armstrong, "Natural and Unnatural Communities: Spinoza beyond Hobbes," *British Journal for the History of Philosophy* 17, no. 2 (2009): 279–305.

29. See also Vardoulakis, "Spinoza's Empty Law: The Possibility of Political Theology," in *Spinoza Beyond Philosophy*, ed. Beth Lord (Edinburgh: Edinburgh University Press, 2012), 135–48.

30. Moira Gatens and Genevieve Lloyd, *Collective Imaginings: Spinoza, Past and Present* (London: Routledge, 1999), 92.

31. According to Alexandre Lefebvre, Deleuze also creates a positive image of the law, or what he calls "jurisprudence," by developing a similar conception of its parallel contingency and necessity; see Lefebvre, *The Image of Law: Deleuze, Bergson, Spinoza* (Stanford: Stanford University Press, 2008), 58–59.

32. For these two different conceptions of duty—either as adherence to rules or as linked to responsibility—see Vardoulakis, "Spectres of Duty: The Politics of Silence in Ibsen's *Ghosts*," *Orbis Litterarum* 64, no. 1 (2009): 50–74. It can argued that these two different conceptions of duty mirror the distinction between ethics and morality that Gilles Deleuze draws, for instance, in Deleuze, *Spinoza: Practical Philosophy*, trans. Robert Hurley (San Francisco: City Lights, 1988).

33. Deleuze is correct to observe that the use of the word or the image "God" can offer one the possibility of "maximum emancipation" form religion; see Deleuze's seminar on Spinoza delivered on November 25, 1980, available at www .webdeleuze.com, accessed August 2010. Louis Althusser explains Spinoza's use of the term "God" as a strategic ruse: "He began with God, and deep down inside . . . he was . . . an atheist. A supreme strategy: he began by taking over the stronghold of his adversary, or rather he established himself as if he were his own adversary, therefore not suspected of being the sworn adversary, and redisposed the theoretical fortress in such a way as to turn it completely around, as one turns around cannons against the fortress's own occupant"; Althusser, "The Only Materialist Tradition, Part I: Spinoza," in *The New Spinoza*, ed. Warren Montag and Ted Stolze (Minneapolis: University of Minnesota Press, 1997), 9–10.

34. As I will also explain later, the "necessary rebel" in Spinoza forms part of the tradition of the exigency of participation that characterizes the Greek conception of the political. This exigency entails, first, that political actions are linked to the pursuit of truth and, second, that those who can make true inferences are entitled to rebellion. As Aristotle encapsulates this point in *Politics*, "of all men those who excel in virtue would most justifiably stir up rebellion"; Aristotle, *Politics*, trans. H. Rackham (Cambridge, Mass.: Harvard University Press, 1998), 1301a–b. Spinoza's necessary rebel is Aristotle's man of virtue (*areti*). H. L. A. Hart fully recognizes the centrality of this tradition for any conception of the law: "At any given moment the life of any society which lives by rules, legal or not, is likely to consist in a tension between those who, on the one hand, accept and voluntarily cooperate in maintaining the rules . . . and those who, on the other hand, reject the rules. . . . One of the difficulties facing any legal theory anxious to do justice to the complexity of the facts is to remember the presence of both these points of view"; H. L. A. Hart, *The Concept of Law* (Oxford: Oxford University Press, 1982), 88. Needless to say, such assertions by Spinoza and Aristotle are incompatible with the liberal insistence on tolerance, as it is expressed, for instance, in Locke's "Letter on Toleration."

35. For a more detailed argument about the notion of political theology in Spinoza, as well as a comparison to the discipline of political theology that arose through Carl Schmitt's work, see Vardoulakis, "Spinoza's Empty Law."

36. Étienne Balibar, *Spinoza and Politics*, trans. Peter Snowdon (London: Verso, 1998), 68.

37. The way that power is articulated in terms of the distinction between natural and man-made law is crucial for what Hasana Sharp calls "the politics of renaturalization"; see her *Spinoza and the Politics of Renaturalization* (Chicago: University of Chicago Press, 2011).

38. Power as possibility refers to potentia, not to potestas. For the distinction between the two senses of power, see Antonio Negri's *The Savage Anomaly, The*

Savage Anomaly: The Power of Spinoza's Metaphysics and Politics, trans. Michael Hardt (Minneapolis: University of Minnesota Press, 2002).

39. See Deleuze, *Expressionism in Philosophy: Spinoza*, trans. Martin Joughin (New York: Zone Books, 1992).

40. Alexandre Matheron, "The Theoretical Function of Democracy in Spinoza and Hobbes," in *The New Spinoza*, ed. Warren Montag and Ted Stolze (Minneapolis: University of Minnesota Press, 1997), 216.

41. For an important work on the relation between freedom and necessity that looks at Spinoza, see Genevieve Lloyd, *Providence Lost* (Cambridge, Mass.: Harvard University Press, 2008). Lloyd discovers the roots of the nexus of freedom and necessity in Stoic thought.

42. Warren Montag has also shown how the nexus of freedom and necessity links the arguments of the *Tractatus Theologico-Politicus* and the *Ethics*; see, e.g., Montag, *Bodies, Masses, Power: Spinoza and his Contemporaries* (London: Verso, 1999), 56–58.

43. Negri has been the most important philosopher who has argued for the privileging of *potentia* over *potestas*. Cesare Casarino challenges Negri to clarify this position in Casarino and Negri, *In Praise of the Common: A Conversation on Philosophy and Politics* (Minneapolis: University of Minnesota Press, 2008).

44. References to the *Tractatus Politicus* in the *Collected Works* are by chapter number, followed by paragraph number. Warren Montag has persuasively shown that the insistence in Chapter 16 of the *Tractatus Theologico-Politicus* that "right equals power displaces the individual from the center of political analysis." Montag continues that the "argument breaks off in chapters 16 and 17 [of the *Tractatus Theologico-Politicus*], pauses, and then resumes only at [the *Tractatus Politicus*]"; Montag, "Who's Afraid of the Multitude? Between the Individual and the State," *South Atlantic Quarterly* 104, no. 4 (2005): 659.

45. For a discussion of this proposition, see Alexander García Düttmann, "A Matter of Life and Death: Spinoza and Derrida," in *Spinoza Now*, ed. Vardoulakis, 351–62.

46. Edwin Curley correctly observes that this position is a challenge to the entire contractarian tradition: "If no contract is binding unless it is useful, then the supposed social contract can play no real part in founding the sovereign's right to command"; Curley, Kissinger, "Spinoza and Genghis Khan," in *The Cambridge Companion to Spinoza*, ed. Don Garrett (Cambridge: Cambridge University Press, 1997), 324.

47. Immanuel Kant, *Groundwork of the Metaphysics of Morals*, trans. Mary Gregor (Cambridge: Cambridge University Press, 2002), 15.

48. It has often being pointed out that this discussion in the *Tractatus Theologico-Politicus* contradicts Proposition 72 from Part IV of the *Ethics*, where Spinoza writes, "The Free man never acts deceitfully, but always in good faith"

(357); see, e.g., Henry E. Allison, *Benedict de Spinoza: An Introduction* (New Haven: Yale University Press, 1987), 158–59; and Firmin DeBrabander, *Spinoza and the Stoics: Power, Politics and the Passions* (London: Continuum, 2008), 81–82. However, as the Scholium to the same proposition of the *Ethics* makes clear, Spinoza's argument views lying in terms of the means that it affords both the individual and society—it does not rely on any kind of adherence to an ideal. For a discussion of this point, as well as a more extensive discussion of lying in Spinoza compared to Kant's account of lying, see Dimitris Vardoulakis, "The Freedom to Lie," forthcoming.

49. Arthur Jacobson has observed the elimination of justification in Spinoza's theory of right: "Spinoza's approach [propels his] account of the nature and foundation of right entirely away from justification"; Jacobson, "Law Without Authority: Sources of the Welfare State in Spinoza's *Tractatus Theologico-Politicus*," *Cardozo Law Review* 25, no. 2 (2003): 675.

50. Derrida, *Rogues: Two Essays on Reason*, trans. Pascale-Anne Brault and Michael Nass (Stanford: Stanford University Press, 2005), xiv.

51. Derrida, *Rogues*, 30–31.

52. Heinrich von Kleist, "Michael Kohlhaas," in *The Marquise of O—And Other Stories*, trans. David Luke and Nigel Reeves (Harmondsworth, UK: Penguin, 1978). I have been using the German edition of the Kleist-Archiv Sembdner edition, published on March 24, 2003, http://www.kleist.org/texte/MichaelKohlhaasL.pdf, accessed May 2009. All page references parenthetically. When there is a reference to the German edition, it is separated by a forward slash, and it follows the reference to the English edition.

53. Cf. Andreas Gailus, *Passions of the Sign: Revolution and Language in Kant, Goethe, and Kleist* (Baltimore: Johns Hopkins University Press, 2006), 110.

54. Carl Schmitt, *The Theory of the Partisan: A Commentary/Remark on the Concept of the Political*, trans. A. C. Goodson, *The New Centennial Review* 4, no. 3 (2004): 65.

55. Schmitt, *Partisan*, 5. Schmitt's argument can, of course, be used by any revolutionary to *justify* his actions—it is an argument about justification. For instance, Yasser Arafat used the same principle to distinguish between a revolutionary and a terrorist in his famous address to the United Nations on November 13, 1974: "The difference between the revolutionary and the terrorist lies in the reason for which each fights. For whoever . . . fights for freedom and liberation of his land . . . cannot possibly be called terrorist"; downloaded from http://www.mideastweb.org/arafat _at_un.htm, accessed October 8, 2010.

56. Schmitt, *The Concept of the Political*, trans. George D. Schwab (Chicago: University of Chicago Press, 1996).

57. Christiane Frey observes, *pace* Schmitt, that "it is difficult to image in a text that better exemplifies the paradox of the state of exception" (9); Frey, "The Excess

of Law and Rhetoric in Kleist's Michael Kohlhaas," *Phrasis: Studies in Language and Literature* 47, no. 1 (2006): 9–18.

58. Wolfgang Wittkowski has argued that the background to the decision to take the law into his own hand was the Prussian law reforms; Wittkowski, "Is Kleist's Michael Kohlhaas a Terrorist? Luther, Prussian Law Reform and the Accountability of Government," *Historical Reflections* 26, no. 3 (2000): 471–86.

59. As J. Hillis Miller observes, the "interview with Luther is profoundly ironic" (94), given that Kohlhaas had been acting the way the young Luther had acted; Miller, "Laying Down the Law in Literature: Kleist," in *Topographies* (Stanford: Stanford University Press, 1995).

60. If that is the case, if there is indeed a desire in Kohlhaas to be placed within the law, then the opposite of what Hélène Cixous avers is in fact the case—namely, that Kohlhaas does not resist "castration in an absolute way" (45), but rather desires to be castrated, desires to be placed under the law; in Hélène Cixous, *Readings: The Poetics of Blanchot, Joyce, Kafka, Kleist, Lispector, and Tsvetayeva*, trans. Verena Andermatt Conley (Minneapolis: University of Minnesota Press, 1991).

61. This accords with Kohlhaas himself issuing "an edict [to the Junker] in which, by virtue of the authority inborn in him [*kraft der ihm angebotenen Macht*]" (137/16–17) for the restoration of his two horses to their previous state, or "what he called a 'Declaration under the Writ of Kohlhaas'" in which he called upon the country to withhold all aid and comfort from Junker Wenzel von Tronka" (140). In the second part of the novella Kohlhaas presents himself as a sovereign, as a "foreign invading power," and not as a warrior of a just cause.

62. Henry Sussman, *The Aesthetic Contract: Statutes of Art and Intellectual Work in Modernity* (Stanford: Stanford University Press, 1997), 112–13; see also 132–33.

63. Carol Jacobs refers to this parallel narrative as "a tale within a tale"; Jacobs, *Uncontainable Romanticism: Shelley, Bronte, Kleist* (Baltimore: Johns Hopkins University Press, 1989), 221. I would rather avoid this expression, because it is analogous to "a state within a state" that would usually refer to different written or religious laws within a single state. The different space indicated here, however, is not simply legal, but rather the contingency that makes law possible.

64. In the secondary literature, the majority of criticism castigates the last part of the novella as poor writing because all the accidents appear as ad hoc. For instance, to refer to only one example, see Robert E. Helbling, "The Search for Justice," in *The Major Works of Heinrich von Kleist* (New York: New Directions, 1975), 193–209. Even though it is true that too many accidents do not make for a good plot, as anyone who has taught or attended a creative writing class knows, still Kleist can be seen here to subvert this law of narrative in order to make a political point about sovereignty.

65. Cf. Gailus, *Passions of the Sign*, 128.

5. DEMOCRACY AND ITS OTHER: BIOPOLITICAL SOVEREIGNTY

1. Walter Benjamin, "On the Concept of History," *Selected Writings*, ed. Michael W. Jennings, et al. (Cambridge, Mass.: Belknap, 2003), 4:392.

2. Carl Schmitt, *Political Theology: Four Chapters on the Concept of Sovereignty*, trans. George D. Schwab (Cambridge, Mass.: MIT Press, 1985), 5.

3. For a comparison on Benjamin and Schmitt's use of the exception, see Samuel Weber, "Taking Exception to the Decision: Walter Benjamin and Carl Schmitt," *Diacritics* 22 (1992): 5–18. For a discussion about their relation, see Horst Bredekamp, "From Walter Benjamin to Carl Schmitt via Thomas Hobbes," trans. Melissa Thorson Hause and Jackson Bond, *Critical Inquiry* 25 (1999): 247–66.

4. The term "biopolitics" has received different definitions in the hands of different philosophers. I will concentrate here primarily on Michael Foucault. The reason is not only that he invented the name "biopolitics"; moreover, I believe that he holds the more complex position about biopolitics—perhaps because that position was never fully developed, but presented provisionally mostly through his lectures. For a significant overview of the most important contribution to biopolitics, see Thomas Lemke, *Biopolitics: An Advanced Introduction* (New York: New York University Press, 2011).

5. Michael Foucault, *The Will to Knowledge*, vol. 1 of *The History of Sexuality*, trans. Robert Hurley (London: Penguin, 1990).

6. Roberto Esposito, *Bíos: Biopolitics and Philosophy*, trans. Timothy Campbell (Minneapolis: University of Minnesota Press, 2008), 145.

7. E.g., see Giorgio Agamben, *Homo Sacer: Sovereign Power and Bare Life*, trans. Daniel Heller-Roazen (Stanford: Stanford University Press, 1998), 178–80.

8. David Hume, *Dialogues Concerning Natural Religion and Other Writings*, ed. Dorothy Coleman (Cambridge: Cambridge University Press, 2007), 69.

9. Agamben, *Homo Sacer*, 37.

10. Foucault, *Discipline and Punish: The Birth of the Prison*, trans. Alan Sheridan (Harmondsworth, UK: Penguin, 1979).

11. This sense of the inescapability of biopolitics is described very well in Tiqqun's *Introduction to Civil War*, trans. Alexander R. Galloway and Jason E. Smith (Los Angeles: Semiotext(e), 2010).

12. See, e.g., Agamben, *State of Exception*, trans. Kevin Attell (Chicago: University of Chicago Press, 2005).

13. Agamben, *Remnants of Auschwitz: The Witness and the Archive*, trans. Daniel Heller-Roazen (New York: Zone, 2002), 156.

14. Jacques Derrida, *The Beast and the Sovereign*, trans. Geoffrey Bennington (Chicago: University of Chicago Press, 2009), 1:330–31. For a critique of this apocalyptic rhetoric in Agamben, see also Jacques Rancière, "Who Is the Subject of the Rights of Man?" *South Atlantic Quarterly* 103, nos. 2–3 (2004): 297–310.

15. Walter Benjamin, "On the Concept of History," 392.

16. Walter Benjamin, *The Arcades Project*, trans. Howard Eiland and Kevin McLaughlin (Cambridge, Mass.: Belknap, 1999).

17. See Charles Rice, *The Emergence of the Interior: Architecture, Modernity, Domesticity* (London: Routledge, 2007).

18. Schmitt, *The Crisis of Parliamentary Democracy*, trans. Ellen Kennedy (Cambridge, Mass.: MIT Press, 1988), 51.

19. Karl Marx, *The Eighteenth Brumaire of Louis Bonaparte*, trans. Clemens Dutt, in *Collected Works*, vol. 11 (New York: International Publishers, 1976). All references to this edition in-text parenthetically.

20. In the reading of the *Eighteenth Brumaire* here I will avoid addressing altogether the complex question of whether the text presents a causality of events amounting to a "scientific" Marxism, as Engels wants to insist in his prologue, or conversely whether themes such as alienation are predominant. These are important questions for a study of Marx, but I would like to concentrate here on how sovereignty is registered in the text. For an analysis of the ambiguous relation between a scientific Marxism and the exuberant rhetoric of Marx in the *Eighteenth Brumaire*, see Dominick LaCapra, *Rethinking Intellectual History: Texts, Contexts, Language* (Ithaca: Cornell University Press, 1983), 268–90. Also, for a useful history of the reception of the *Eighteenth Brumaire*, see Donald Reid, "Inciting Readings and Reading Cites: Visits to Marx's *The Eighteenth Brumaire of Louis Bonaparte*," *Modern Intellectual History* 4, no. 3 (2007): 545–70.

21. Kojin Karatani, *Transcritique: On Kant and Marx*, trans. Sabu Kohso (Cambridge, Mass.: MIT Press, 2003), 144.

22. Karatani, *Transcritique*, 149.

23. Karatani, *Transcritique*, 151.

24. Naomi Klein has recently described how neoliberalism has used the same technique in order to implement economic reforms that, under normal circumstances, would have been unpalatable to the population. Naomi attributes this "shock doctrine" to Milton Friedman, who argued that "Only a crisis—actual or perceived—produces real change"; Friedman, quoted in Klein, *The Shock Doctrine: The Rise of Disaster Capitalism* (New York: Metropolitan Books and Henry Holt, 2007), 140.

25. Marx, *The Class Struggles in France 1848 to 1850*, in *Collected Works* (New York: International Publishers, 1976), 10:62.

26. Marx, *The Class Struggles in France*, 62

27. Marx, *The Class Struggles in France*, 63.

28. On Roman fashion and the French revolution, cf. Walter Benjamin's Thesis XIV from "On the Concept of History," 395. For a reading, see Andrew Benjamin, "Being Roman Now," *Thesis Eleven* 75 (2003): 39–53.

29. See also Derrida, *Spectres of Marx: The State of Debt, the Work of Mourning, and the New International*, trans. Peggy Kamuf (New York: Routledge, 1994).

30. On the relation between Marx and Spinoza, see Cesare Casarino, "Marx Before Spinoza: Notes Toward an Investigation," in *Spinoza Now*, ed. Dimitris Vardoulakis (Minneapolis: University of Minnesota Press, 2011), 179–234; and Eugene Holland, "Spinoza and Marx," *Cultural Logic* 2, no. 1 (1998), http://clogic.eserver.org/2-1/holland.html, accessed June 2006.

31. See Kiarina Kordela, *$urplus: Spinoza, Lacan* (New York: SUNY, 2007).

32. There is a complex history to the use of the term "dictatorship of the proletariat" by Marx. The phrase is used for the first time in *Class Struggles in France*, published in installments in 1850. Weydemeyer adopted this expression as the title of an article that he wrote for *Turn-Zeitung*, a New York periodical. The article was published in January 1, 1852; see Joseph Weydemeyer, "The Dictatorship of the Proletariat," trans. Horst Duhnke and Hal Draper, *Labor History* 3, no. 2 (1962): 214–17. Hal Draper argues that "Weydemeyer did not grasp the idea of a class dictatorship, however many times Marx had underlined that term," and that's what motivated Marx to return to the term in the March 1852 letter in the context of discussing the *Eighteenth Brumaire*; Draper, *The "Dictatorship of the Proletariat" from Marx to Lenin* (New York: Monthly Review Press, 1987), 28.

33. In fact, it was Lenin's *The State and Revolution* that was responsible for the popularization of the concept of the dictatorship of the proletariat; see Vladimir Lenin, *Essential Works of Lenin: "What Is to Be Done?" and Other Writings*, ed. Henry M. Christman (New York: Dover, 1987). For a reading of Lenin's book, see Étienne Balibar, *On the Dictatorship of the Proletariat*, trans. Grahame Lock (London: NLB, 1977).

34. Karl Kautsky, *The Dictatorship of the Proletariat*, trans. H. J. Stenning (Westport, Conn.: Greenwood Press, 1981), 43.

35. Marx to Josef Weydemeyer, 5 March 1852, in Marx, *Collected Works* (New York: International Publishers, 1976), 39:62.

36. Marx to Josef Weydemeyer, 62–63.

37. For a discussion of the institution of dictatorship as opposed to tyrannical government, see Andreas Kalyvas, "The Tyranny of Dictatorship: When the Greek Tyrant Met the Roman Dictator," *Political Theory* 35, no. 4 (2007): 412–42. For instance, Kalyvas writes: "The dictator denoted a legal and regular though extraordinary magistracy intended to protect the public good in moments of crisis and danger; tyranny designated an unjust and violent power, the destruction of the common interest, and the downfall of legality and freedom" (416).

38. I borrow the figure of awakening from Walter Benjamin; see *The Arcades Project*, trans. Howard Eiland and Kevin McLaughlin (Cambridge, Mass.: Belknap, 1999), "Konvolut K," for instance: "The compelling—the drastic—experience, which refutes everything 'gradual' about becoming and shows all seeming 'development' to be dialectical reversal, eminently and thoroughly composed, is the awakening from dream" (K1, 3).

39. In fact, Shakespeare's text says "said," instead of "burrowed." Marx's mistakes indicate that he was concerned with the position of the Ghost beneath the stage.

40. Marx to Josef Weydemeyer, 63.

41. For the utopian potential of a stage where everyone is invited, see my analysis of the last chapter of Kafka's *America* in Dimitris Vardoulakis, "'The Fall Is the Proof of Our Freedom': Mediated Freedom in Kafka," in *Freedom and Confinement in Modernity: Kafka's Cages*, ed. Kiarina Kordela and Dimitris Vardoulakis (New York: Palgrave, 2011), 87–106.

42. A transcript of the debate can be read online at "Human Nature: Justice versus Power—Noam Chomsky Debates with Michel Foucault," http://www.chomsky .info/debates/1971xxxx.htm; accessed September 2009.

43. Foucault, *The Will to Knowledge*, 135.

44. As Keith Baker summarizes this point, a "democratized sovereignty serves the ends of surveillance by destroying the obstacles hindering the development of disciplinary society"; Baker, "A Foucauldian Account of the French Revolution?" in *Foucault and the Writing of History*, ed. Jan Goldstein (Oxford: Blackwell, 1994), 204. I will argue later, however, that a different notion of the democratic can be gleaned from Foucault's writings—perhaps, even, despite Foucault's reservations.

45. Foucault, "Nietzsche, Genealogy, and History," in *The Essential Works of Foucault, Volume II: 1954–84*, ed. James Faubion (London: Penguin Books, 2000), 369.

46. Foucault, "What Is Enlightenment?" in *Essential Works of Foucault 1954–1984*, vol. 1, *Ethics*, trans. R. Hurley, et al., ed. Paul Rabinow (Harmondsworth, UK: Penguin, 1997), 316.

47. The case becomes more complex if we also consider Foucault's activism, interviews, and a series of public addresses that he made. For instance, Paul Patton makes a persuasive argument about Foucault's use of a human right's discourse by looking at such writings; see Patton, "Foucault, Critique and Rights," *Critical Horizons* 6, no. 1 (2005): 268–87. However, even in Patton's account, Foucault is not presented as making a positive description of a democratic conception of power. Rather, the discourse of rights is described in oppositional terms. For instance, Patton argues that Foucault's conception of right "is normative in the sense that these should provide *effective counter-arguments* to the techniques, justifications and goals of disciplinary power" (283, emphasis added). Patton further elaborates: "[T]he normative bases of the critique of disciplinary power must come from within the liberal tradition of government. . . . [A]ppeals to new rights or new forms of right will always rely upon concepts that may be found within or derived from existing discourses of moral or political right. Critical appeals to new rights or new forms of right will always be incremental and experimental" (284). In this account, any democratic appeal to rights is seen as a reaction to established

relations of power that are oppressive. Thus critique is an effect of sovereignty. In the argument I pursue here, I want to explore the possibility of reversing this relation. Is it possible to argue that sovereignty is an effect of critique and of the democratic?

48. Foucault, "Governmentality," in *The Foucault Effect: Studies in Governmentality*, ed. Graham Burchell, Colin Cordon, and Peter Miller (Chicago: Chicago University Press, 1991), 95. This is in fact a lecture that Foucault delivered as part of his course *Security, Territory, Population* in 1977–78, which was published only recently in its entirety; see Foucault, *Security, Territory, Population: Lectures at the Collège de France, 1977–1978*, trans. Graham Burchell, ed. Michel Senellart (New York: Palgrave Macmillan, 2007). I am quoting from the earlier edition, which has been the reference of the extensive discussions on governmentality in the secondary literature. Governmentality here is used as a synonym of biopolitics. Even though it is not in dispute that Foucault's conception of biopolitics is related to that of governmentality, it is much harder to say exactly what the difference between the two might be. Paul Rabinow and Nikolas Rose suggest that the name changes as Foucault refines his theory, especially as he "distanced himself from the view that such power over life is unambiguously nefarious"; Rabinow and Rose, "Biopower Today," *BioSocieties* 1 (2006): 200.

49. Foucault, "Governmentality," 102. For a discussion of the implications of this passage, see Ben Golder and Peter Fitzpatrick, *Foucault's Law* (London: Routledge, 2009), 33–34.

50. Foucault, *The Will to Knowledge*, 142.

51. Mark Bevir also argues in "Foucault and Critique: Deploying Agency against Autonomy," *Political Theory* 27, no. 1 (1999): 65–84, that biopower "incorporates all of sovereignty" (71).

52. Foucault, *Society Must Be Defended: Lectures at the Collège de France 1975–1976*, trans. David Macey (New York: Picador, 2003). All references are provided parenthetically within the text.

53. For a philosophical account of the genesis of the modern conception of the pathological, see Georges Canguilhem, *The Normal and the Pathological*, trans. Carolyn R. Fawcett (New York: Zone Books, 1991); see also Nikolas Rose, "Life, Reason and History: Reading Georges Canguilhem Today," *Economy and Society* 27, nos. 2–3 (1998): 154–70.

54. Ian Hacking, *The Taming of Chance* (Cambridge: Cambridge University Press, 1990).

55. A number of influential philosophers, including Charles Taylor, Jürgen Habermas, and Nancy Fraser, have criticized Foucault on the grounds that he collapses the distinction between power and knowledge. For an examination of these critiques as well as a reply, see Tom Keenan, "The 'Paradox' of Knowledge and Power: Reading Foucault on a Bias," *Political Theory* 15, no. 1 (1987): 5–37.

56. As Walter Benjamin puts it, "The true goal of Haussmann's projects was to secure the city against civil war. He wanted to make the erection of barricades in Paris impossible for all time"; Benjamin, *The Arcades Project*, 12.

57. Foucault has been criticized for failing to reconcile the skepticism of this theoretical works with the optimistic, affirmative rhetoric of his political engagement. For instance, Rebecca Comay laments: "Ironically, the outcome of Foucault's regionalism [that is, the critique of particular technologies of power] may prove to be a kind of isolation and ultimately another form of confinement"; Comay, "Excavating the Repressive Hypothesis: Aporias of Liberation in Foucault," in *Michel Foucault: Critical Assessments*, ed. Barry Smart (London: Routledge, 1994), 3:247. In the terms of the present study, dejustification does not offer an adequate account of the political. It is possible, nonetheless, to read Foucault in such as way as to show that he insisted on the primacy of agonism and resistance over biopower. For instance, Bevir argues that power according to Foucault "can exist only where people have the capacity to act freely, and so only where they can resist that power"; Bevir, "Foucault and Critique," 73. This observation implies the move that I am making here—namely, that agonistic resistance implies a space that is more primary than sovereignty in either of its three forms outlined here—or, differently put, sovereignty is an effect of the agonistic and the democratic.

58. Cosima Marriner, "Abortion Couple Not Aware They Broke Law," *Sydney Morning Herald*, September 19, 2009, available at http://www.smh.com.au/national/abortion-couple-not-aware-they-broke-law-20090918-fvcg.html, accessed September 2009.

59. "Queensland Criminal Code ACT 1899," section 225, 121–22, available at www.legislation.qld.gov.au/legisltn/current/c/crimincode.pdf, accessed October 2010.

60. George Williams, "Abortion Law Stuck in the 19th Century," *Sydney Morning Herald*, 12 October 2010, available at http://www.smh.com.au/opinion/society-and-culture/abortion-law-stuck-in-the-19th-century-20101011-16fwq.html, accessed 12 October 2010. Williams is Professor of Law at the University of New South Wales.

61. To be more precise, the Federal Parliament voted to give control of the regulation of RU486 to the Therapeutic Goods Administration, the body that regulates pharmaceuticals in Australia.

62. It should be noted that, according to traditional Christian dogma, the soul does not enter the body until forty days after birth, and does not leave the earth until forty days after death—recall Jesus's ascension forty days after his death (*Acts* 1:9–11).

63. Quoted in Stephanie Small, "Abortion Trial Sparks Legislation Debate," ABC News, 14 October 2010, http://www.abc.net.au/news/stories/2010/10/14/3038708.htm.

64. Foucault, *Will to Knowledge*, 59. For a review of the use of confession in Foucault's work in general, see Graham Burchell, "Confession, Resistance, Subjectivity," *Journal for Cultural Research*, 13, no. 2 (2009): 159–77.

65. Sergei Prozorov makes a similar argument about a Foucaultian conception of political freedom in *Foucault, Freedom and Sovereignty* (Aldershot, UK: Ashgate, 2007). According to Prozorov, "what renders freedom political is its a priori antagonistic nature with regard to every positive form of order" (9). In other words, it is the antagonism between life and control that makes freedom possible. Prozorov continues: "If freedom is political in this sense, then it must logically precede any positive order of politics" (10). As Prozorov makes clear, this logical priority does not refer to a renewed search for foundations, but rather to an ontological understanding of the political. Lois McNay recognizes this dual aspect of freedom in Foucault—both antagonistic and ontological: "The freedom of the individual from the government of individualization is not grounded in metanarratives of justice or morality but must take the form of a principle of permanent self-critique and experimentation. This relation to self is in no sense a recovery of authentic experience or an assertion of genuine identity, rather it is a liminal process which seeks to explore ways of being beyond the already known"; McNay, "Self as Enterprise: Dilemmas of Control and Resistance in Foucault's *The Birth of Biopolitics*," *Theory, Culture and Society* 26, no. 6 (2009): 67. Prozorov and McNay agree that Foucaultian resistance can be ontologically grounded without thereby lapsing into counter-resistance.

66. Foucault, "Revolutionary Action: 'Until Now,'" in *Language, Counter-Memory, Practice*, ed. Donald L. Bouchard (Ithaca: Cornell University Press, 1977), 230.

67. Foucault himself has often been accused of having been a victim of counter-resistance. Kevin Thompson has proposed that Foucault solves this problem in his later work, when he shifts to the model of the "care of the self"; see Thompson, "Forms of Resistance: Foucault on Tactical Reversal and Self-formation," *Continental Philosophy Review* 36 (2003): 113–38.

68. Elizabeth Stewart puts the biopolitical transformation of Michael Kohlhaas in Michael K. as follows: "Coetzee quotes Kleist's fire, I believe, and transforms it into the fire of cremation that symbolizes the state of emergency that has become continuous: not in the sense of the threat to political sovereignty (as in Kleist), but rather in the sense of the state asserting continuously and rhythmically its total and annihilating authority by way of a totally pervasive 'management' of the lives (and deaths) of creatures"; Stewart, "Broken Sovereignties: J. M. Coetzee's Ethics of Anxiety and Disarray," *The International Journal of the Humanities* 3, no. 5 (2005/2006): 157–64 (here, 158); see also Peter Horn, "Michael K.: Pastiche, Parody or the Inversion of Michael Kohlhaas," *Current Writing* 17, no. 2 (2005): 56–73.

69. Michael Hardt and Antonio Negri, *Empire* (Cambridge, Mass.: Harvard University Press, 2000), 203.

70. Hardt and Negri, *Empire*, 204.

71. Hardt and Negri, *Empire*, 204.

72. See, e.g., the last part of Hardt and Negri, *Multitude: War and Democracy in the Age of Empire* (New York: Penguin, 2004).

73. Hardt and Negri, *Empire*, 205 and 393.

74. I discuss this theological vision of a community without restrictions in relation to Kafka's "Nature Theatre of Oklahoma" in Vardoulakis, "'The Fall Is the Proof of Our Freedom': Mediated Freedom in Kafka," in *Freedom and Confinement in Modernity: Kafka's Cages*, ed. Kiarina Kordela and Dimitris Vardoulakis (New York: Palgrave, 2011), 87–106.

75. Catherine Mills, in "Life Beyond Law: Biopolitics, Law and Futurity in Coetzee's *Life and Times of Michael K.*," *Griffith Law Review* 15, no. 1 (2006): 177–95, also conducts a reading of the novella through biopolitics, but she relies on Agamben's, instead of Foucault's, conception of biopolitics.

76. On the relation of the civil war and racism in Foucault, see David Macey, "Some Reflections on Foucault's *Society Must Be Defended* and the Idea of 'Race'," in *Foucault in the Age of Terror: Essays on Biopolitics and the Defence of Society*, ed. Stephen Norton and Stephen Bygrave (New York: Palgrave, 2008), 118–32; on the same topic, see also Simon Dawes's interview with Macey on Fanon, Foucault and Race, on the *Theory, Culture and Society* blog, http://theoryculturesociety.blogspot .com/2011/01/interview-with-david-macey-on-fanon.html, published 5 January 2011, accessed June 2011.

77. J. M. Coetzee, *Life and Times of Michael K.* (London: Vintage, 2004). All references to this edition are included parenthetically in the text.

78. David Attwell, *J. M. Coetzee: South Africa and the Politics of Writing* (Berkeley: University of California Press, 1993), 92–93, references a range of articles that accused *Life and Times of Michael K.* of not referring explicitly enough to the political situation of its time.

79. Even though there are no explicit references to the color of the characters' skin throughout the novel, there are implicit references. I have identified the following ones:

> The climb brought a flush to his [Visagie's grandson] skin. (62)
> the captain, the big blonde man. (91)
> a florid-faced woman in a polka-dot dress, the wife, I think, of one of the NCOs. (133)
> "Where were you brought up, monkey?" shouted the farmer. (87)
> "And I'm locking up these monkeys with you!" (92)
> "Otherwise why would they leave this monkey here?" K overheard. (123)
> "So, what's this about, monkey?" he said. (124)

> They want to hear about all the cages I have lived in, as if I were a budgie or a
> white mouse or a monkey. (181)

All these references are to figures of power who want to control Michael K. But these are too allusive to make this the main topic. Even the uses of the pejorative "monkey" are not emphasized. Instead, what is emphasized is Michael K's lip and his "idiocy." (I will come back to this in a moment.)

80. Coetzee, quoted in David Attwell, *J. M. Coetzee: South Africa and the Politics of Writing*, 91. Derek Attridge offers an explanation that is close to the position that I hold here: "What, though, of the features of these novels that seem to invite the allegorical reading that I am resisting? Why is one novel set in an indeterminate time and place, and the other in the future, for instance? [I.e., readings that seek to find a correspondence between the events in the fiction and the historical reality.] Rather than accepting the carping answer that was common when these works appeared—that Coetzee wished to avoid having the novels read as pertaining closely to the South Africa of his time . . . I would argue that his aim is to put his characters, and therefore his readers, in situations of peculiar intensity, stripped of the often distracting detail of historical reference. These situations are nevertheless entirely relevant to the South Africa of the time of writing, though not only to that time and place. . . . K's hare lip is less an allegorical indicator of the handicaps suffered by certain sectors of the South African population than an important part of the causal chain that has produced the particular individual he is revealed to be during the events of the novel"; Attridge, *J. M. Coetzee and the Ethics of Reading: Literature in the Event* (Chicago: University of Chicago Press, 2004), 58–59. For a critical engagement with Attridge's position, see Gert Buelens and Dominik Hoens, "'Above and Beneath Classification': *Bartleby, Life and Times of Michael K.*, and Syntagmatic Participation," *Diacritics* 37, nos. 2–3 (2007): 157–70.

81. King James Bible, 1 Cor. 3:18–19. For a discussion of the holy fool, see John Saward, *Perfect Fools: Folly for Christ's Sake in Catholic and Orthodox Spirituality* (Oxford: Oxford University Press, 1980). There are several remarkable literary presentations of the holy fool in Dostoevsky.

82. This is a discourse that even distorts the name—the doctor says "Michaels"—of its subject.

83. King James Bible, Gen. 1:28.

84. The politico-legal concept of terra nullius registers this theological dimension. Terra nullius arises out of the reference in the Genesis that is taken to mean that any uncultivated territory can become the "dominion" of whichever sovereign power claims it. This was a crucial theologico-political justification for the colonialist project; see, for instance, Andrew Fitzmaurice, "The Genealogy of *Terra Nullius*," *Australian Historical Studies* 129 (2006), 1–15.

85. Jean-Jacques Rousseau, *Discourse on the Origin of Inequality*, trans. Franklin Philip (Oxford: Oxford University Press, 1994), 55.

86. The concept of deterritorialization develops in a number of texts that Gilles Deleuze and Felix Guattari coauthored, such as *Anti-Oedipus: Capitalism and Schizophrenia*, trans. Robert Hurley, et al (London: Athlone Press, 2000)—the first book in which the term is used.

87. For another reading of the novella that emphasizes the importance of the now, see Sarah Dove Heider, "The Timeless Ecstasy of Michael K.," in *Black/White Writing: Essays on South African Literature*, ed. Pauline Fletcher (Lewisburg, Penn.: Bucknell University Press, 1993), 83–98.

88. Catherine Mills provides a similar interpretation of the end of the novella. According to Mills, Michael K.'s stance brings "about the conditions under which life can be maintained." Mills further contends that the conception of temporality at the end of the novella "allows no figuration of the form of the future—not even the romanticism of gardening—but instead can only gesture toward a space in which there is indeed 'time enough for everything,' in which what comes may be happy or it may be monstrous, but in any case it is always 'to-come' in the Derridean sense, unbidden, unforeseen and undetermined"; Mills, "Life Beyond Law," 193.

BIBLIOGRAPHY

Aeschylus. *Agamemnon; Libation-Bearers; Eumenides*. Translated and edited by Alan H. Sommerstein. Cambridge, Mass: Harvard University Press, 2008.

Agamben, Giorgio. *Homo Sacer: Sovereign Power and Bare Life*. Translated by Daniel Heller-Roazen. Stanford: Stanford University Press, 1998.

———. *Remnants of Auschwitz: The Witness and the Archive*. Translated by Daniel Heller-Roazen. New York: Zone, 2002.

———. *State of Exception*. Translated by Kevin Attell. Chicago: University of Chicago Press, 2005.

Agnew, John. *Globalization and Sovereignty*. Lanham, Md.: Rowman and Littlefield, 2009.

Alcaeus, "Fragments." Edited and translated by D. A. Campbell. In *Greek Lyric: Sappho and Alcaeus*. Cambridge. Mass.: Harvard University Press, 1982.

Allison, Henry E. *Benedict de Spinoza: An Introduction*. New Haven: Yale University Press, 1987.

Althusser, Louis. *Politics and History: Montesquieu, Rousseau, Marx*. Translated by Ben Brewster. London: NLB, 1972.

———. "The Only Materialist Tradition, Part I: Spinoza." In *The New Spinoza*, ed. Warren Montag and Ted Stolze, 3–19. Minneapolis: University of Minnesota Press, 1997.

Anidjar, Gil. *The Jew, the Arab: A History of the Enemy*. Stanford: Stanford University Press, 2003.

Arafat, Yasser. "Speech Before the United Nations. November 13, 1974." Downloaded from http://www.mideastweb.org/arafat_at_un.htm. Accessed 8 October 2010.

Arendt, Hannah. *Love and Saint Augustine*. Chicago: University of Chicago Press, 1996.

———. *On Revolution*. London: Penguin, 2006.

———. *On Violence*. New York: Harcourt, 1970.

Aristotle. *The "Art" of Rhetoric.* Translated by J. H. Freese. Cambridge, Mass.: Harvard University Press, 1926.

———. *The Athenian Constitution; The Eudemian Ethics; On Virtues and Vices.* Translated by H. Rackham. Cambridge, Mass.: Harvard University Press, 1935.

———. *Politics.* Translated by H. Rackham. Cambridge, Mass.: Harvard University Press, 1998.

Armstrong, Aurelia. "Natural and Unnatural Communities: Spinoza beyond Hobbes." *British Journal for the History of Philosophy* 17, no. 2 (2009): 279–305.

Attridge, Derek. *J. M. Coetzee and the Ethics of Reading: Literature in the Event.* Chicago: University of Chicago Press, 2004.

Attwell, David. *J. M. Coetzee: South Africa and the Politics of Writing.* Berkeley: University of California Press, 1993.

Augustine. *The City of God Against the Pagans.* Translated and edited by R.W. Dyson. New York: Cambridge University Press, 1998.

———. *St. Augustine's Confessions.* Translated by William Watts. Cambridge, Mass.: Harvard University Press, 1912.

Baker, Keith. "A Foucauldian Account of the French Revolution?" In *Foucault and the Writing of History,* edited by Jan Goldstein, 187–205. Oxford: Blackwell, 1994.

Bakhtin, Mikhail. *Rabelais and His World.* Translated by Hélène Iswolky. Bloomington: Indiana University Press, 1984.

Balibar, Étienne. "Gewalt." In *Historisch-kritisches Wörterbuch des Marxismus,* edited by W. F. Haug, 5:1270–1307. Berlin: Argument, 2001.

———. *On the Dictatorship of the Proletariat.* Translated by Grahame Lock. London: NLB, 1977.

———. *Spinoza and Politics.* Translated by Peter Snowdon. London: Verso, 1998.

———. "Subjection and Subjectivation." In *Supposing the Subject,* edited by Joan Copjec, 1–15. London: Verso, 1994.

Barbour, Charles. "The Sovereign Without Domain: Georges Bataille and the Ethics of Nothing." In *The Politics of Nothing: Sovereignty and Modernity,* edited by Clare Monagle and Dimitris Vardoulakis, 37–49. London: Routledge, 2013.

Barmash, Pamela. *Homicide in the Biblical World.* Cambridge: Cambridge University Press, 2005.

Bartelson, Jens. *A Genealogy of Sovereignty.* Cambridge: Cambridge University Press, 1995.

Bataille, Georges. *The Accursed Share: An Essay on General Economy.* Translated by Robert Hurley. Vols. 1–3. New York: Zone Books, 1988–1991.

Bauman, Zygmunt. *Modernity and Ambivalence.* Cambridge: Polity, 1991.

Beaulac, Stéphane. *The Power of Language in the Making of International Law: The Word Sovereignty in Bodin and Vattel and the Myth of Westphalia.* Leiden: Martinus Nijhoff, 2004.

Benjamin, Andrew. "Being Roman Now." *Thesis Eleven* 75 (2003): 39–53.
———. *Place, Commonality and Judgment: Continental Philosophy and the Ancient Greeks*. London: Continuum, 2011.
———. "Placing Speaking: Notes on the First Stasimon of Sophocles' Antigone." *Angelaki* 9, no. 2 (2004): 55–66.
———. *The Plural Event: Descartes, Hegel, Heidegger*. London: Routledge, 1993.
Benjamin, Walter. *The Arcades Project*. Translated by Howard Eiland and Kevin McLaughlin. Cambridge, Mass.: Belknap, 1999.
———. "Critique of Violence." Translated by Edmund Jephcott. In *Selected Writings*, edited by Marcus Bullock and Michael W. Jennings, 1:236–52. Cambridge, Mass.: Belknap, 2002.
———. "On the Concept of History." In *Selected Writings*, edited by Michael W. Jennings, et al., 4:389–400. Cambridge, Mass.: Belknap, 2003.
———. *The Origin of German Tragic Drama*. Translated by John Osborne. London: Verso, 2003.
———. "The Task of the Translator." In *Selected Writings*, edited by Marcus Bullock and Michael W. Jennings, 1:253–63. Cambridge, Mass.: Belknap, 1997.
Bernstein, J. M. "Love and Law: Hegel's Critique of Morality." *Social Research* 70, no. 2 (2003): 393–432.
———. "Promising and Civil Disobedience: Arendt's Political Modernism." In *Thinking in Dark Times: Hannah Arendt on Ethics and Politics*, edited by Roger Berkowitz, Jeffrey Katz, and Thomas Keenan, 115–27. New York: Fordham University Press, 2010.
Bevir, Mark. "Foucault and Critique: Deploying Agency against Autonomy." *Political Theory* 27, no. 1 (1999): 65–84.
Blair, Ann. *The Theater of Nature: Jean Bodin and Renaissance Science*. Princeton: Princeton University Press, 1997.
Blumenberg, Hans. "An Anthropological Approach to the Contemporary Significance of Rhetoric." Translated by Robert M. Wallace. In *After Philosophy: End or Transformation?* edited by Kenneth Baynes, James Bohman, and Thomas A. McCarthy, 429–58. Cambridge, Mass.: MIT Press, 1987.
———. *Shipwreck with Spectator: Paradigm of a Metaphor for Existence*. Translated by Steven Rendall. Cambridge, Mass.: MIT Press, 1997.
"boat-people.org," http://www.boat-people.org/. Accessed July 2011.
Bobbio, Noberto. *Thomas Hobbes and the Natural Law Tradition*. Translated by Daniela Gobetti. Chicago: University of Chicago Press, 1993.
Bodin, Jean. *On Sovereignty: Four Chapters from the Six Books of the Commonwealth*. Translated and edited by Julian H. Franklin. Cambridge: Cambridge University Press, 1992.
Borradori, Giovanna. *Philosophy in a Time of Terror: Dialogues with Jürgen Habermas and Jacques Derrida*. Chicago: University of Chicago Press, 2003.

Bredekamp, Horst. "From Walter Benjamin to Carl Schmitt via Thomas Hobbes." Translated by Melissa Thorson Hause and Jackson Bond. *Critical Inquiry* 25 (1999): 247–66.

————. "Thomas Hobbes's Visual Strategies." In *The Cambridge Companion to Hobbes's Leviathan*, edited by Patricia Springborg, 29–60. Cambridge: Cambridge University Press, 2007.

Breyfolge, Todd. "Citizenship and Signs: Rethinking Augustine on the Two Cities." In *A Companion to Greek and Roman Political Thought*, edited by Ryan K. Balot, 501–25. Oxford: Blackwell, 2009.

Brook, Peter. *The Empty Space*. New York, Atheneum, 1968.

Brown, Peter. *The Body and Society: Men, Women and Sexual Renunciation in Early Christianity*. New York: Columbia University Press, 1988.

Brown, Wendy. *Walled States, Waning Sovereignty*. New York: Zone Books, 2010.

Buelens, Gert, and Dominik Hoens. "'Above and Beneath Classification': *Bartleby, Life and Times of Michael K.*, and Syntagmatic Participation." *Diacritics* 37, nos. 2–3 (2007): 157–70.

Bull, Hedley. *The Anarchical Society: A Study of Order in World Politics*. 3rd ed. New York: Palgrave, 2002.

Burchell, Graham. "Confession, Resistance, Subjectivity." *Journal for Cultural Research* 13, no. 2 (2009): 159–77.

Burton, Anthony J. "An Unrecognized Theme in *Hamlet*: Lost Inheritance and Claudius's Marriage to Gertrude." *The Shakespeare Newsletter* (Fall 2000): 75–82.

Butler, Judith. *Antigone's Claim: Kinship Between Life and Death*. New York: Columbia University Press, 2000.

————. "Critique, Coercion, and Sacred Life in Benjamin's 'Critique of Violence.'" In *Political Theologies: Public Religions in a Post-Secular World*, edited by Hent de Vries and Lawrence E. Sullivan, 201–19. New York: Fordham University Press, 2006.

————. "Indefinite Detention." In *Precarious Life: The Powers of Mourning and Violence*, 50–100. London: Verso, 2004.

Calderwood, James L. *To Be and Not To Be: Negation and Metadrama in Hamlet*. New York: Columbia University Press, 1983.

Canguilhem, Georges. *The Normal and the Pathological*. Translated by Carolyn R. Fawcett. New York: Zone Books, 1991.

Casarino, Cesare. "Marx Before Spinoza: Notes Toward an Investigation." In *Spinoza Now*, edited by Dimitris Vardoulakis, 179–234. Minneapolis: University of Minnesota Press, 2011.

Casarino, Cesare, and Antonio Negri. *In Praise of the Common: A Conversation on Philosophy and Politics*. Minneapolis: University of Minnesota Press, 2008.

Chanter, Tina. *Ethics of Eros*. London: Routledge, 1995.

Charney, Maurice. *Hamlet's Fictions*. London: Routledge, 1988.

Chomsky, Noam, and Michel Foucault. "Human Nature: Justice versus Power. Noam Chomsky Debates with Michel Foucault, 1971." Transcript of debate at http://www.chomsky.info/debates/1971xxxx.htm. Accessed September 2009.

Cicero. *On Duties*. Edited by M. T. Griffin and E. M. Atkins. Cambridge: Cambridge University Press, 1991.

Cixous, Hélène. *Readings: The Poetics of Blanchot, Joyce, Kafka, Kleist, Lispector, and Tsvetayeva*. Translated by Verena Andermatt Conley. Minneapolis: University of Minnesota Press, 1991.

Clemens, Justin. "Spinoza's Ass." In *Spinoza Now*, edited by Dimitris Vardoulakis, 65–95. Minneapolis: University of Minnesota Press, 2011.

Coetzee, J. M. *Life and Times of Michael K*. London: Vintage, 2004.

Colish, Marcia L. "Cicero's *De Officiis* and Machiavelli's *Prince*." *Sixteenth Century Journal* 9, no. 4 (1978): 80–93.

Collins, Jeffrey R. *The Allegiance of Thomas Hobbes*. Oxford: Oxford University Press, 2005.

———. "Interpreting Thomas Hobbes in Competing Contexts." *Journal of the History of Ideas* 70, no. 1 (2002): 165–80.

Collins, Stephen L. *From Divine Cosmos to Sovereign State: An Intellectual History of Consciousness and the Idea of Order in Renaissance England*. New York: Oxford University Press, 1989.

Comay, Rebecca. "Excavating the Repressive Hypothesis: Aporias of Liberation in Foucault." In *Michel Foucault: Critical Assessments*, edited by Barry Smart, 3:242–50. London: Routledge, 1994.

———. "The Sickness of Tradition: Between Melancholia and Fetishism." In *Walter Benjamin and History*, edited by Andrew Benjamin, 88–101. London: Continuum, 2005.

Connolly, William E. *The Augustinian Imperative*. Newbury Park, Calif.: Sage, 1993.

Curley, Edwin. "Kissinger, Spinoza and Genghis Khan." In *The Cambridge Companion to Spinoza*, edited by Don Garrett, 313–42. Cambridge: Cambridge University Press, 1997.

Curtofello, Andrew. "'Hamlet Could Never Know the Peace of a "Good Ending"': Benjamin, Derrida and the Melancholy of Critical Theory." In *Nostalgia for a Redeemed Future: Critical Theory*, edited by Stefano Giacchetti Ludoviski, 199–216. Rome: John Cabot University Press, 2009.

Dawes, Simon. "Interview with David Macey on Fanon, Foucault and Race." *Theory, Culture and Society* blog: http://theoryculturesociety.blogspot.com/2011/01/interview-with-david-macey-on-fanon.html. Published 5 January 2011. Accessed June 2011.

DeBrabander, Firmin. *Spinoza and the Stoics: Power, Politics and the Passions*. London: Continuum, 2008.

Deleuze, Gilles. *Expressionism in Philosophy: Spinoza.* Translated by Martin Joughin. New York: Zone Books, 1992.

———. Seminar on Spinoza, 25 November 1980, available at www.webdeleuze.com. Accessed August 2010.

———. *Spinoza: Practical Philosophy.* Translated by Robert Hurley. San Francisco: City Lights, 1988.

Deleuze, Gilles, and Felix Guattari. *Anti-Oedipus: Capitalism and Schizophrenia.* Translated by Robert Hurley, et al. London: Athlone Press, 2000.

Derrida, Jacques. "Autoimmunity: Real and Symbolic Suicides." In *Philosophy in a Time of Terror: Dialogues with Jürgen Habermas and Jacques Derrida,* by Giovanna Borradori, 85–136. Chicago: University of Chicago Press, 2003.

———. *The Beast and the Sovereign.* Vol. 1. Translated by Geoffrey Bennington. Chicago: University of Chicago Press, 2009.

———. "Force of Law: The 'Mystical Foundation of Authority.'" Translated by Mary Quaintance. *Gardozo Law Review* 11 (1990): 919–1045.

———. *Of Grammatology.* Translated by Gayatri Chakravorty Spivak. Baltimore: Johns Hopkins University Press, 1997.

———. *Of Hospitality: Anne Dufourmantelle Invites Jacques Derrida to Respond.* Translated by Rachel Bowldy. Stanford: Stanford University Press, 2000.

———. *Politics of Friendship.* Translated by George Collins. Verso: London, 1997.

———. *Rogues: Two Essays on Reason.* Translated by Pascale-Anne Brault and Michael Nass. Stanford: Stanford University Press, 2005.

———. *Spectres of Marx: The State of Debt, the Work of Mourning, and the New International.* Translated by Peggy Kamuf. New York: Routledge, 1994.

———. "Unconditionality or Sovereignty: The University at the Frontiers of Europe." Translated by Peggy Kamuf. *Oxford Literary Review* 31, no. 2 (2009): 115–31.

———. "Violence and Metaphysics: An Essay on the Thought of Emmanuel Levinas." In *Writing and Difference,* translated by Allan Bass, 97–192. London: Routledge, 2002.

Detienne, Marcel. "The Gods of Politics in Early Greek Cities." In *Political Theologies: Public Religions in a Post-Secular World,* edited by Hent de Vries and Lawrence E. Sullivan, 91–101. New York: Fordham University Press, 2006.

Dolan, Chris J. *In War We Trust: The Bush Doctrine and the Pursuit of Just War.* Burlington, Vt.: Ashgate, 2005.

Doueihi, Milad. *Augustine and Spinoza.* Translated by Jane Marie Todd. Cambridge, Mass.: Harvard University Press, 2010.

Draper, Hal. *The "Dictatorship of the Proletariat" from Marx to Lenin.* New York: Monthly Review Press, 1987.

Dumm, Thomas L. "The Problem of 'We': Or, The Persistence of Sovereignty." *Boundary 2* 26, no. 3 (1999): 55–61.

Durkheim, Emile. *The Elementary Forms of Religious Life*. Translated by Carol Cosman. Oxford: Oxford University Press, 2001.

Düttmann, Alexander García. "A Matter of Life and Death: Spinoza and Derrida." In *Spinoza Now*, edited by Dimitris Vardoulakis, 351–62. Minneapolis: University of Minnesota Press, 2011.

———. *At Odds with AIDS: Thinking and Talking About a Virus*. Translated by Peter Gilgen and Conrad Scott-Curtis. Stanford: Stanford University Press, 1996.

Esposito, Roberto. *Bíos: Biopolitics and Philosophy*. Translated by Timothy Campbell. Minneapolis: University of Minnesota Press, 2008.

Fenves, Peter. *The Messianic Reduction: Walter Benjamin and the Shape of Time*. Stanford: Stanford University Press, 2011.

Fitzmaurice, Andrew. "The Genealogy of *Terra Nullius*." *Australian Historical Studies* 129 (2006): 1–15.

Fohrmann, Jürgen. "Enmity and Culture: The Rhetoric of Political Theology and the Exception in Carl Schmitt." Translated by Dimitris Vardoulakis. *Theory, Culture and Critique* 51, no. 2 (2010): 129–44.

Foucault, Michel. *Discipline and Punish: The Birth of the Prison*. Translated by Alan Sheridan. Harmondsworth, UK: Penguin, 1979.

———. "Governmentality." In *The Foucault Effect: Studies in Governmentality*, edited by Graham Burchell, Colin Cordon, and Peter Miller, 87–104. Chicago: University of Chicago Press, 1991.

———. *History of Madness*. Translated by J. Murphy, edited by Jean Khalfa. London: Routledge, 2006.

———. "Nietzsche, Genealogy, and History." In *The Essential Works of Foucault, Volume II: 1954–84*, edited by James Faubion, 369–93. London: Penguin Books, 2000.

———. *The Order of Things: An Archaeology of the Human Sciences*. London: Routledge, 2002.

———. "Revolutionary Action: 'Until Now.'" In *Language, Counter-Memory, Practice*, edited by Donald L. Bouchard, 218–34. Ithaca: Cornell University Press, 1977.

———. *Security, Territory, Population: Lectures at the Colle'ge de France, 1977–1978*. Translated by Graham Burchell, edited by Michel Senellart. New York: Palgrave Macmillan, 2007.

———. *Society Must Be Defended: Lectures at the Collège de France 1975–1976*. Translated by David Macey. New York: Picador, 2003.

———. "What Is Enlightenment?" Translated by R. Hurley, et al. In *Essential Works of Foucault 1954–1984*, vol. 1, *Ethics*, edited by Paul Rabinow, 303–19. Harmondsworth, UK: Penguin, 1997.

———. *The Will to Knowledge*, Vol. 1 of *The History of Sexuality*. Translated by Robert Hurley. London: Penguin, 1990.

Freud, Sigmund. *Civilization and its Discontents*. In *The Standard Edition of the Complete Psychological Works*, edited and translated by James Strachey, 21:57–146. London: Hogarth, 1953–74.

———. "Mourning and Melancholia." In *Penguin Freud Library*, 11:251–68. Harmondsworth, UK: Penguin, 1991.

Frey, Christiane. "The Excess of Law and Rhetoric in Kleist's Michael Kohlhaas." *Phrasis: Studies in Language and Literature* 47, no. 1 (2006): 9–18.

Frost, Samantha. *Lessons from a Materialist Thinker: Hobbesian Reflections on Ethics and Politics*. Stanford: Stanford University Press, 2008.

Frydman, Benoit. "Divorcing Power and Reason: Spinoza and the Founding of Modern Law." *Cardozo Law Review* 25, no. 2 (2003): 607–25.

Gailus, Andreas. *Passions of the Sign: Revolution and Language in Kant, Goethe, and Kleist*. Baltimore: Johns Hopkins University Press, 2006.

Gamboni, Dario. "Composing the Body Politic: Composite Images of Political Representation, 1651–2004." In *Making Things Public: Atmospheres of Democracy*, edited by Bruno Latour and Peter Weibel, 162–95. Karlsruhe: ZKM; Cambridge, Mass.: MIT Press, 2005.

Gatens, Moira, and Genevieve Lloyd. *Collective Imaginings: Spinoza, Past and Present*. London: Routledge, 1999.

Geulen, Eva. *Giorgio Agamben zur Einführung*. Hamburg: Junius, 2005.

Goethe, Johann Wolfgang von. *Wilhelm Meister's Apprenticeship*. In *The Collected Works*. Translated and edited by Eric Blackall, in cooperation with Victor Lange. Princeton: Princeton University Press, 1995.

Golder, Ben, and Peter Fitzpatrick. *Foucault's Law*. London: Routledge, 2009.

Goodrich, Peter. *The Laws of Love: A Brief Historical and Practical Manual*. New York: Palgrave, 2006.

Gourgouris, Stathis. *Does Literature Think? Literature as Theory for an Antimythical Era*. Stanford: Stanford University Press, 2003.

———. "The Present of a Delusion." In *Paul and the Philosophers*, ed. Ward Blanton, Creston Davis, and Hent de Vries. New York: Fordham University Press, 2013.

Gurnham, David. "'The Otherness of the Dead': The Fates of Antigone, Narcissus, and the Sly Fox, and the Search for Justice." *Law and Literature* 16, no. 3 (2005): 327–51.

Hacking, Ian. *The Taming of Chance*. Cambridge: Cambridge University Press, 1990.

Hamacher, Werner. "Afformative Strike: Benjamin's 'Critique of Violence.'" In *Destruction and Experience*, edited by Andrew Benjamin and Peter Osborne, 108–36. Manchester, UK: Clinamen, 2000.

Hanssen, Beatrice. *Critique of Violence: Between Structuralism and Critical Theory*. London: Routledge, 2000.

Hardt, Michael, and Antonio Negri. *Empire*. Cambridge, Mass.: Harvard University Press, 2000.

———. *Multitude: War and Democracy in the Age of Empire*. New York: Penguin, 2004.

Hart, H. L. A. *The Concept of Law*. Oxford: Oxford University Press, 1982.

Haverkamp, Anselm. "*Richard II*, Bracton, and the End of Political Theology." *Law and Literature* 16, no. 3 (2005): 313–26.

Hegel, Georg Wilhelm Friedrich. *Lectures on the Philosophy of Religion*. Translated by R. F. Brown, et al. Berkeley: University of California Press, 1987.

———. *Phenomenology of Spirit*. Translated by A. V. Miller. Oxford: Oxford University Press, 1977.

Heidegger, Martin. *Introduction to Metaphysics*. Translated by Gregory Fried and Richard Polt. New Haven: Yale University Press.

Heider, Sarah Dove. "The Timeless Ecstasy of Michael K." In *Black/ White Writing: Essays on South African Literature,* edited by Pauline Fletcher, 83–98. Lewisburg: Bucknell University Press, 1993.

Helbling, Robert E. "The Search for Justice." In *The Major Works of Heinrich von Kleist,* 193–209. New York: New Directions, 1975.

Hesiod. *Theogony, Works and Days, Testimonia*. Translated and edited by Glenn W. Most. Cambridge, Mass.: Harvard University Press, 2006.

Hobbes, Thomas. *Behemoth: The History of the Causes of the Civil Wars of England, and of the Counsels and Artifices By Which They Were Carried On From the Year 1640 to the Year 1660*. In *The English Works of Thomas Hobbes of Malmesbury,* edited by William Molesworth. Vol. 6. London: John Bohn, 1839–45.

———. *De Cive*. In *The Clarendon Edition of the Philosophical Works of Thomas Hobbes*. Vol. 3, edited by Howard Warrender. Oxford: Clarendon, 1983.

———. *Leviathan*. Edited by Richard Tuck. Cambridge: Cambridge University Press, 1999.

———. "Of the Life and History of Thucydides." In *The English Works of Thomas Hobbes of Malmesbury,* edited by William Molesworth, 8:xiii–xxii. London: John Bohn, 1839.

Hölderlin, Friedrich. *Essays and Letters*. Translated by Jeremy Adler and Charlie Louth. London: Penguin, 2009.

———. *Sämtliche Werke: Briefe und Dokumente*. Edited by D. E. Sattler. Bremer Augabe. Darmstadt: Wissenschaftliche Buchgesellschaft, 2004.

Holland, Eugene. "Spinoza and Marx." *Cultural Logic* 2, no.1 (1998): http://clogic.eserver.org/2-1/holland.html. Accessed June 2006.

Honig, Bonnie. "Antigone's Laments, Creon's Grief: Mourning, Membership, and the Politics of Exception." *Political Theory* 37, no. 1 (2009): 5–43.

———. "Antigone's Two Laws: Greek Tragedy and the Politics of Humanism." *New Literary History* 41 (2010): 1–33.

———. *Democracy and the Foreigner*. Princeton: Princeton University Press, 2001.

———. *Emergency Politics: Paradox, Law, Democracy*. Princeton: Princeton University Press, 2009.

Horn, Peter. "Michael K.: Pastiche, Parody or the Inversion of Michael Kohlhaas." *Current Writing* 17, no. 2 (2005): 56–73.

Howard, John. "John Howard's Policy Speech," 28 October 2001. A transcript available at *AustralianPolitics.com*: http://australianpolitics.com/news/2001/01 -10-28.shtml. Accessed July 2011.

Hull, Gordon. *Hobbes and the Making of Modern Political Thought*. London: Continuum, 2009.

Hume, David. *Dialogues Concerning Natural Religion and Other Writings*. Edited by Dorothy Coleman. Cambridge: Cambridge University Press, 2007.

Irigaray, Luce. *An Ethics of Sexual Difference*. Translated by Carolyn Burke and Gillian C. Gill. Ithaca: Cornell University Press, 1993.

———. *Sexes and Genealogies*. Translated by Gillian C. Gill. New York: Columbia University Press, 1993.

———. *Speculum of the Other Woman*. Translated by Gillian C. Gill. Ithaca: Cornell University Press, 1994.

———. *Thinking the Difference: For a Peaceful Revolution*. Translated by Karin Montin. London: Routledge, 1994.

Jackson, Robert. *Sovereignty: Evolution of an Idea*. Cambridge: Polity, 2007.

Jacobs, Carol. "Dusting Antigone."*Modern Language Notes* 111 (1996): 889–917.

———. *Uncontainable Romanticism: Shelley, Bronte, Kleist*. Baltimore: Johns Hopkins University Press, 1989.

Jacobson, Arthur. "Law Without Authority: Sources of the Welfare State in Spinoza's Tractatus Theologico-Politicus." *Cardozo Law Review* 25, no. 2 (2003): 669–714

James, Susan. *Spinoza on Philosophy, Religion, and Politics: The Theologico-Political Treatise*. Oxford: Oxford University Press, 2012.

Kahn, Paul. *Sacred Violence: Torture, Terror, and Sovereignty*. Ann Arbor: University of Michigan Press, 2008.

Kalyvas, Andreas. *Democracy and the Politics of the Extraordinary: Max Weber, Carl Schmitt, and Hannah Arendt*. Cambridge: Cambridge University Press, 2009.

———. "The Tyranny of Dictatorship: When the Greek Tyrant Met the Roman Dictator." *Political Theory* 35, no. 4 (2007):412–42.

Kant, Immanuel. *Groundwork of the Metaphysics of Morals*. Translated by Mary Gregor. Cambridge: Cambridge University Press, 2002.

———. "Perpetual Peace." Translated by H. B. Nisbet. In *Political Writings*, edited by Hans Reiss, 93–130. Cambridge: Cambridge University Press, 1991.

Kantorowicz, Ernst H. *The King's Two Bodies: A Study in Mediaeval Political Theology*. Princeton, N.J.: Princeton University Press, 1970.

Karatani, Kojin. *Transcritique: On Kant and Marx*. Translated by Sabu Kohso. Cambridge, Mass.: MIT Press, 2003.

Kautsky, Karl. *The Dictatorship of the Proletariat*. Translated by H. J. Stenning. Westport, Conn.: Greenwood Press, 1981.

Keenan, Tom. "The 'Paradox' of Knowledge and Power: Reading Foucault on a Bias." *Political Theory* 15, no. 1 (1987): 5–37

Klein, Naomi. *The Shock Doctrine: The Rise of Disaster Capitalism*. New York: Metropolitan Books and Henry Holt, 2007.

Kompridis, Nikolas. *Critique and Disclosure: Critical Theory Between Past and Future*. Cambridge, Mass.: MIT Press, 2006.

Kordela, Kiarina. *$urplus: Spinoza, Lacan*. New York: SUNY, 2007.

Krasner, Stephen D. *Sovereignty: Organized Hypocrisy*. Princeton: Princeton University Press, 1999.

Kurland, Stuart M. "Hamlet and the Scottish Succession?" *Studies in English Literature, 1500–1900* 34, no. 2 (1994): 279–300.

LaCapra, Dominick. *Rethinking Intellectual History: Texts, Contexts, Language*. Ithaca: Cornell University Press, 1983.

Landes, Joan B. "Novus Ordo Saeclorum: Gender and Public Space in Arendt's Revolutionary France." In *Feminist Interpretations of Hannah Arendt*, edited by Bonnie Honig, 195–219. University Park: Pennsylvania State University Press, 1995.

Lefebvre, Alexandre. *The Image of Law: Deleuze, Bergson, Spinoza*. Stanford: Stanford University Press, 2008.

Lemke, Thomas. *Biopolitics: An Advanced Introduction*. New York: New York University Press, 2011.

Lenin, Vladimir. *Essential Works of Lenin: "What Is to Be Done?" and Other Writings*. Edited by Henry M. Christman. New York: Dover, 1987.

Lezra, Jacques. *Wild Materialism: The Ethics of Terror and the Modern Republic*. New York: Fordham University Press, 2010.

Lloyd, Genevieve. *Providence Lost*. Cambridge, Mass.: Harvard University Press, 2008.

Loraux, Nicole. *The Divided City: On Memory and Forgetting in Ancient Athens*. Translated by Corinne Pache and Jeff Fort. New York: Zone, 2006.

———. *The Invention of Athens: The Funeral Oration in the Classical City*. Translated by Alan Sheridan. Cambridge, Mass.: Harvard University Press, 1986.

Lupton, Julia. "Hamlet, Prince: Tragedy, Citizenship, Political Theology." In *Alternative Shakespeares*, edited by Diana Henderson, 3:181–203. London: Routledge, 2007.

Lyotard, Jean-François. *The Confession of Augustine*. Translated by Richard Beardsworth. Stanford: Stanford University Press, 2000.

Macey, David. "Some Reflections on Foucault's *Society Must Be Defended* and the Idea of 'Race'." In *Foucault in the Age of Terror: Essays on Biopolitics and the Defence of Society*, edited by Stephen Norton and Stephen Bygrave, 118–32. New York: Palgrave, 2008.

Machiavelli, Niccolò. *Discourses on Livy.* Translated by H. Mansfield and N. Tarcov. Chicago: University of Chicago Press, 1996.

———. *The Prince.* Translated by Peter Bondanella. Oxford: Oxford University Press, 2005.

Mack, Michael. *Spinoza and the Specters of Modernity: The Hidden Enlightenment of Diversity from Spinoza to Freud.* London: Continuum, 2010.

———. "Toward an Inclusive Universalism: Spinoza's Ethics of Sustainability." In *Spinoza Now,* edited by Dimitris Vardoulakis, 99–134. Minneapolis: University of Minnesota Press, 2011.

Macpherson, C. B. *The Political Theory of Possessive Individualism: Hobbes to Locke.* Oxford: Clarendon Press, 1962.

Mansfield, Nick. *The God Who Deconstructs Himself: Sovereignty and Subjectivity Between Freud, Bataille, and Derrida.* New York: Fordham University Press, 2010.

———. *Theorizing War: From Hobbes to Badiou.* New York: Palgrave, 2008.

Maritain, Jacques. *Three Reformers: Luther, Descartes, Rousseau.* New York: Thomas Crowell, 1970.

Marr, Andrew, and Mirian Wilkinson. *Dark Victory.* Crows Nest, NSW: Allen and Unwin, 2004.

Marriner, Cosima. "Abortion Couple Not Aware They Broke Law." *Sydney Morning Herald,* September 19, 2009. Available at http://www.smh.com.au/national/abortion-couple-not-aware-they-broke-law-20090918-fvcg.html. Accessed September 2009.

Martel, James. *Subverting the Leviathan: Reading Thomas Hobbes as a Radical Democrat.* New York: Columbia University Press, 2007.

Martinich, A. P. "Hobbes's Erastianism and Interpretation." *Journal of the History of Ideas* 70, no. 1 (2002): 43–63.

Marx, Karl. *The Class Struggles in France 1848 to 1850.* In *Collected Works.* Vol. 10. New York: International Publishers, 1976.

———. *The Eighteenth Brumaire of Louis Bonaparte.* Translated by Clemens Dutt. In *Collected Works.* Vol. 11. New York: International Publishers, 1976.

Matheron, Alexandre. "The Theoretical Function of Democracy in Spinoza and Hobbes." In *The New Spinoza,* edited by Warren Montag and Ted Stolze, 206–17. Minneapolis: University of Minnesota Press, 1997.

McNay, Lois. "Self as Enterprise: Dilemmas of Control and Resistance in Foucault's *The Birth of Biopolitics.*" *Theory, Culture and Society* 26, no. 6 (2009): 55–77.

McNeal, Andrew W. "Cutting off the King's Head: Foucault's *Society Must Be Defended* and the Problem of Sovereignty." *Alternatives* 29 (2004): 373–98.

Milbank, John. *Theology and Social Theory: Beyond Secular Reason.* Oxford: Blackwell, 2006.

Miller, J. Hillis. "Laying Down the Law in Literature: Kleist." In *Topographies.* Stanford: Stanford University Press, 1995.

Mills, Catherine. "Life Beyond Law: Biopolitics, Law and Futurity in Coetzee's *Life and Times of Michael K.*" *Griffith Law Review* 15, no. 1 (2006):177–95.

Monagle, Clare. "A Sovereign Act of Negation: Schmitt's Political Theology and Its Ideal Medievalism." In *The Politics of Nothing: Sovereignty and Modernity*, edited by Clare Monagle and Dimitris Vardoulakis, 7–19. London: Routledge, 2012.

Montag, Warren. *Bodies, Masses, Power: Spinoza and his Contemporaries*. London: Verso, 1999.

———. "Who's Afraid of the Multitude? Between the Individual and the State." *South Atlantic Quarterly* 104, no. 4 (2005): 655–73.

Montag, Warren, and Ted Stolze, eds. *The New Spinoza*. Minneapolis: University of Minnesota Press, 1997.

Montesquieu. *The Spirit of the Laws*. Translated by Anne M. Cohler, Basia Carolyn Miller, and Harold Samuel Stone. Cambridge: Cambridge University Press, 1989.

Moretti, Franco. *Signs Taken for Wonders: Essays in the Sociology of Literary Forms*. Translated by Susan Fischer, et al. London: Verso, 1988.

Mouffe, Chantal. "Deliberative Democracy or Agonistic Pluralism?" *Social Research* 66, no. 3 (1999): 745–58.

Muslow, Martin. "The Libertine's Two Bodies: Moral *Persona* and Free Thought in Early Modern Europe." *Intellectual History Review* 18, no. 3 (2008): 337–47.

Nederman, Cary J. *Lineages of European Political Thought: Explorations Along the Medieval/Modern Divide from John of Salisbury to Hegel*. Washington, D.C.: The Catholic University of America Press, 2009.

Negri, Antonio. *Insurgencies: Constituent Power and the Modern State*. Translated by Maurizia Boscagli. Minneapolis: University of Minnesota Press, 1999.

———. *The Savage Anomaly: The Power of Spinoza's Metaphysics and Politics*. Translated by Michael Hardt. Minneapolis: University of Minnesota Press, 2002.

Neocleous, Mark. *The Fabrication of Social Order: A Critical Theory of Police Power*. London: Pluto Press, 2000.

The New Testament. Greek edition. London: British and Foreign Bible Society, 1904.

Nietzsche, Friedrich. *On the Genealogy of Morality and Other Writings*. Translated by Carol Diethe. Edited by Keith Ansell-Pearson. Cambridge: Cambridge University Press, 2006.

Papadopoulos, Dimitris, and Vassilis Tsianos. "How to Do Sovereignty without People? The Subjectless Condition of Postliberal Power." *Boundary 2* 34, no. 1 (2007): 135–72.

Patton, Paul. "Foucault, Critique and Rights." *Critical Horizons* 6, no. 1 (2005): 268–87.

Philpott, Daniel. *Revolutions in Sovereignty: How Ideas Shaped Modern International Relations*. Princeton: Princeton University Press, 2001.

---. "Westphalia, Authority, and International Society." *Political Studies* 48 (1999): 566–89.

Plato. *Republic*. Translated by Paul Shorey. Cambridge, Mass.: Harvard University Press, 2003.

Plutarch. "Solon." In *Lives I*, translated by Bernadotte Perrin. Cambridge, Mass.: Harvard University Press, 1998.

Prosser, Eleanor. *Hamlet and Revenge*. Stanford: Stanford University Press, 1971.

Prozorov, Sergei. *Foucault, Freedom and Sovereignty*. Aldershot, UK: Ashgate, 2007.

"Queensland Criminal Code ACT 1899." Available at www.legislation.qld.gov.au/legisltn/current/c/crimincode.pdf. Accessed October 2010.

Quinones, Ricardo J. *The Changes of Abel: Violence and the Lost Brother in Cain and Abel Literature*. Princeton: Princeton University Press, 1991.

Rabinow, Paul, and Nikolas Rose. "Biopower Today." *BioSocieties* 1 (2006): 195–217.

Rancière, Jacques. *Disagreement: Politics and Philosophy*. Translated by Julie Rose. Minneapolis: University of Minnesota Press, 1999.

---. "Who Is the Subject of the Rights of Man?" *South Atlantic Quarterly* 103, nos. 2–3 (2004): 297–310.

Rasch, William. *Sovereignty and Its Discontents: On the Primacy of the Conflict and the Structure of the Political*. London: Birkbeck Law Press, 2004.

Reid, Donald. "Inciting Readings and Reading Cites: Visits to Marx's *The Eighteenth Brumaire of Louis Bonaparte*." *Modern Intellectual History* 4, no. 3 (2007): 545–70.

Rice, Charles. *The Emergence of the Interior: Architecture, Modernity, Domesticity*. London: Routledge, 2007.

Riley, Patrick. *The General Will before Rousseau: The Transformation of the Divine into the Civic*. Princeton: Princeton University Press, 1986.

Rose, Nikolas. "Life, Reason and History: Reading Georges Canguilhem Today." *Economy and Society* 27, nos. 2–3 (1998): 154–70.

Rousseau, Jean-Jacques. *Discourse on the Origin of Inequality*. Translated by Franklin Philip. Oxford: Oxford University Press, 1994.

---. *Discourse on Political Economy* and *The Social Contract*. Translated by Christopher Betts. Oxford: Oxford University Press, 1994.

Roy, Olivier. *The Failure of Political Islam*. Translated by Carol Volk. Cambridge, Mass.: Harvard University Press, 1994)

---. *The Politics of Chaos in the Middle East*. Translated by Ros Schwartz. London: Hurst, 2007.

Rust, Jennifer. "Political Theology and Shakespearean Studies." *Literature Compass* 6, no. 1 (2009): 175–90.

---. "Wittenberg and Melancholic Allegory: The Reformation and Its Discontents in *Hamlet*." In *Shakespeare and the Culture of Christianity in Early Modern England*, edited by Dennis Taylor and David N. Beauregard, 260–84. New York: Fordham University Press, 2003.

Santner, Eric. *On Creaturely Life: Rilke, Benjamin, Sebald*. Chicago: University of Chicago Press, 2006.

——. *The Royal Remains: The People's Two Bodies and the Endgames of Sovereignty*. Chicago: University of Chicago Press, 2011.

Saward, John. *Perfect Fools: Folly for Christ's Sake in Catholic and Orthodox Spirituality*. Oxford: Oxford University Press, 1980.

Schlegel, August. *Lectures on Dramatic Art and Literature*. Translated by John Black. London: G. Bell and Sons, 1902.

Schmitt, Carl. *The Concept of the Political*. Translated by George D. Schwab. Chicago: University of Chicago Press, 1996.

——. *The Crisis of Parliamentary Democracy*. Translated by Ellen Kennedy. Cambridge, Mass.: MIT Press, 1988.

——. *Hamlet or Hecuba: The Intrusion of Time into the Play*. Translated by David Pan and Jennifer Rust. New York: Telos, 2009.

——. *Legality and Legitimacy*. Translated by Jeffrey Seitzer. Durham: Duke University Press, 2004.

——. *The Leviathan in the State Theory of Thomas Hobbes: Meaning and Failure of a Political Symbol* [1938]. Translated by George Schwab and Erna Hilfstein. Westport, Conn.: Greenwood Press, 1996.

——. *The Nomos of the Earth in the International Law of the Jus Publicum Europaeum*. Translated by G. L. Ulmen. New York: Telos Press, 2003

——. *Political Theology: Four Chapters on the Concept of Sovereignty*. Translated by George D. Schwab. Cambridge, Mass.: MIT Press, 1985.

——. *The Theory of the Partisan: A Commentary/Remark on the Concept of the Political*. Translated by A. C. Goodson. *The New Centennial Review* 4, no. 3 (2004): 65.

Shakespeare, William. *Hamlet*. Edited by Burton Raffel. New Haven: Yale University Press, 2003.

Shapiro, Kam. *Sovereign Nations, Carnal States*. Ithaca: Cornell University Press, 2003.

Sharp, Hasana. *Spinoza and the Politics of Renaturalization*. Chicago: University of Chicago Press, 2011.

Shulman, George M. "The Myth of Cain: Fratricide, City Building and Politics." *Political Theory* 14, no. 2 (1986): 215–38.

Sissa, Giulia, and Marcel Detienne. *The Daily Life of the Greek Gods*. Translated by Janet Lloyd. Stanford: Stanford University Press, 2000.

Skinner, Quentin. *The Age of Reformation*. Vol. 2 of *The Foundations of Modern Political Thought*. Cambridge: Cambridge University Press, 1978.

——. "Hobbes on Persons, Authors and Representatives." In *The Cambridge Companion to Hobbes's Leviathan*, edited by Patricia Springborg, 157–80. Cambridge: Cambridge University Press, 2007.

———. *Reason and Rhetoric in the Philosophy of Hobbes*. Cambridge: Cambridge University Press, 1996.

Small, Stephanie. "Abortion Trial Sparks Legislation Debate." ABC News, 14 October 2010, http://www.abc.net.au/news/stories/2010/10/14/3038708.htm. Accessed 14 October 2010.

Sophocles. *Antigone; Women of Trachis; Philosctetes; Oedipus at Colonus*. Translated by Hugh Lloyd-Jones. Cambridge, Mass.: Harvard University Press, 1994.

Spinoza, Baruch. *Complete Works*. Translated by Samuel Shirley, edited by Michael L. Morgan. Indianapolis: Hackett, 2002.

———. *Opera quae supersunt omnia*, ed. Carolus Hermannus Bruder (Leipzig: Bernhardi Tauchnitz, 1843–1846).

Spruyt, Hendrik. *The Sovereign State and Its Competitors: An Analysis of Systems Change*. Princeton: Princeton University Press, 1994.

Sreedhar, Suzanne. *Hobbes on Resistance: Defying the Leviathan*. Cambridge: Cambridge University Press, 2010.

States, Bert O. *Hamlet and the Concept of Character*. Baltimore: John Hopkins University Press, 1992.

Steiner, Georg. *Private Lives, Public Deaths: Antigone and the Invention of Individuality*. New Haven: Yale University Press, 1996.

Stewart, Elizabeth. "Broken Sovereignties: J. M. Coetzee's Ethics of Anxiety and Disarray." *The International Journal of the Humanities* 3, no. 5 (2005/2006):157–64.

Strauss, Jonathan. *Antigone*. New York: Fordham University Press, 2013.

Strauss, Leo. *Natural Right and History*. Chicago: University of Chicago Press, 1953.

———. "On Thucydides' War of the Peloponnesians and the Athenians." In *The City and Man*, 138–241. Chicago: University of Chicago Press, 1978.

———. *The Political Philosophy of Hobbes: Its Basis and Its Genesis* [1936]. Translated by Elsa M. Sinclair. Chicago: University of Chicago Press, 1963.

Sullivan, Vickie. *Machiavelli, Hobbes, and the Formation of Liberal Republicanism in England*. Cambridge: Cambridge University Press, 2004.

Sussman, Henry. *The Aesthetic Contract: Statutes of Art and Intellectual Work in Modernity*. Stanford: Stanford University Press, 1997.

Szendy, Peter. *Prophesies of Leviathan*. Translated by Gil Anidjar. New York: Fordham University Press, 2010.

Thompson, Kevin. "Forms of Resistance: Foucault on Tactical Reversal and Self-formation." *Continental Philosophy Review* 36 (2003): 113–38.

Thucydides. *History of the Peloponnesian War*. Vol. 1. Translated by Charles Foster Smith. Loeb edition. Cambridge, Mass.: Harvard University Press, 1956.

Tillyard, E. M. W. *The Elizabethan World Picture*. Harmondsworth, UK: Penguin, 1982.

Tiqqun, *Introduction to Civil War*. Translated by Alexander R. Galloway and Jason E. Smith. Los Angeles: Semiotext(e), 2010.

Tralau, Johan, "Leviathan, the Beast of Myth: Medusa, Dionysos, and the Riddle of Hobbes's Sovereign Monster." In *The Cambridge Companion to Hobbes's Leviathan*, edited by Patricia Springborg, 61–81. Cambridge: Cambridge University Press, 2007.

Turchetti, Mario. "Jean Bodin." In the *Stanford Encyclopedia of Philosophy*. Revision 14 June 2010, http://plato.stanford.edu/entries/bodin/. Accessed August 2011.

United Nations High Commission for Refugees. "Convention and Protocol Relating to the Status of Refugees." UNHCR. Available at http://www.unhcr.org/protect/PROTECTION/3b66c2aa10.pdf. Accessed July 2011.

Vardoulakis, Dimitris. *Critical Praxis: Or, Is Everything Political?* Edited by Dimitris Vardoulakis. *Parallax* 16, no. 4 (special issue) (2010).

———. *The Doppelgänger: Literature's Philosophy*. New York: Fordham University Press, 2010.

———. "The Ends of Stasis: Spinoza as a Reader of Agamben." *Culture, Theory and Critique* 51, no. 2 (2010): 145–56.

———. "'The Fall Is the Proof of Our Freedom': Mediated Freedom in Kafka." In *Freedom and Confinement in Modernity: Kafka's Cages*, edited by Kiarina Kordela and Dimitris Vardoulakis, 87–106. New York: Palgrave, 2011.

———. "The Freedom to Lie." Forthcoming.

———. "A Matter of Immediacy: The Artwork and the Political in Walter Benjamin and Martin Heidegger." In *"Sparks Will Fly": Benjamin and Heidegger*, edited by Andrew Benjamin and Dimitris Vardoulakis. New York: SUNY, forthcoming.

———. "Spectres of Duty: The Politics of Silence in Ibsen's *Ghosts*." *Orbis Litterarum* 64, no. 1 (2009): 50–74.

———."Spinoza's Empty Law: The Possibility of Political Theology." In *Spinoza Beyond Philosophy*, edited by Beth Lord, 135–48. Edinburgh: Edinburgh University Press, 2012.

———. "Stasis: Beyond Political Theology?" *Cultural Critique* 73 (2009): 125–47.

———. "War and Its Other." *Cultural Studies Review* 16, no. 1 (2010): 267–72.

Vatter, Miguel. "Strauss and Schmitt as Readers of Hobbes and Spinoza: On the Relation between Political Theology and Liberalism." *New Centennial Review* 4, no. 3 (2004): 161–214.

Villani, Arnaud. "Figures of Duality: Hölderlin and Greek Tragedy." In *The Solid Letter: Readings of Friedrich Hölderlin*, edited by Aris Fioretos, 175–99. Stanford: Stanford University Press, 1999.

von Kleist, Heinrich. "Michael Kohlhaas." Translated by David Luke and Nigel Reeves. In *The Marquise of O—And Other Stories*. Harmondsworth. UK: Penguin, 1978.

———. "Michael Kohlhaas." Kleist-Archiv Semdbner edition. Published on 24 March 2003; http.www.kleist.org/texte/MichaelKohlhaasL.pdf. Accessed May 2009.

Weber, Samuel. "Taking Exception to the Decision: Walter Benjamin and Carl Schmitt." *Diacritics* 22 (1992): 5–18.

Weizman, Eyal. *Hollow Land: Israel's Architecture of Occupation.* London: Verso, 2007.

Weydemeyer, Joseph. "The Dictatorship of the Proletariat." Translated by Horst Duhnke and Hal Draper. *Labor History* 3, no. 2 (1962): 214–17.

Williams, George. "Abortion Law Stuck in the 19th Century." *Sydney Morning Herald*, 12 October 2010. Available at http://www.smh.com.au/opinion/society -and-culture/abortion-law-stuck-in-the-19th-century-20101011-16fwq.html. Accessed 12 October 2010.

Wittgenstein, Ludwig. *On Certainty.* Translated by Denis Paul and G. E. M. Anscombe. Edited by G. E. M. Anscombe and G. H. von Wright. Oxford: Blackwell, 1998.

Wittkowski, Wolfgang. "Is Kleist's Michael Kohlhaas a Terrorist? Luther, Prussian Law Reform and the Accountability of Government." *Historical Reflections* 26, no. 3 (2000): 471–86.

Wyduckel, Dieter. *Princeps Legibus Solutus: Eine Untersuchung zur frühmodernen Rechts- und Staatslehre.* Berlin: Duncker und Humblot, 1979.

Zagorin, Perez. *Hobbes and the Law of Nature.* Princeton: Princeton University Press, 2010.

Žižek, Slavoj. *Violence.* London: Profile Books, 2009.

Žižek, Slavoj, Eric L. Santner, and Kenneth Reinhard. *The Neighbor: Three Inquiries in Political Theology.* Chicago: University of Chicago Press, 2005.

INDEX

243n72; *Empire*, 3, 190, 207n14, 209n27,
210n5, 212n23, 213n40, 243nn69–71, 243n73
Hart, H. L. A., 232n34
Haverkamp, Anselm, 224n41
Hegel, Georg Wilhelm Friedrich, 54, 54–59,
162, 209n24, 216n9, 217nn24–25, 219n37;
Phenomenology of the Spirit, 56, 217n21,
217n23
Heidegger, Martin, 16, 213n35, 217n25
Heider, Sarah Dove, 245n87
Helbling, Robert E., 235n64
Hesiod, *Theogony*, 47, 215n5
Hobbes, Thomas, 46, 77–78, 84–100, 102,
105–6, 108, 112–15, 119–20, 127–29, 131, 134,
140–41, 144, 153, 158, 168, 193, 211n20,
215n4, 222n22, 222n24, 223n25, 223nn32–
34, 224nn34–35, 225nn42–44, 229n4,
229n18, 231n28; *Leviathan*, 77, 84–85,
87–88, 90–94, 102, 107–8, 220n2, 222n21,
223n33, 224n42, 229n5
Hölderlin, Friedrich, 54–59, 216n12,
216nn14–17, 217n18
Holland, Eugene, 238n30
Honig, Bonnie, 16, 54, 58–59, 116–17, 119, 122,
207n11, 214n48, 218nn27–28, 227n62,
229n4, 229n22, 229nn14–17
Horn, Peter, 242n68
Howard, John, 8–9, 209n31
Hull, Gordon, 223n32
Hume, David, *Dialogues on Religion*, 158,
236n8
Hussein, Saddam, 26

Irigaray, Luce, 217n24

Jackson, Robert, 206n7
Jacobs, Carol, 216n9, 217n20, 235n63
Jacobson, Arthur, 234n49
James, Susan, 230n24
Job, 90, 94, 224n35
John of Salisbury, 222n23

Kahn, Paul, 208n21
Kalyvas, Andreas, 17, 210n7, 238n37
Kant, Immanuel, 20–21, 138, 209n24, 211n17,
234n48; *Groundwork on the Metaphysics
of Morals*, 138, 233n47
Kantorowicz, Ernst, 93–94, 224n40; *The
King's Two Bodies: A Study in Mediaeval
Political Theology*, 93, 224nn38–39;
Richard II, 94, 224n41
Karatani, Kojin, 162, 163, 237nn21–23
Kautsky, Karl, 171, 238n34
Keenan, Tom, 240n55
King James Bible, 69, 224n81, 224n83

Klein, Naomi, 237n24
Kleist, Heinrich von, 17, 19, 35, 36, 140–44,
147–50, 154, 156, 182, 202, 234n52, 235n64,
242n68; "Michael Kohlhaas," 17, 19, 35–36,
140–52, 154, 156–57, 182, 188–90, 194–95,
234n52, 235nn59–61, 242n68
Kompridis, Nikolas, 16, 210n4
Kordela, Kiarina, 238n31
Krasner, Stephen D., 206n5
Kurland, Stuart M., 226n53

LaCapra, Dominick, 237n20
Laclau, Ernesto, 16
Landes, Joan B., 229n11
Leach, Teagan, 184–88
Lefebvre, Alexandre, 231n31
Lemke, Thomas, 236n4
Lenin, Vladimir, 238n33
Levinas, Emmanuel, 214n48
Levine, Judge, 184
Lezra, Jacques, 211n15, 214n44
Lincoln, Abraham, 215n7
Lloyd, Genevieve, 233n41
Locke, John, 232n34
Loraux, Nicole, 47, 215n7, 218n34
Louis Phillipe, 164
Lupton, Julia, 227n64, 228n64
Lyotard, Jean-François, 16, 73, 219n46

Macey, David, 243n76
Machiavelli, Niccolò, 4, 25, 77–81, 83–84,
110–11, 139, 210n3, 220n4, 228n2; *The
Prince*, 4, 25, 79, 139, 221n5
Mack, Michael, 231n26
Macpherson, C. B., 222n22
Mansfield, Nick, 21, 212nn25–26, 214n52
Maritain, Jacques, 229n13
Marr, Andrew and Mirian Wilkinson,
209n33
Marriner, Cosima, 241n58
Martin, Teresa, 185
Martinich, A. P., 223n25
Martle, James, 222n22
Marx, Karl, 156–57, 159, 161–75, 192–93,
237nn19–20, 238n30, 238nn35–36; *The
Class Struggles in France 1848 to 1850*, 166,
237nn25–27; *The Eighteenth Brumaire of
Louis Bonaparte*, 155–57, 161–64, 167–73,
175–76, 237nn19–20, 238n32
Matheron, Alexandre, 133, 233n40
McNay, Lois, 242n65
McNeal, Andrew, 205n3
Milbank, John, 211n20
Miller, J. Hillis, 235n59
Mills, Catherine, 243n75, 245n88

Monagle, Clare, 207n12, 217n22
Montag, Warren, 232n33, 233nn42–44
Montesquieu, 228n1
Moretti, Franco, 101, 226n58
Mouffe, Chantal, 16–17, 211n12
Muslow, Martin, 230n19

Nederman, Cary J., 222n23
Negri, Antonio, 16, 207n15, 208n17, 233n38, 233n43
Neocleous, Mark, 223n27
Nietzsche, Friedrich, 2, 22, 70, 195, 209n25, 219n39

Papadopoulos, Dimitris and Vassilis Tsianos, 208n21
Patton, Paul, 239n27
Pericles, 46–51, 58, 63, 73, 79, 198, 215n7
Philpott, Daniel, 206n6
Plato, 60–62, 65–67, 83, 89, 134, 166, 218n31; Republic, 60–61, 83, 166, 218n31, 221n19; Timaeus, 83
Plowden, Edmund, 93
Plutarch, 213n42
Prosser, Eleanor, 227n61
Prozorov, Sergei, 242n65
Pufendorf, 230n19

Quinones, Ricardo J., 219n44, 225n52

Rabelais, 226n60
Rabinow, Paul, 240n48
Rancière, Jacques, 223n28, 236n14
Rasch, William, 207n11
Rawls, John, 15
Realpolitik, 20
Reid, Donald, 231n20
Rice, Charles, 237n17
Riley, Patrick, 229n13, 230n19
Rose, Nikolas, 240n48, 240n53
Rousseau, Jean-Jacques, 84, 109, 111–22, 131–34, 137–38, 140–41, 144, 157–58, 168, 197, 228n3, 229n4, 229nn12–13, 229n18, 230n18, 230n20, 245n85; Discourse on the Origin of Inequality, 113, 228n3, 229n12, 245n85; Social Contract, 111–14, 116, 118, 120–22, 228n3
Roy, Olivier, 33, 214n45
Rust, Jennifer, 225n50, 226n60

Santner, Eric, 98, 225n46, 230n20
Saward, John, 244n81
Schlegel, August, 226n57
Schmitt, Carl, 16–17, 19–21, 33, 56, 81, 83, 88, 142–43, 145, 154, 158, 161, 163, 176, 206n6,

207n11, 210n6, 211n14, 217n22, 222n22, 223n31, 226n53, 227n64, 228n64, 232n35, 236n12, 237n18; The Concept of the Political, 33, 143, 207n11, 211n19, 214n46, 234n54, 234n56; Political Theology, 19, 163, 211n14, 211n16, 217n22, 221n18, 236n2; Theory of the Partisan, 142, 234n54
Shakespeare, William, 17, 93, 100, 102–3, 173, 225n50, 225n51, 226n53, 239n39; Hamlet, 17, 78, 86, 94, 99–107, 147, 173–74, 181, 225n51, 226n53, 226nn59–61, 227nn62–63, 227n64, 228n64, 228n66
Shapiro, Kam, 219n43
Sharp, Hasana, 232n37
Shulman, George M., 210n3
Sissa, Giulia and Marcel Detienne, 215n6
Skinner, Quentin, 221n10, 224n34, 224n42
Small, Stephanie, 241n63
Socrates, 60, 61, 83
Solon, 31, 34–35, 41, 46, 52, 54, 67–69, 74, 86, 88, 101, 119, 125, 139, 172, 177, 183, 203, 213n42, 214n44
Sophocles, 17, 52, 58, 216nn10–11; Antigone, 17, 52–68, 100, 105–6, 115, 202, 215n8, 216nn9–12, 217n18, 217nn24–25, 227n62
Spinoza, Baruch, 3, 23, 122–40, 142, 148–50, 151, 155–57, 170, 176–77, 183, 186–88, 198–99, 203, 208n22, 230n23, 231nn24–27, 232nn33–35, 233n48, 234n49, 238n30; Ethics, 23, 122, 131, 136, 233n48, 234n48; Tractatus Theologico-Politicus, 23, 123–25, 130–32, 134–37, 148, 155, 233n42, 233n44, 233n48, 234n49
Spruyt, Hendrik, 206n5
Sreedhar, Suzanne, 225n43
States, Bert O., 227n61
Steiner, Georg, 217n18
Stewart, Elizabeth, 242n68
Strauss, Jonathan, 215n8
Strauss, Leo, 21, 41, 212n23, 215n1, 222n22, 224n34
Sullivan, Vickie, 222n22
Sussman, Henry, 147, 235n62
Szendy, Peter, 218n29

Taylor, Charles, 240n55
Thompson, Kevin, 242n67
Thucydides, 41–47, 52, 54, 64, 88, 99, 213n38, 215n2, 223n32; History of The Peloponnesian War, 41, 43–44, 46–47, 51, 54, 88, 215n2
Tillyard, E. M. W., 227n63
Tiqqun, 236n11

COMMONALITIES

TIMOTHY C. CAMPBELL, SERIES EDITOR

CPSIA information can be obtained
at www.ICGtesting.com
Printed in the USA
BVHW031415181219
567071BV00001B/14/P

9 781646 960101